Eugenio Montale

Swinburne's Early Poetry (1956)

Leopardi and the Theory of Poetry (1964)

Le opere di Rabindranath Tagore, selected and introduced by G. Singh (1966)

Le poesie di Kabir, translated into Italian by Ezra Pound and G. Singh, with a preface by G. Singh (1966)

Contemporary Italian Verse, selected, edited, and translated by G. Singh, (1968)

Leopardi e l'Inghilterra (1968)

Poesie di Hardy, selected, translated into Italian, and introduced by G. Singh, with a preface by Eugenio Montale (1968)

The Butterfly of Dinard, translated by G. Singh (1970; American edition, 1971)

Xenia, translated by G. Singh (1970)

Eugenio Montale, *Selected Poems,* edited with introduction, notes, and vocabulary by G. Singh. Preface by Eugenio Montale (1973)

Eugenio Montale

A CRITICAL STUDY OF HIS
POETRY, PROSE, AND CRITICISM

by G. Singh

NEW HAVEN AND LONDON
YALE UNIVERSITY PRESS, 1973

Designed by Sally Sullivan
and set in Linotype Granjon type.
Printed in the United States of America by
Vail-Ballou Press, Inc., Binghamton, N.Y.

Distributed in Great Britain, Europe, and Africa by
Yale University Press, Ltd., London; in Canada by
McGill-Queen's University Press, Montreal; in Latin
America by Kaiman & Polon, Inc., New York City; in India by
UBS Publishers' Distributors Pvt., Ltd., Delhi; in
Japan by John Weatherhill, Inc., Tokyo.

Contents

Preface

In what happens to be, not simply in English, the first critical study of Eugenio Montale's works I have followed certain basic assumptions. The first is that this book is primarily intended for English-speaking readers who have at least a certain familiarity with English literature and criticism as well as with Italian. The second is that, however searching and illuminating some Italian criticism of Montale's poetry may be—and I have in mind first and foremost the criticism of Sergio Solmi, and then of Alfredo Gargiulo, Giuseppe De Robertis, and Gianfranco Contini—it is not always, because of its peculiarly abstract and theoretical nature, of much help to an English reader even when translated. And my last assumption is that while this book tries to take into account the various aspects of Montale's poetry in all its complexity, it doesn't purport to offer any specialized thesis or exegesis concerning any one particular aspect. Its aim is to provide a general critical account of Montale's *oeuvre* in its totality. There is no doubt that Montale's poetry is not, as he himself admits in his preface to my annotated edition of his poems (published by Manchester University Press, 1973), "transparent at first reading, which is not due to any deliberate attempt to fool the reader, but to the intrinsic difficulties that a modern poet finds himself up against today . . . (especially) at a time when it is generally boasted that art is dead and that any new poetry cannot be other than the epicedium of a miracle that will never be repeated. To my mind poetry has always been dead and has always arisen from its ashes." [1] In any case only a critic walking roughshod

1. "Sia ben chiaro che se io non sono stato sempre trasparente a una prima lettura ciò non è da attribuirsi a una mia deliberata 'fumisteria' ma alle intrinseche difficoltà che oggi incontra un poeta moderno. Come tanti altri poeti d'oggi (italiani e anche inglesi) io sono nato in tempi poco propizi al tradizionale bel canto (poetico); in tempi in cui si afferma addirittura con orgoglio che l'arte è morta e che ogni nuova poesia non può essere altro che l'epicedio di un miracolo che non si ripeterà più. A mio avviso la poesia è sempre morta ed è sempre risorta dalle sue ceneri." Eugenio Montale, in his preface to *Selected Poems,* ed. and intro. by G. Singh with notes and vocabulary (Manchester, Eng.: Manchester University Press, 1973).

over Montale's poetry and mechanically analyzing and dismembering it would try to extricate any particular component of it—let us say, symbolism—from the closely knit pattern of imagery, concepts, and analogies that it represents. For Montale's symbolism can no more be abstracted from his poetry for paraphrase or discussion—as some critics, both in Italy and out, have tried to do—than its moral or metaphysical ethos can be separated from the poetic pattern within which it operates.

As to my own method of approach I have, in the course of writing this book, been conscious of what F. R. Leavis said more than thirty years ago. In his preface to *Revaluation* (1936) he wrote:

> no treatment of poetry is worth much that does not keep very close to the concrete: there lies the problem of method. The only acceptable solution, it seemed to me, lay in the extension and adaptation of the method appropriate in dealing with individual poets as such. In dealing with individual poets the rule of the critic is, or should (I think) be, to work as much as possible in terms of particular analysis—analysis of poems or passages, and say nothing that cannot be related immediately to judgments about producible texts. Observing this rule and practising this self-denial, the critic limits, of course, his freedom; but there are kinds of freedom he should not aspire to, and the discipline, while not preventing his saying anything that he should in the end find himself needing to say, enables him to say it with a force of relevance and an edged economy not otherwise attainable.

I have tried to achieve this goal as well as I could; I may have failed, but at least that was my aim.

Another thing that I have had in mind is what T. S. Eliot says about Matthew Arnold. Praising Arnold's essay on "The Study of Poetry," he observes: "To be able to quote as Arnold could is the best evidence of taste." I have made abundant use of quotations from Montale's poetry. And in selecting what to quote, I have been guided not only by what are generally accepted to be some of Montale's best poems, but also by my own critical judgment.

Lastly the question of translations. Translating what one admires in a poet is in my opinion itself a form of literary criticism. I have ventured to offer my own translations as an integral part of the critical discussion and context. There are as many as sixty poems, representing a fairly wide selection of Montale's poetry and translated in full, besides some other poems and short stories from *Farfalla di Dinard* that are translated partially. Some of the poems have never been translated before; in the case of those that have been, I have still preferred to use my own translations rather than others that for one reason or another I found unsatisfactory.

In my translations of Montale's poetry I have been fully aware that his distinctive and decisive originality depends on and is, in fact, inseparable from his ability to create his "poetic" out of the living, spoken Italian language. This inevitably means that the translator should, as far as possible, try to achieve this quality in his translations. For the question of the living, spoken language used as a poetic diction is not merely a linguistic one; it embraces the much more complex factors of tone, rhythm, and inflection that determine the texture of a poet's verse and display the subtlety and suppleness of control with which he not only uses the language but also places his caesuras, internal rhymes, assonance, and alliteration, while at the same time regulating the length of the lines and stanzas. Thus, fidelity to a poet's material is in the deepest sense unattainable without fidelity to his tone and rhythm. For, as Pound—who, besides being a great poet was also a great translator, perhaps the greatest since Edward FitzGerald—has observed, "the perception of the intellect is given in the words, that of the emotions in the cadence." [2]

In his best poems Montale weds the rhythm and the structure in such a way as to produce an effect of spontaneous naturalness as well as of exquisitely accomplished art. Thus, besides analyzing and evaluating these traits of his art and style, I have tried to bring them out in my own translations, which are meant not only to ease the reader's path to familiarity with the Italian text but also to serve as an integral part of my critical evaluation of what the poems mean. For, to quote Pound again, "Tain't what a man *sez*, but wot he *means* that the traducer has got to bring out. The *implication* of the word." [3] However, except in rare and fortuitous cases, I have deliberately refrained from trying to reproduce Montale's rhymes, internal rhymes, assonances, and alliteration. Such an effort would inevitably result, not only in a certain departure from the meaning of the original text, but also in tampering with the natural flow and inflection of the English idiom. I have adhered all the more closely to this criterion in view of the fact that many of Montale's English translators have yielded to this temptation, with resultant loss in terms of spontaneity, flexibility, and inevitability in their use of the English language. I therefore assume (or hope) that my translations will be taken as a relevant part of my critical assessment of Montale's poetry, and that the reader will

2. See Ezra Pound's introduction to Cavalcanti's poems in *The Translations of Ezra Pound*, ed. Hugh Kenner (London: Faber & Faber, 1953), p. 23.
3. Pound's letters to W. H. D. Rouse, *Letters of Ezra Pound* (London: Faber & Faber, 1951), p. 360.

be able to see for himself that there is a certain correlation between the inherent merit of a particular poem as I see it and my translation of it.[4]

I am grateful to Montale himself for the various kinds of help he has given me, especially in explaining certain difficulties in the interpretation as well as

4. Some of my translations quoted here have been published before. *Xenia* I and II were brought out by Black Sparrow Press (Los Angeles) and New Directions (New York) in 1970. The book also included translations of some other poems—"Il repertorio," "Laggiù," and "Nel fumo"—then unpublished but now included in *Satura.*
My other translations appeared in the following publications:
"Oboe," *Times Literary Supplement,* September 12, 1968
"Gli uomini che si voltano," *Times Literary Supplement,* January, 23, 1969.
"Götterdämmerung 1968," *London Magazine,* no. 100 (1969), p. 151
"Provo rimorso" and "Refrain dell'onorevole professore," *London Magazine* 9, no. 7 (October 1969) : 52.
"Intercettazione telefonica," "Surrogati," "Leggendo il giornale," and "La madre di Bobi B.," *London Magazine* 10, no. 1 (April 1970) : 70–73
"Botta e risposta," *Forum Italicum* 4, no. 4 (December 1970) : 572–75
"A pianterreno," *London Magazine* (August / September 1971), p. 94
The following poems also appeared in my translation in the special W. B. Yeats / Eugenio Montale issue of *Agenda,* vol. 9, no. 4-vol. 10, no. 1 (Autumn-Winter, 1971–72).
From *Ossi di seppia:*
"Spesso il male di vivere ho incontrato"
From *Le occasioni:*
"Non recidere, forbice",
From *La bufera e altro:*
"A mia madre"
"Ballata scritta in una clinica"
"Due nel crepuscolo"
"Finestra fiesolana"
"Luce d'inverno"
"Nubi color magenta"

From *Satura:*

"A tarda notte"
"Divinità in incognito"
"Ex voto"
"La belle dame sans merci"
"L'Arno a Rovezzano"
"Rebecca"
My English translation of Montale's *Farfalla di Dinard,* with a preface by Eugenio Montale, was published by Alan Ross (London) in 1968, and the American edition brought out by Kentucky University Press (Lexington) in 1971.
To appear in the *Mediterranean Review* for summer of 1972 are translations of the following poems:
From *Satura:*
"A tarda notte"
"Dalle finestre si vedevano dattilografe"
"Il primo gennaio"
From *Diario del '71:*
"I nascondigli"
"Lettera a Bobi"

translation of his poetry; to F. R. Leavis for having taken the trouble to read my manuscript and for his invaluable comments and suggestions; and to Professor Filippo Donini, Director of the Italian Institute in London, for his unstinted help and advice. Thanks are also due to Mondadori in Milan for permission to quote extensively from Montale's prose and poetry.

1: Introduction: Biography and Literary Background

Eugenio Montale is the most important living poet in Italy, and also the most influential. His impact on modern Italian poetry has been hardly less profound than that of Pound or Eliot on English verse. As in the case of Eliot's poetry, one can trace influences such as John Donne or the Jacobean dramatists, Pound or Laforgue; so also can one refer to Dante, Leopardi, Pascoli, and D'Annunzio as possible influences on Montale. Yet neither Donne nor Laforgue on the one hand, nor Dante, Pascoli, or D'Annunzio on the other, could account for the unmistakable originality of such poems as Eliot's "Portrait of a Lady," or Montale's "Arsenio" or "Casa sul mare." There was nothing quite like these before either in English or in Italian. The break from the poetic conventions of the more or less immediate past has as impressive a finality about it in Montale as in Pound or Eliot.

The first published volume of Montale's verse, *Ossi di seppia,* came out in 1925.[1] The high degree of creative maturity and technical accomplishment of a great many poems in this volume marks an epoch in Italian poetry just as *Hugh Selwyn Mauberley* and *The Waste Land* do in English. No doubt Ungaretti's early poetry as well as Gozzano's pointed the way to a reaction against D'Annunzianism; but it is Montale's poetry that by virtue of the depth and complexity underlying the language, images, and symbols offers a richer and more compact body of achieved poetry. This is, of course, not to deny Ungaretti's originality as a poet, nor the historical significance of his poetic innovations, but merely to stress the conspicuous degree of originality in Montale's verse and to show how it represents a more sustained and more complex creativeness, as well as a more subtle and sophisticated mode of questioning and exploring one's own experience, than is the case with Ungaretti's poetry.

1. Concerning earlier poems by Montale that appeared before the publication of *Ossi di seppia,* see Appendix 1.

Whatever literary comparisons, particularly comparisons from other cultures and literatures may be worth, one can say that, so far as poetry is concerned, if the first half of the twentieth century in England was dominated by Pound and Eliot, in Italy it was dominated by D'Annunzio, Ungaretti, and Montale. Montale's influence, however, has not been confined to poetry alone; he is also an influential literary critic, as well as a journalist who has written some fifteen hundred articles. Nevertheless it is through *Ossi di seppia* that he made the greatest impact. *Le occasioni* followed in 1939, *La bufera e altro* in 1956, and *Satura* in 1971. Montale has also published a book of prose called *Farfalla di Dinard* (1956). And as a critic, he has given us some very cogent and perceptive evaluations of modern Italian writers —Croce, Svevo, Saba, Campana, Palazzeschi, Cardarelli, Cecchi, and Moravia. He has also done some very effective translations from Shakespeare, Marlowe, Blake, Hopkins, Hardy, Yeats, Joyce, and Eliot (see Appendix 2). In fact he is the first major Italian poet to take such a deep interest in English literature: Italian writers in the past having been mostly, if not exclusively, concerned with French literature and, in a very few cases (for instance, Carducci), with German literature.

Wherein does Montale's originality as a poet lie? What is the precise nature of his impact and achievement? Questions like these invite us to examine his poems, his literary style, and his thought. It is not enough to repeat what has often been said, namely, that Montale's lyric poetry—and unlike Eliot, Montale is essentially, indeed almost exclusively, a lyric poet—is the finest blend of the three most significant influences on modern poetry: French symbolism, "Hermetism," and the Italian, or to be more precise, the Montalian version of the "objective correlative." During the early stages of his poetic career Montale was to some extent influenced by these movements. But he soon evolved an altogether different and conspicuously personal mode of expression.

In a way which is only indirectly symbolical, Montale's poetry expresses the moral and intellectual dilemmas of our times, without being overladen with any philosophy as such. And the real essence of his modernity lies in his feeling for objects, including the phenomena of nature—objects that are simultaneously charged with a personal sentiment and an impersonal symbolism. Sometimes as mute but not insentient listeners or participants in a lyric monologue or reverie, sometimes as disinterested but not indifferent spectators of the poet's inner drama, the objects in Montale's poetry are depicted as having an autonomous existence.

The person addressed as "tu" in Montale's poetry stands for a woman loved, but at the same time also for something vaster, more impersonal, and more complex, embodying, as it does, the poet's ethical or philosophical alter ego.[2] Thus Montale is both a love poet and a philosophical poet; and even when he strikes a highly personal vein, the depth and solemnity of an impersonal and universal sentiment almost invariably comes out or is felt to be in the background.

Montale has also created a new poetic mythology—a mythology that includes dogs, kitchen utensils, maid servants, moles, crickets, bats, drills, tapes, ribbons—giving it the same pride of place as Wordsworth gave to rocks, stones, and trees. There is something challengingly fresh about such realism: it is not, as often happens in avant-garde or neo-avant-garde art, a substitute for a genuine creative urge, but is firmly rooted in and inspired by such an urge. Lastly, Montale has delved deep into the hitherto unexplored resources of the Italian language and has shown that a poet need not escape from personal emotions in order to convey the quality and essence of a universal emotion.

Few Italian poets have celebrated their birthplaces or the places associated with their childhood and adolescence as passionately as has Montale. In this he may be regarded as the very antithesis of Leopardi with his famous diatribes against Recanati. The youngest of five children—he had three brothers and one sister—Montale was born at Genoa on 12 October 1896. His father, Domingo Montale, owned an import firm and came from Monterosso, one of the five small towns on the Liguarian coast, collectively called Cinque Terre; his mother, Giuseppina Ricci, came from Nervi. The poet's family owned a villa at Monterosso where he spent his summers up to the age of thirty. It is not surprising, then, that the charm and appeal of the magnificent coastline that stretches from Genoa to La Spezia should have been in Montale's blood. In fact one may well wonder if Montale's poetry in general, and *Ossi di seppia* in particular, would have been the same had he been born anywhere else.

At the time of his birth, Montale tells us, Genoa was "one of the most beautiful and characteristic cities in Italy . . . a city of winding streets, with a center inhabited by rich and poor alike . . . a beehive of stalls and commercial offices." During the last half-century, however, like many other cities, it has undergone considerable change. It is now "a twenty-mile strip from Voltri to Nervi," and seen from an airplane it must look like "a serpent that has swallowed a rabbit and is unable to digest it." However, Montale tells us: "I

2. In his poem "Il tu" (*Satura*) Montale points out how, according to his critics, "il mio *tu* è un istituto" and adds: "in me i tanti sono uno anche se appaiono / moltiplicati dagli specchi."

couldn't forget Genoa. I know the Genoese dialect. I have spoken it at home and outside, I even know the two dialects of Vernazza and Monterosso. When I go back I still find much of its past there and I watch with a mixture of admiration and dismay the signs of its present and future".[3] But it is the Cinque Terre, especially Monterosso, forming "an enchanting arc of rocks and sky"[4] that has left the deepest mark on Montale's writings. Some of the autobiographical pieces in *Farfalla di Dinard* are set in Liguria. They describe the impact his early life and surroundings made on his mind and art. For instance, in "La regata" the description of Verdaccio, a tiny coastal town, may be regarded as offering a typical glimpse into the Ligurian life and landscape of that time:

> Verdaccio—a tiny seaport protected by high rocks, in the heart of a semicircle of old houses huddled together or merely divided by narrow passages and winding alleys—was almost in line with Zebrino's room on the third floor of the Montecorvo villa where his family used to spend the summer months. But it was on the opposite side of the inlet, about three miles as the crow flies; and in consequence of the ragged and picturesque bustle of the place one would have needed a pair of binoculars to bring into sharper focus the soot of that lair of pirates and hawks, which not even the Saracens had ever dared to approach. No trains stopped there, nor was it accessible by any usable road. There were neither hotels nor rooms to let. If by any chance a stranger happened to land there and ventured out in those lanes he was sure to have full chamber pots emptied on his head from the top floors, without even the ritual warning "vitta ch'er beuttu!" (Watch out, I am going to throw!)—a cry reserved only for persons of consequence.

In "La casa delle due palme" the house described is Montale's own family home at Monterosso:

> It was a yellowish, rather drab pagoda, and one could have a side view of it from the train, as well as of the two palm trees in front of it, which were both symmetrical but not identical. They were planted as twins in the year of grace 1900. But one grew faster and soon out-topped the other. There was no way of checking its growth or accelerating that of the other. That day it was a slow train and so, although half-hidden by more recent constructions, the villa had long been visible. On the western side,

3. See Montale's preface, entitled "Genova nei ricordi di un esule," to the volume *Genua urbs maritima* published by the Pubbliche Relazioni Italsider, Genoa, 1968.
4. "Un incantevole arco di rocce e di cielo." "Le cinque terre," in *Fuori di casa* (Milan: Ricciardi, 1969), p. 11.

at the top of a small flight of stairs and hidden by a pittosporum hedge, someone (mother, aunt, cousin, or nephew) used to stand and wave a handkerchief or a towel in order to greet whoever happened to be arriving, and above all to rush (if the person responded by waving back) to put the "gnocchi" in the pot. The guest in question would then arrive, duly tired and hungry, within six or seven minutes. Five hours of train and smoke!

Montale did not receive a university education. His early passion was for music and he took up singing as a profession. But the death of his *maestro di canto*, Ernesto Sivori, as well as his father's desire that he should do something more practical, induced him to change his mind. Moreover, he must have realized, as he himself tells us, that "to be a singer one has really to get down to the business of singing. I had other interests. And then perhaps I wasn't stupid enough, for in order to be a good singer one has to have a mixture of talent and stupidity."[5] In "Racconto d'uno sconosciuto," Montale explains how the problem of settling upon a career remained unsolved:

in a family like ours, as a matter of course, one son, usually the youngest, was supposed to be the favorite; from him no serious occupation was expected. The youngest son of a widower, who had been in poor health since infancy, but who had nevertheless plenty of vague and indefinable ideas about extracommercial vocations, I had reached the age of fifteen, then twenty, then twenty-five without ever having taken any decision. I was snatched from home by the War. And with its aftermath came the crisis of the great revolution which was to save us from the horrors of bolshevism.

In 1917 Montale was called up for military service and sent to Parma where he met his earliest and one of his most important critics, Sergio Solmi. After the training period he went to the front at Vallarsa in Trentino. In "Valmorbia, discorrevano il tuo fondo" (*Ossi di seppia*), he reminisces about those days. At the end of the war he came back to Genoa where he remained until 1927. It was during this period that he met such literary figures as Angelo Barile, Adriano Grande (to whom he dedicated the first two editions of *Ossi di seppia*), and Camillo Sbarbaro (who is the subject of two poems in *Ossi di seppia*). In 1925 the publication of *Ossi di seppia* made him famous, but he was still without a job. He spent most of his time in libraries or in the company of friends. He also read a lot. His earliest readings were in

5. Montale's observation, quoted by Giulio Nascimbeni in his biographical study *Eugenio Montale* (Milan: Longanesi, 1969), p. 51.

Baudelaire, Mallarmè, Maurice de Guèrin, Henry James, Valéry, and such philosophers as Croce, Boutroux, and Bergson. He started contributing poems, articles, and reviews to newspapers as well as to the literary periodicals of the day: *Primo tempo, Il Baretti, L'Esame, Il Convegno, Il Quindicinale,* and *La fiera letteraria.* It was, for example, in *L'Esame* that Montale's first article "Omaggio a Italo Svevo," an article which made Svevo famous in Italy, appeared in 1925.

However, in 1927, partly in order to look for a job and partly to get away from the provincial atmosphere of Genoa, Montale set out for Florence. (He would actually have liked to live in Milan, but this desire was not to be fulfilled until some twenty years later.) In Florence he first worked for the publisher Bemporad, but after a year or so he was appointed director of the well-known literary and scientific library called Gabinetto Vieusseux. One reason he succeeded in getting this post was that he was the only candidate who was not a member of the Fascist party. In 1938, however, when fascism was in full swing, it was for precisely that reason that he had to resign from this position.[6] In 1939 his second book of poems, *Le occasioni,* was published by Einaudi. In the meantime he was writing for such famous Florentine periodicals as *Solaria, Pegaso,* and *Il Mondo.* Thus the years spent in Florence were just as important and fruitful in his career as was his later life in Milan or his earlier life in Liguria. The Monterosso period, he tells us, "was a very formative period. However, it led to the habit of introspection, which amounted to a feeling of imprisonment within the cosmos. . . . But as far as cultural development is concerned, it is the twenty years spent in Florence that have been the most important. For it was there that I discovered that there is not only sea, but also dry land: the land of culture, ideas, tradition, humanism.[7]

During his long stay in Florence, Montale wrote part of his third volume of poems, *La bufera e altro* (1956).[8] He also wrote reviews and articles for journals and translated into Italian such works as Marlowe's *Dr. Faustus,* Corneille's *Le Cid,* the three intermezzi by Cervantes, and Shakespeare's *Julius Caesar, Hamlet, The Comedy of Errors, The Winter's Tale,* and *Timon of Athens.* Some of Montale's best-known poems, for instance "Ballata scritta in una clinica," as well as some of the prose pieces in *Farfalla di Dinard* refer to

6. The story "Il colpevole" by Montale (originally published in the Triestine periodical *Ponte rosso* in 1847 and now included, both in the later Mondadoi editions of *Farfalla di Dinard* and in the English and American editions of my English translation, *The Butterfly of Dinard*) is indirectly autobiographical.

7. Quoted by Nascimbeni, *Eugenio Montale,* p. 31.

8. The poems that Montale wrote between 1940 and 1942 were published in Lugano in 1943 under the title *Finisterre.*

his Florentine period before and during the war. He had also started writing for *Corriere della sera* in 1946, although it was only in 1948 that he got a permanent job on its editorial staff. This was due to a particular circumstance.

On 30 January 1948, Montale happened to be in Milan and went to see the editor of *Corriere della sera,* Guglielmo Emanuel. The editor was apparently worried. He had received the news of Gandhi's assassination but had nobody on hand who could do a piece on him for the paper. He asked Montale if he would try. Montale agreed, and within two hours the article was ready. Next day it came out anonymously, entitled "Missione interrotta." Montale not only paid tribute to Gandhi ("Gandhi will remain among the greatest spirits of our age, one of the most difficult to study and an example of inimitable moral greatness") but also to England:

> To Gandhi's doctrine of "nonresistance" to violence, to the spiritual position which he created, one could almost say invented, namely, that of passive disobedience, England opposed, in a conflict that moved the whole world, a force of moral persuasion that was at times worthy of its antagonist.[9]

The editor was so impressed by this article, which is indeed one of the best examples of Montale's journalism, that he offered him a permanent post with *Corriere della sera.* As a result Montale moved to Milan where he has lived ever since. From 1955 to 1967 he also worked as a music critic for *Corriere d'informazione,* the evening edition of *Corriere della sera.* He has been awarded the honorary degree of Doctor of Letters by the universities of Rome, Milan, and Cambridge, and in 1967 Giuseppe Saragat, the then president of Italy, made him a senator for life.

As to his literary background, Montale himself has furnished all the essential data pertaining to his development as a poet and the literary influences and affinities that may have molded his poetry in "Intenzioni: intervista immaginaria." [10] Regarding his early attitude to poetry, for instance, he tells us that he was

> never particularly fond of poetry, nor had I any desire to "specialize" in that field. In those days hardly anybody seemed to be interested in poetry. The latest success that I remember having heard about was Gozzano, but the influential critics spoke ill of him, and I too (quite wrongly)

9. "Missione interrotta," *Corriere della sera,* January 31, 1948.
10. This imaginary interview originally appeared in *Rassegna d'Italia* in January 1946, and was later included in *Poesia italiana contemporanea,* ed. G. Spagnoletti (Parma: Guanda, 1961) to serve as a preface to the selection of Montale's poems in this anthology.

was of their opinion. The most important literary men of the day, who collaborated with the periodical *La Ronda,* thought that from then on poetry should be written in prose. I remember having published my earliest poems in *Primo Tempo,* edited by Debenedetti, and that my friends' attitude toward me was rather ironic. Those friends were completely engrossed in politics and were more or less antifascist. Gobetti himself, who published my first book of poems in 1925, was not very happy with a political article of mine which I had submitted to his periodical, *Rivoluzione liberale.* He, too, thought that a poet can't and mustn't have anything to do with politics. He was wrong. Moreover, I wasn't even sure that I was a poet.

Nor does Montale believe that a poet is superior to any other man who really lives his life:

> poetry is only one of the many positive activities of life. I don't think a poet is superior to anybody else who really lives, or that he is anyone in particular. In my time I got a smattering of psychoanalysis. . . . I soon came to see for myself that art is a form of life for those who do not really live: a compensation or a substitute. This doesn't, however, justify any deliberate *turris eburnea:* a poet needn't renounce life. It is life that makes a point of escaping him.[11]

Montale's interest in poetry developed side by side with his interest in painting and music. However, it was poetry that increasingly dominated his interests. He gives us a valuable insight into the nature of the kind of poetry at which he tried from the very outset to excell:

> I was aware even then of the distinction between poetry and description; but at the same time I knew that poetry cannot function in a vacuum and that one cannot achieve concentration except in the wake of diffusion, by which of course I don't mean dissipation. A poet mustn't spoil his voice by sol-faing too much, mustn't lose that timbre which he will never find again. He needn't write a series of poems when a single one can exhaust a particular psychological situation or occasion. . . . I do not mean that a poet cannot or should not train himself in his *métier* as such, but the best training is the inner one, consisting of reading and introspection. All sorts of reading, not simply poetry. There is no need for him to spend his time reading others' poetry, but at the same time it is inconceivable that he should be unaware of what has already been achieved in his art from the technical point of view.[12]

11. Ibid., pp. 341–42.
12. Ibid., p. 343.

As to the relationship between prose and poetry, Montale thinks that prose is "the great seedbed of every poetic invention," and that at one time "everything was expressed in verse, and these verses seemed, and at times were, poetry. Today only certain things are expressed in verse." Poetry is increasingly becoming "more a means of knowledge than of representation." To the extent to which Montale himself has written poetry that is rich in philosophical and metaphysical as well as symbolic undertones, what he says about the nature of poetic truth is both relevant and characteristic. The poet's need, he tells us,

> is the search for a precise truth, not for the general truth. In other words, truth about the poet-subject that does not sacrifice the truth about the empirical man-subject. A poet may well sing about that which unites man to other men, but he should not deny that which distinguishes and differentiates him from others and renders him unique and unrepeatable.[13]

This is something quite different from what is generally understood by philosophical poetry, namely, poetry "that propagates ideas" and for which Montale didn't have much use.[14] Nor did he have much use for what was commonly understood in Italy as "pure poetry." Or rather he had his own opinion of what pure poetry ought to be like and what some of his own poems aptly illustrate. Pure poetry, he tells us, doesn't mean

> a play of sonorous suggestions; but rather a fruit that must contain its motifs without revealing them, or better still without blurting them out. Conceding that in art there exists a balance between the internal and the external, between the occasion and the resultant work, what was needed was to express the object and to say nothing about the stimulus for the occasion. A new way, as distinguished from the Parnassian, of immersing the reader *in medias res,* a total merging of the intentions with the objective results. Even here I was guided by instinct, and not by any theory (I don't think that the Eliotian theory of the "objective correlative" yet existed in 1928 when my *Arsenio* appeared in *Criterion*).[15]

As to his own mode of writing poetry, Montale has the same attitude to it as Leopardi had. "I have written very few and very short poems," Leopardi wrote in a letter to Giuseppe Melchiorri:

13. Ibid., p. 344.
14. However, of some of the poems in *Satura*—for instance, "La storia," "A un gesuita moderno," "Fanfara," and "Realismo non magico"—one can say that they do "propagate ideas" and that their value as poetry is consequently limited.
15. "Intenzioni: intervista immaginaria," p. 346. As to Eliot's theory of the "objective correlative" existing in 1928 or not, perhaps what Montale means is that at that time it was not yet known in Italy. Eliot, however, discussed it in his essay "Hamlet and His Problems" (1919), which appeared in *The Sacred Wood* (1920).

In writing them I have followed nothing but a certain inspiration (or
frenzy), in the wake of which I can form the outline and distribution
of the whole composition in two minutes. Having done this, I always
wait for another moment. When it comes (which ordinarily does not
happen except after a period of a few months), I sit down to compose,
but so slowly that it is not possible for me to finish a poem, however
short it may be, in less than two or three weeks. This is my method, and
if inspiration does not come of its own accord, it would be easier for
water to issue out of a tree-trunk than a single line of verse to come out
of my head.[16]

And this is how Montale describes his method:

I do not go in search of poetry; I wait for poetry to visit me. I write
little and with few revisions when it seems to me that I cannot do without
them. If even then one cannot avoid rhetoric, it means that it is, at least
for me, indispensable.[17]

But creative inspiration in Montale, as in all major artists, coexists with a
critical awareness of moral and intellectual pressures and challenges which
constitute, as it were, a sort of deterministic force. An artist, Montale tells
us, "is a man who works by necessity; he does not have a free choice. In this
field, more than in any other, there exists an effective determinism. I have
followed the way imposed upon me by my times; tomorrow others will
follow different ways; I myself may change." [18]

All in all, "Intenzioni: intervista immaginaria" may be regarded as a
résumé of Montale's poetics—a résumé to which can be added some of his
more pregnant critical pronouncements on other poets and writers. Among the
classic Italian writers Dante has been cited more often than any other poet as
having been a vital influence on Montale. Other influences are Leopardi,
Pascoli, D'Annunzio, Sbarbaro, Govoni, Boine, and Ceccardi. Among foreign
poets one could mention Eliot and Pound as being more obvious influences
on Montale than any other comparable major poet.

As to Dante's influence on Montale, one can to some extent compare it
with the sort of influence that Eliot acknowledged and analyzed in his own
verse with regard to Dante. In his lecture "What Dante Means to Me" [19]

---

16. *Le Lettere* of Giacomo Leopardi, ed. Francesco Flora (Milan: Mondadori, 1949), pp.
477–78.
17. "Intenzioni: intervista immaginaria," p. 347.
18. Ibid., p. 348.
19. A talk given by Eliot at the Italian Institute, London, on July 4, 1950, and now
included in *To Criticize the Critic* (London: Faber & Faber, 1965), pp. 125–35.

Eliot describes how he tried to imitate Dante (in *Little Gidding*) and to achieve some of the essential characteristics of Dante's art and style, namely the "very bare and austere style, in which every word has to be 'functional' " and from which the slightest degree of vagueness or imprecision has to be purged,—the absolute spareness and directness of Dante's language, in which every single line or word is "completely disciplined to the purpose of the whole," so that "no poet convinces one more completely that the word he has used is the word he wanted, and that no other will do." [20] Eliot then proceeds to evaluate what he admires most in Dante. First of all he is impressed by the fact that "of the very few poets of similar stature . . . none, not even Virgil . . . has been a more attentive student of the *art* of poetry, or a more scrupulous, painstaking, and *conscious* practitioner of the craft" than Dante. Then there is Dante's "lesson of width of emotional range." And lastly, it is the fact that Dante has passed on to posterity his own language in a "more highly developed, more refined, and more precise" form than it was before he wrote, which itself constitutes "the highest possible achievement of the poet as poet." [21]

Now in respect of all these qualities Montale himself seems to have come closer to Dante than any other Italian poet of the twentieth century, although he hasn't, like Eliot, consciously tried to imitate him. As he himself tells us, he did not write with *The Divine Comedy* lying open at his side,[22] although the very effort on his part to attain those qualities and characteristics which Eliot associates with and admires in Dante's poetry brought out, significantly enough, his own characteristic originality of style and diction. Montale's use of Dante's vocabulary, style, and imagery not only fitted well with his own aim of achieving the vividness, spareness, and concreteness of an antieloquent diction, but it also served to focus the radical difference between Dante's sensibility and his own. And this difference is no less felt even when Montale is trying, like Dante, to blend the physical and the transcendental, and to postulate the theme of spiritual and moral salvation in terms of love which is both human and divine. All this, however, is not a matter of mere borrowing or adaptation from Dante. For, if while deliberately using a distinctly Dantesque word or phrase, Montale succeeds in making it do something quite different, it is because his thought and sensibility, his mode of analyzing and assessing his own experience, and the nature of his explorations into reality are as profoundly different from Dante's as they are characteristically

20. Ibid.
21. Ibid.
22. Quoted by T. Comello in "Dante e Montale," *Dimensioni,* Pescara, nos. 5–6 (1961), pp. 13–19.

modern. In a word, whatever Montale takes from Dante becomes a challenge for him—a challenge through which to assert his own individuality.

Petrarch's influence, too, has been a significant factor in the development of the lyric tradition of nineteenth- and twentieth-century Italian poetry, including Montale's. However, both on the stylistic and the linguistic levels, Petrarch has made a less significant impact on Montale's poetry than on the work of such poets as Leopardi, Saba and Ungaretti, for example. In fact, by virtue of his avowed aim which, while echoing Verlaine ("Art poetique") he defines as being that of wringing the neck of "our courtly language," Montale represents as antithetical a position to Petrarch as, for example, Donne does to Spenser, or Hopkins to Tennyson, substituting prosaic ruggedness and essentiality of diction for Petrarch's elegance and smoothness. Nevertheless, in spite of the linguistic and stylistic barriers between them, what brings Montale close to Petrarch is the mode and direction that his sensibility takes while dealing with the theme of love and exploiting the psychological and emotional situations it involves. Thus while recollecting the various features, episodes, and aspects of the woman loved—a woman separated from him either by death or distance—Montale idealizes her more or less along Petrarchan lines. And this is what he means when he refers to his "Petrarchan experience" as embodied in the *Finisterre* poems.[23] However, this experience is often expressed in terms of style, diction, and imagery that are characteristically un-Petrarchan or even anti-Petrarchan.

The poet to whom Montale is even closer than to Petrarch, and in quite a different way, is Leopardi. The verbal echoes and reminiscences from Leopardi in Montale's poetry are something more than mere echoes and reminiscences. They represent Montale's awareness of the immediacy and complexity of the relevance that the *Canti* have had to the development of modern Italian poetry, especially in the wake of the impetus provided by the periodical *La Ronda*.[24] Montale's own laconic comment apropos the significance of Leopardi is revealing. "After Leopardi," he tells us, "it was almost impossible to write poetry during the rest of the century." [25] To take poetry beyond the stage where Leopardi had left off and at the same time to do something conspicuously different from what had been done by Pascoli,

23. In "Intenzioni: intervista immaginaria," p. 347.

24. *La Ronda* (1919–23) was the most important and influential periodical of its time and was edited by Vincenzo Cardarelli, Emilio Cecchi, and Riccardo Bacchelli, who were also among its most important contributors. Its aim was to renovate Italian literature through a fuller consciousness of, and inspiration derived from, tradition and to merge the spirit of modernity with that of classicism. Perhaps the most important influence on the ethos of this periodical was Leopardi, especially as a prose writer.

25. Domenico Porzio, "Dialogo con Montale sulla poesia," *Quaderni Milanesi* (Milan, Autumn 1960).

D'Annunzio, and Gozzano was a formidable challenge, and Montale acquitted himself impressively in meeting it.

In "Intenzioni: intervista immaginaria" Montale again mentions Leopardi as presenting, in some of his earlier "idylls," that kind of contrast or dualism which was to be a characteristic of his own poetry; the contrast, that is to say, between "lyricism and commentary, between poetry and the preparation or stimulus for poetry." Together with the awareness of the nature and significance of Leopardi's poetry, which had been so eloquently and passionately proclaimed by *La Ronda* and especially by one of its founders, Cardarelli, at a time when Montale was at the most formative stage of his poetic development, there are the Leopardian echoes, reminiscences, and tones in Montale's poetry—especially in *Ossi di seppia*—which constitute both a semantic and a conceptual basis for an affinity between Leopardi and Montale. In his essay "Montale e Leopardi"[26] Filippo Donini lists some of these echoes and reminiscences, to which even more could be added.[27] The link between such verbal echoes and conceptual affinity bcomes more evident —and is indeed stronger—when Montale is dealing with "the evil of living," or with such themes as human destiny, the sense of philosophical or metaphysical determinism, and moral and historical pessimism. In other words, it is that aspect of Leopardi's perennial modernity which is firmly rooted in a moral, philosophical, and metaphysical view of life, which could not but have appealed to a poet like Montale. Hence, despite his avowed predilection for

---

26. In *La Cultura*, no. 3 (1963), pp. 328–31.

27. For instance, compare "la carriera / del sole e la mia, breve" ("Fuscello teso dal muro") and "ove tende / Questo vagar mio breve" ("Canto notturno di un pastore errante dell'Asia"); "che il tuo cuore disumano / ci spaura" ("Giunge a volte") and "ove per poco / il cuor non si spaura" ("L'Infinito"); "Questo pezzo di suolo non erbato" ("Giunge a volte") and "questo arido suolo" ("Alla sua donna"); "un discendere / fino al vallo estremo, / nel buio" ("Noi non sappiamo") and "Abisso orrido, immenso, / ov'ei precipitando, il tutto obblia" ("Canto notturno di un pastore errante dell'Asia"); "la vita è questo scialo / di triti fatti, vano / più che crudele" or "la vita è crudel più che vana" ("Flussi") and "veder che tutto è vano altro che il duolo" ("Ad Angelo Mai"); "il tempo precipita" ("Flussi") or "ecco precipita / il tempo" ("Crisalide") and "In peggio / precipitano i tempi" ("Bruto minore"); "e poi non restano / neppure le nostre orme sulla polvere" ("Crisalide") and "A pensar come tutto al monda passa, / E quasi orma non lascia" ("La sera del dì di festa"); "ch'io scenda senza viltà" ("Incontro") and "Non io / con tal vergogna scenderò sotterra" ("La ginestra"); "le campane / d'argento sopra il borgo" ("Carnevale di Gerti") and "Viene il vento recando il suon dell'ora / Dalla torre del borgo" ("Per ricordanze"); "Ricerco invano il punto onde si mosse / il sangue" ("Stanze") and "Per tornar sempre là donde son mosse" ("Canto notturno di un pastore errante dell'Asia"); "Tutto è uguale" ("Costa San Giorgio") and "Tutto è simile" ("Ad Angelo Mai"); "il dio / del caso" ("Nuove stanze") and "cieco / Dispensator de'casi" ("Ultimo Canto di Saffo"); "alluccioliò / della galassia, la fascia d'ogni tormento" ("Notizie dall'Amiata") and "A noi le fasce / Cinse il fastidio" ("Ad Angelo Mai"); "crudi / noviluni annebbiati" ("Personae separatae") and "il crudo sol" ("Io qui vagando"), etc.

Foscolo as opposed to Leopardi, there are closer verbal, thematic, and conceptual links between Montale and Leopardi than between Montale and any other poet after Dante.

It is when we come to the twentieth-century poets Pascoli, D'Annunzio, Sbarbaro, Govoni, Boine, Campana, and Cardarelli that it becomes all the more difficult to sift conscious or unconscious verbal echoes and reminiscences from direct or indirect influence.

Pascoli is generally credited with having initiated the process of renewing poetic diction; with having introduced into Italian poetry the element of the particular as opposed to the general, the vague, and the indeterminate; and above all with having created what is called "the poetry of objects" with its naturalistic and symbolic undertones. To the extent to which Montale's own poetry shares these characteristics, although operating and developing them in a more personal and complex manner, he may be said to have something in common with, if not to have been actually influenced by, Pascoli. However, it is not so much what Montale and Pascoli have in common as what they differ about that brings out the essential originality of Montale's art. Even so, whatever is characteristically Montalian is itself rooted in the soil prepared by Pascoli, D'Annunzio, and Gozzano. Critics like De Robertis, Contini, and Bonfiglioli [28] have, for instance, drawn attention to the verbal, metrical, and imagistic similarities between Pascoli and Montale—similarities that form an integral part of Montale's linguistic and poetic realism. However, one should draw a sharp distinction, as indeed Bonfiglioli does, between what Montale could find in Pascoli and what he could discover only in himself. And the difference can be summed up in Montale's own words. While criticizing Pascoli for the fact that "rarely does one of his poems become something detached, something that can live on its own," [29] Montale indirectly hints at what his own poetic mode and technique aim to do and what in his best poems he does succeed in doing. Thus what he achieves in these poems differs conspicuously from Pascoli's achievement in spite of his use of some typically Pascolian words and images.

More or less the same applies to what Montale consciously or unconsciously borrowed or learnt from D'Annunzio, especially in the field of linguistic and prosodic innovations and experiments, as Montale himself is the first to admit. D'Annunzio, he tells us, "has experimented or touched upon all the linguistic and prosodic possibilities of our time . . . not to have learnt anything from

28. See Bibliography.
29. In his article "La fortuna del Pascoli," *Corriere della sera,* November 30, 1955. See also chapter 7. For echoes from Pascoli as well as D'Annunzio, see Pier Vincenzo Mengaldo's essay "Da D'Annunzio a Montale," in *Ricerche sulla lingua poetica contemporanea,* Padua, 1966.

him would be a very bad sign." [30] The most exhaustive treatment of the connection between D'Annunzio and Montale is to be found in Pier Vincenzo Mengaldo's essay "Da D'Annunzio a Montale," which incidently also examines echoes and reminiscences in Montale's poetry from poets like Sbarbaro, Govoni, Gozzano, and Corazzini.[31] However, these echoes and reminiscences, far from detracting from the originality of Montale's poetry, simply attest to a critically perceptive awareness on his part of the cultural milieu in which he grew and developed as a poet. Without this awareness, which entailed his being fully alive to the poetic tradition in Italy from Dante to D'Annunzio, and without his sure and discriminating grasp of what he could profitably borrow from that tradition and what he couldn't, it is doubtful that Montale would have made the mark he did on his epoch, still less have achieved that distinction and status of a classic poet which is undoubtedly his.

However, Montale himself observes that "there is no need for a poet to spend his time reading others' poetry, but at the same time it is inconceivable that he should be unaware of what has been achieved in his art from the technical point of view." [32] And this last is precisely what Montale has done. Thus he learnt from Gozzano—who had undergone many literary influences, having been "a D'Annunzian at the age of twenty and even later," and having subsequently prayed God in verses "that he might be delivered from the pestilence of D'Annunzianism"—how to "give sparkle to the language by juxtaposing the courtly and the prosaic," and how to write poetry that is also prose, which, as Montale points out, "has been the dream of every modern poet from Browning on." [33] He learnt from Cardarelli to value the quality of low

---

30. Quoted by Pier Vincenzo Mengaldo in "Da D'Annunzio a Montale," p. 181.
31. Ibid.
32. "Intenzioni: intervista immaginaria," p. 343.
33. See Montale's introductory essay on Gozzano in *Le poesie di Guido Gozzano* (Milan: Garzanti, 1960) and also chapter 7. Apart from Gozzano and Browning, and to a far greater and more revolutionary extent, it is Pound who both used colloquial as well as prose style in his poetry. He expatiated upon its significance and utility in modern poetry as early as 1914, in his essay on Ford Madox Ford entitled "The Prose Tradition in Verse" (*Literary Essays,* ed. T. S. Eliot [London: Faber & Faber, 1954], pp. 371–77). One can find in Montale's poetry, including *Xenia* and *Satura,* traces of Pounds's colloquial style, idiom, and inflexion—or at least traces of close affinity with them. Compare, for instance, such lines as "uomo intento che riguarda / in sè, in altrui il bollore / della vita fugace" ("Avrei voluto sentirmi") and "Eternal watcher of things, / of men, of passions" (Canto 7); "un filtro / fa spogli suoni" ("Carnevale di Gerti") and "or only the husk of talk" (Canto 7); "è linfa che disegna le tue mani, / ti batte ai polsi inavvertita e il volto / t'infiamma o doscolora" ("Stanze") and "The tree has entered my hands, / The sap has ascended my arms, / The tree has grown in my breast" ("A Girl," *Personae*); "fili su cui s'impligli / il fiocco della vita s'incollani / in ore e in anni" ("Su una lettera non scritta") and "But you never string two days upon one wire" ("Au Jardin," *Personae*); "Visse ancora

tone and prosaic verse and the intensity of reflection which "burns away the prosaic basis and nourishes that hammering repetitiveness, the monologue which is rightly called dramatic." [34] From Campana he was to learn the importance of the synthesis between artistic control and spontaneity, which Campana himself could achieve only in his prose. A poet like Sbarbaro was to teach him the significance of what is exemplified in his best poetry: the almost physical weight of the metaphysical sense of melancholy and solitude coupled with a sense of determinism which he accepts with virile stoicism and aristocratic reserve. By virtue of these qualities as well as the vivid concreteness with which he describes the Ligurian landscape, Sbarbaro comes closer to Montale than has been recognized. Montale himself was to praise Sbarbaro's

---

qualche anno e morendo due volte / ebbe il tempo di leggere le sue necrologie" ("Il Farfarella garrulo portiere," *Satura*) and "Metevsky died and was buried, i.e. officially, / And sat in the Yeiner Kafé watching the funeral" (Canto 18); "le luci erano a tratti / scancellate dal crescere dell'onde / invisibili al fondo della notte" ("Vecchi versi") and "From the long boats they have set lights in the water, / The sea's claw gathers them outward" (Canto 47); "l'ombra non ha più peso della tua" ("Voce giunta con le folaghe") and "Thy weight less than the shadow" (Canto 47).

Similarly, there are many affinities and correspondences between Eliot and Montale. For instances, compare "il punto morto del mondo" ("I limoni") and "the still point of the turning world" ("Burnt Norton," *Four Quartets*); "il falco alto levato" ("Spesso il male di vivere") and "The Eagle soars in the summit of Heaven" (*Choruses from the Rock*, I); "bruciare, / questo, non altro, é il mio significato" ("Dissipa tu se lo vuoi") and "But a life-time burning in every moment" ("East Coker," *Four Quartets*); "e ritorna / ad ogni accordo che esprima / l'armonia guasta" ("Dora Markus," II) and "the voice returns like the insistent out-of-tune / of a broken violin" ("Portrait of a Lady"); "è linfa che disegna le tue mani, / ti batte ai polsi inavvertita e il volto / t'infiamma e discolora" ("Stanze") and "The dance along the artery / The circulation of the lymph / Are figured in the drift of stars / Ascend to summer in the tree" ("Burnt Norton," *Four Quartets*); "crolli di altane e di ponti" ("Ballata scritta in una clinica") and "the city over the mountains / Cracks and reforms and bursts in the violet air / Falling towers" or "London Bridge is falling down falling down falling down" ("What the Thunder Said," *The Waste Land*); "Le parole / se si ridestano / rifiutano la sede / più propizia, la carta / di Fabriano, l'inchiostro / di china, la cartella / di cuoio o di velluto / che le tenga in segreto" ("Le parole") and "Words strain, / Crack and sometimes break, under the burden, / Under the tension, slip, slide, perish, / Decay with imprecision, will not stay in place, / Will not stay still" ("Burnt Norton," *Four Quartets*).

34. See Montale's essay on Cardarelli in *Corriere della sera*, June 16, 1959, and also chapter 7. There are some echoes from Cardarelli in Montale's poetry. For instance, compare "La mia malinconia / di fanciullo invecchiato che non doveva pensare" (Potessi almeno costringere") and "Un fanciullo / che si duole di essere cresciuto" ("Adolescente"); "Tutto ignoro di te fuor del messaggio / muto che mi sostenta sulla via" ("Delta") and "Poi più nulla di te, fuorchè il tuo spettro, / assiduo compagno, il tuo silenzio / pauroso come un pozzo senza fondo" ("Crudele addio"); "Se parlo ascolto quella voce attonito, / scendere alla sua gamma più remota / o spenta all'aria che non la sostiene" ("Due nel crepuscolo") and "e tutto il mio passato / mi frana addosso. / Inorridisco al suono / della mia voce" ("Partenza mattutina"); "questo mare / infinito di creta e di mondiglia" ("Proda di Versilia") and "questo fango che non ha mai fine" ("Non basta morire").

"landscapes full of music and color" and to note how Sbarbaro "has a center, a vein of his own and that he can therefore write entire pages—something quite rare nowadays—which, even if they seem to be externally fragmentary, are in fact governed and animated by an emotional consistency." [35] Montale, Anceschi points out in his introduction to the anthology *Lirica del Novecento*, (edited by him and Sergio Antonielli), "recovers a material that was dear to Sbarbaro, but he exalts it by dint of moral and artistic force, augments the authority of the verse, and strengthens the element of subjectivity." [36] This is indeed a fair summing-up of what Sbarbaro's poetry meant to Montale and what he made of it in his own writing.

Critics have also noted verbal echoes and reminiscences from Corrado Govoni in Montale's poetry.[37] One can say that at least during the initial stages of his poetic formation Montale had read Govoni, especially the group of poems entitled *Armonia in grigio et in silenzio* (1903) and *L'Inaugurazione della primavera* (1915). Images and impressionistic evocations such as "stagnant water / with a worn-out bark" ("La strada è tutta erbosa"), "The trees seem convulsed / in the gardens and avenues" ("Temporale estivo"), "Among the leaves one hears the crackle / of the sleigh-bells of a robin" ("Patina di bronzo"), or "The wind combs its ruffled hair / with the poplars' long combs" ("La siesta del micio") may have served Montale as poetic tips on the basis of which he was to achieve an altogether different effect through the same notation of natural phenomena and to show a greater degree of incisiveness and evocative richness than Govoni had done. In his obituary article on the latter, Montale referred to his "explosive naturalism," in which the "most extraordinary images are only just held together by means of an imperceptible thread" and form "poetic carpets that are unrivaled in any literature." [38]

35. See Montale's essay on Sbarbaro, which serves as an introduction to *"Il Nostro" e nuove gocce*, ed. Vanni Scheiwiller (Milan: All'Insegna del Pesce d'Oro, 1964). It had originally appeared as a review of Sbarbaro's *Trucioli* in *L'azione* (Genoa), November 10, 1970, and is one of Montale's earliest critical pieces. See also Montale's article "Ricordo di Sbarbaro," *Corriere della sera*, November 5, 1967. The following are among possible echoes from Sbarbaro. Compare "Piove in petto una dolcezza inquieta" ("I limoni") and "Pioveva dalle cose indistinte intorno una dolcezza che mi strangolava" (*Trucioli*, 1914–18, l. 8); "in questa valle / non è vicenda di buio e di luce" ("Dove se ne vanno") and "La vicenda di gioia e di dolore" (*Pianissimo* I); "la patria sognata" ("Ho sostato talvolta nelle grotte") and "trasognato paese" ("Versi a Dina").

36. See *Lirica del Novecento* (Florence: Vallecchi, 1963).

37. See Mengaldo, "Da D'Annunzio a Montale," and Sergio Solmi, *Scrittori negli anni* (Milan: Il Saggiatore, 1963), p. 285.

38. See Montale's article on Govoni in *Corriere della sera*, October 22, 1965. Other echoes from Govoni in Montale's poetry are: "specchio annerito che ti vide / diversa una storia di errori / imperturbati" and "sguardi / di uomini che hanno fedine altere e deboli in grandi / ritratti d'oro" ("Dora Markus"); cf. "I ritratti che sanno tante storie / sono disposti a ventaglio di memorie" ("Crepuscolo ferrarese"); "La banderuola / affumicata gira senza

However, of all the Ligurian poets it is Giovanni Boine who comes closest to anticipating in a significant way some aspects of the style and ethos of Montale's poetry, even though he himself was not really a poet. From the literary and creative point of view *Frantumi* is his most important book, consisting of prose pieces with a philosophical lyricism and poetic intuitionalism. The affinity between Boine and Montale lies in the fact that they both render their thoughts, perceptions, and intuitions, however subtle and profound they may be, into a language that is at once concrete and figurative, picturesque and speculative, metaphorical and metaphysical. Hence there are in Montale's poetry a number of echoes from, and correspondences or affinities with, Boine.[39]

And yet despite all these echoes, reminiscences, and affinities, there are two ways in which Montale's poetry distinguishes itself from that of his contemporaries: it combines the expressive liberty of an Ungaretti or a Campana with a disciplined self-control that has nothing to do with the reactionary neoclassicism of *La Ronda*. There is something eclectic about the way Montale makes use of the linguistic and metrical ground prepared for him by the innovations and experiments of Pascoli and D'Annunzio as well as about his way of reacting against the excesses of D'Annunzianism or Pascolism with a view to carving out his own poetic idiom and line of development. The fact remains, however, that Montale's linguistic, technical, and prosodic innovations are more constructive than revolutionary and are dictated by an inner creative need as much as by historical and technical exigencies.

Another way in which Montale's poetry distinguishes itself is through a

---

pietà" ("La casa dei doganieri"); cf. "Solo una ventarola / arrugginata / in alto sulla torre silenziosa / che gira, gira interminatamente" ("Villa chiusa"); la bufera che sgronda sulle foglie" ("La bufera"); cf. "Come, nel sgocciare della gronda, / c'è tutto lo spavento della bufera" ("La trombettina"); "Stende a terra una coltre su cui scricchia / come su zucchero il piede" ("La primavera hitleriana"); cf. "Scricchiolano sotto i piedi / i piccoli obici delle ghiande" ("Poesie elettriche"); "questo lembo / di terra solitario" ("In limine"); cf. "città morta / perduta in una solitaria landa" ("La città morta"); "trema un ricordo nel ricolmo secchio" ("Cigola la carrucola del pozzo"); cf. "Gocce d'acqua che cadono / del colmo secchio in fondo al pozzo" ("La città morta").

39. Compare, for instance, Montale's "un'aria di vetro / arida" ("Forse un mattino andando") or "etra vetrino" ("Egloga") with "pungente ghiaccio dell'aria" ("Resoconto dell'escursione"); "e me n'andrò zitto / tra gli uomini che non si voltano" ("Forse un mattino andando") and "uomini che tengano la loro diritta e non badino in giro" ("Resoconto dell'escursione"); "il buio è rotto a squarci" ("Lungomare") and "tagliano il mio buio rasoiate di luce" ("Resoconto dell'escursione"); "dove il secolo è il minuto" ("Il sogno del prigioniero") and "s'allentano in secoli gli attimi" ("Deliri"); "Ed io riverso / nel potere che grava attorno" ("Due nel crepuscolo") and "In questa apocalittica morgue, inerte sprofondo come in inghiottente pantano" ("Deliri"); "immoto andare" ("Arsenio") and "immobile scivolo nell'immobilità" ("Frantumi"); "quella / eternità d'istante" ("La bufera") and "Ma l'eterno fu un attimo" ("Frammenti"), and so on.

sense of unfaltering poise and self-assurance, both moral and artistic, which informs it from first to last and which is not at all a matter of literary influences. This confidence is something inborn and reveals itself through Montale's probing into the nature of his own experience as well as the essence of things in general. Hence there is a rich metaphysical vein in his poetry and a substantial body of what Matthew Arnold called a "criticism of life." This criticism has an impressive degree of sobriety and profundity which Montale achieves by forging a link between the moral and the metaphysical elements in his experience. It is by virtue of this link that he succeeds in fusing intuitions and observations, images and concepts, objects and symbols.

As to his sense of contemporaneity and the *Zeitgeist*, Montale does not exploit it without subjecting it to rigorous moral criteria. In other words, his creative instinct and his moral perceptiveness go hand in hand; he does not allow one to get the better of the other. While he interprets the political destiny of his age and country in terms of a personal and impersonal destiny, he does not indulge in any form of moral self-complacency or pride. There is a mature sense of prudence and integrity in his assessment of his conduct during the Fascist regime. What he tried to achieve is "everyday decency, the most difficult of virtues" [40]—in other words, living his life "with as little cowardice as possible in view of my weak forces" and without losing sight of the fact that "there are others who have done more, much more, even if they have not published books." [41] Elsewhere he tells us that an "ideological involvement is not a necessary, nor even a sufficient condition for the creation of a poetically vital work; nor is it in itself a negative condition." [42] Thus for Montale there has been no such gulf between ideal existence and everyday reality as there was, for instance, for a poet like Govoni.

In sum, Montale's poetry impresses us both as an artistic triumph and as a moral achievement; and it does so with a firmness and consistency, a modesty and sureness, that betray a high degree of self-knowledge and self-confidence on his part, as well as a profound awareness of the literary and cultural forces and movements around him. Hermetism, futurism, crepuscularism, as well as the impact that such influential periodicals as *La Voce, Solaria,* and *La Ronda* made on the literary scene in the early decades of this century, all had a vital significance for Montale during the early stages of his poetic development—a significance that he both assimilated and transcended in order to realize his own genius.

---

40. In his prose piece "Visita a Fadin," *La Bufera e altro.*
41. "Intenzioni: intervista immaginaria," p. 348.
42. See Montale's answers to "Sette domande sulla poesia," in *Nuovi argomenti,* nos. 55–56 (March–June, 1962), pp. 42–46.

2: *Ossi di seppia*

The most conspicuous characteristic of *Ossi di seppia* is its strikingly uniform level of maturity—a maturity that does not depend on, and cannot therefore be explained in terms of, the stages of development one can often trace in the works and careers of other poets. In other words, insofar as the degree of maturity—moral, psychological, and artistic—is concerned, most of the poems in *Ossi di seppia, Le occasioni* (1939), and *La bufera e altro* (1956) might, in a way, have been written in the same period. Montale illustrates not only the fact that poets are born, but also that some are born mature rather than acquiring maturity gradually. Even when there is a question of technical progress or divergency of style and tone between one volume and another or between one poem and another, the sense of a mature intelligence and sensibility, manifest above all in the language, always impresses us firmly and convincingly. Moreover, that crystalline hardness and precision which one associates with Montale's poetic diction is not so much the result of the influence of other poets as the outcome of his own artistic and technical originality.

Ossi di seppia—the title is reminiscent of D'Annunzio's line "gli ossi delle seppie" in "Il Novilunio" (*Alcyone*)—sets a pattern wherein personal and autobiographical as well as impersonal and philosophical elements are closely interwoven. The note of personal lyricism—love, affection, recollection of the past, memory, search for a personal identity, rapt contemplation of his native Ligurian landscape and especially of the sea that was to haunt Montale "like a passion" all his life—is almost always accompanied by a sharp awareness of the dilemmas and predicaments of his age and country. In poems like "Non chiederci la parola," "Mia vita, a te non chiedo lineamenti," "Ciò che di me sapeste," and "Arsenio," the note of tactiturn stoicism is indicative of the moral and political repression that was felt in Fascist Italy; and so to some extent are Montale's poetic diction and style.

Hence *Ossi di seppia*, no less than his later poetry, can be regarded as an effective commentary on the spirit of Montale's age. And the poems that convey this commentary or "criticism of life" most incisively are those which are rooted in the intimacy of personal experience and feeling. It reveals Montale's originality and at the same time sums up the spirit of the age. It is thus both representative and unique, and made the impact it did because it was symptomatic of the stresses and challenges of the times. In his "Intenzioni: intervista immaginaria," Montale himself has observed that "an artist is a man who works by necessity; not by free choice." [1] Thus a sense of historical as well as metaphysical determinism, a determinism that is evident even in the choice and collocation of words, weighs upon Montale's world as presented in *Ossi di seppia*. Political and metaphysical forebodings and uncertainties merge with a concern for personal identity and determine the search for a pattern or significance underlying the poet's observation of the landscape, his recollection of the past, and his "critical corrosion of existence." [2]

Ossi di seppia opens with "In limine,' which has a prefatory as well as a dedicatory significance. It is addressed to the woman loved, an imaginary interlocutor, or to the poet's alter ego—or to all three rolled into one. And it outlines the moral and philosophical motifs and intentions as well as illustrating the technical devices which characterize *Ossi di seppia*. The typically Montalian landscape is outlined with dynamic vividness, and such impressionistic details as "the wind that enters the apple orchard [il vento ch'entra nel pomario]," "the whir that you hear [il frullo che tu senti]," "this solitary strip of land [questo lembo di terra solitario]," "steep wall [erto muro]," "a broken mesh in the net [una maglia rotta nella rete]," have a subtle and unobtrusive symbolism about them. The wall is a recurrent feature in the Montalian landscape, symbolizing something predetermined, static, and unchangeable, just as the wind and water symbolize change, movement, transformation, and occasionally salvation. Montale's view of salvation is that it is both accidental and dependent on a supernatural agent: "Perhaps you run / into the phantom that saves you [t'imbatti / tu forse nel fantasma che ti salva]." The last two lines in the poem—"Go, I have prayed this for you—now / my thirst will be slaked, the rust less biting [Va per te l'ho pregato,——ora la sete / mi sarà lieve, meno acre la ruggine]"—sum up the unsentimental altruism which forms part of Montale's concept of love.

Along with "In limine," "I limoni" (1921), one of Montale's earliest poems, serves to indicate the direction his poetry was to take. It may be regarded as a

1. "Intenzioni: intervista immaginaria," p. 348.
2. Alfredo Gargiulo, in his introduction to the second edition of *Ossi di seppia* (Turin: Ribet, 1928), which is now included in *Letteratura italiana del Novecento*, new enlarged edition (Florence: Le Monnier, 1958), p. 453.

sort of poetic manifesto—Contini calls it "the dialectic of sentiments" [3]—expounding the kind of language, imagery, and rhythms that he was to use in his poetry, thereby differentiating it from the classical or crepuscular poets who "move only among plants / with unusual names [si muovono soltanto fra le piante / dai nomi poco usati]," and who always aim at achieving the effect of the sublime. Gargiulo's characterization of Montale's poetic diction as "stony" is as significant as his characterization of the ethos and spirit of his poetry as representing "the critical corrosion of existence." And yet behind the stony nature of Montale's diction, as behind the critical corrosion of existence, there is something positively vital and creative. If he manages to transform what Gargiulo calls "desperate critical material' [4] into lyric poetry, it is not merely by virtue of his firm hold on and profound feeling for things and objects, but also by his giving an almost palpable form to "what we are *not,* what we *do not* want [ciò che *non* siamo, ciò che *non* vogliamo]," [5] and to his stoicism in the face of a life that cannot be lived. It is this which accounts for the triple facets of Montale's lyricism: the elegiac, the idyllic, and the contemplative. And if Montale often adopts a prosaic tone in his poetry, it is the tone of a poet who is also a master of prose. In other words, he blends with a superb assurance and authority the cadences of prose and poetry, which many poets would consider too risky. Similarly, although Montale's aim was to "wring the neck" of the "old courtly language . . . even at the risk of counter-eloquence," [6] he himself sometimes uses courtly or literary words like *onagri* ("onagers"), *pomario* ("apple-orchard"), *atro* ("dark"), etc.

The poem describes the joy that the sight and smell—particularly the smell—of lemons brings, as well as the peace of the countryside in summer and the immensity of the deep blue sky above. But underlying this description there is a metaphysical curiosity concerning the mystery of life and a feeling of existential sadness and boredom, which are an integral part of the landscape described:

> . . . where in half-dry puddles
> boys catch slender eels; paths
> which wind along the banks, descend
> amidst cluster of reeds, then break
> suddenly into the orchards
> among the lemon trees.

3. "Introduzione a *Ossi di seppia,*" *Esercizi di lettura* (Florence: Le Monnier, 1947), p. 79.
4. *Letteratura italiana del Novecento,* p. 456.
5. "Non chiederci la parola," *Ossi di seppia.*
6. "Intenzioni: intervista immaginaria," p. 345.

> . . . dove in pozzanghere
> mezzo seccate agguantano i ragazzi
> qualche sparuta anguilla;
> le viuzze che seguono i ciglioni,
> discendono tra i ciuffi delle canne
> e mettono negli orti, tra gli alberi dei limoni.

From the observation of these details the poet's mind is drawn to the contemplation of:

> . . . a mistake of Nature's, the dead point
> of the world, the link that doesn't hold,
> the thread to unwind that may
> lead us at last into the heart of a truth.

> . . . uno sbaglio di Natura,
> il punto morto del mondo, l'anello che non tiene,
> il filo da disbrogliare che finalmente ci metta
> nel mezzo di una verità.

One unfailing source of strength in Montale's poetry is his complete mastery of the world of natural phenomena—a mastery by virtue of which he breathes life into what is lifeless, and infuses apparently prosaic or unpoetic objects with a poetic intensity. Moreover, his poetic naturalism is linked, both as a cause and a corollary, to his metaphysical insight or symbolic vision.

"Corno inglese" is one of the eight early poems Montale published in 1922 in *Primo tempo,* a Turin periodical founded and edited by Giacomo Debenedetti, Sergio Solmi, and Mario Gromo (see Appendix 1). The fact that this is the only early poem Montale included in *Ossi di seppia* shows that he thought it to be, not only the most important, but also more akin in spirit and technique to the lyrics included in that volume. His own comment is that it was "the only poem I could have taken out of the group, which I did not like, and which I don't like even now, both because of its general sense and because of its naive pretensions to imitate musical instruments."[7] The wind that plays "the instruments of thick trees, and / sweeps the copper horizon [gli strumenti dei fitti alberi e spazza / l'orizzonte di rame]" ("Corno inglese") and the livid sea that "dashes against the cliffs, / changes colors, and flings / on the shore writhing spirals of foam [che scaglia a scaglia, / livido, muta colore / lancia a terra una tromba / di schiume intorte]" make the poet wish that his heart, a "forgotten instrument [scordato strumento]," might

7. Quoted by Giuliano Manacorda, *Eugenio Montale* (Florence: La Nuova Italia), p. 24.

be used as its lyre. This is one of the very few poems in which one can detect the crepuscular vein in Montale's poetry. But even here such concrete images as "a strong shaking of blades [un forte scotere di lame]" or the "writhing spirals of foam [una tromba / di schiume intorte]" redeem the poem from mere crepuscularism.

With "Quasi una fantasia" we are, however, well within the range of the genuine Montalian inspiration and technique. We find the poet immersed in a characteristic mood—the mood of metaphysical perplexity poetically rendered in minute detail, both evocative and realistic: "The sun's event returns / but doesn't bring back the diffuse voices, / the usual clamor [Torna l'avvenimento del sole e le diffuse / voci, i consueti strepiti non porta]." The sense of time begins to weigh upon his moral and poetic world with a haunting monotony —"rounds of hours that are too alike [giostre d'ore troppo uguali]"—finding its psychological as well as objective correlative in the nostalgic image of "a country of light intact snow / as seen on an arras [un paese d'intatte nevi / ma lievi come viste in un arazzo]," and in the almost Wordsworthian image of woods and hills "soaked in invisible light [gremite d'invisibile luce]." [8] Montale's poetic symbolism, delicately balanced as it is between idyllic charm and a sharp moral awareness, reveals itself through, as well as serving to interpret, memories, hopes, and illusions, or moments of vision and ecstasy:

> Happily shall I read
> the black signs of branches against
> the white like an elemental alphabet.
> The whole past will appear before me
> in one point.
> And no sound will disturb
> this solitary mirth.

> Lieto leggerò i neri
> segni dei rami sul bianco
> come un essenziale alfabeto.
> Tutto il passato in un punto
> dinanzi mi sarà comparso.
> Non turberà suono alcuno
> quest'allegrezza solitaria.

"Falsetto," a poem with rhythmic echoes from D'Annunzio, is a celebration of youth as represented by a girl called Esterina. The poet compares her to

8. Cf. Wordsworth's line "The light that never was, on sea or land" ("Elegiac Stanzas suggested by a picture of Peele Castle").

Diana and looks upon her gaiety with an admiration tinged with envy, in much the same way as Cardarelli does the girl who is the subject of his poem "Adolescente." The poet advises Esterina to enjoy the present, and his prayer is that her twenty years may be "an ineffable concert of bells [concerto ineffabile di sonaglieri]":

> Let not fears cloud your smiling
> present. Your gaiety is already wedded
> to the future
> and with a shrug
> you raze the fortresses of
> your unknown tomorrow.

> . . . Non turbare
> di ubbie il sorridente presente.
> La tua gaiezza impegna già il futuro
> ed un crollar di spalle
> dirocca i fortilizî
> del tuo domani oscuro.

To some extent the poet identifies himself—or that part of himself which has been nurtured by his contact with the sea—with Esterina, as he tells her that the water

> . . . is the force that tempers you,
> in the water you rediscover yourself,
> are renewed; we think of you
> as seaweed, or a pebble, or a marine
> creature which the salt of the sea
> doesn't corrode,
> but returns to the beach, purified.

> . . . è la forza che ti tempra,
> nell'acqua ti ritrovi e ti rinnovi:
> noi ti pensiamo come un'alga, un ciottolo,
> come un'equorea creatura
> che la salsedine non intacca
> ma torna al lito più pura.

In "Caffè a Rapallo," a poem addressed to his fellow Ligurian poet and friend Camillo Sbarbaro, Montale gives us a glimpse of everyday life in the rich concreteness of its physical setting:

> Christmas in the bright tepidarium,
> with its makeup of fumes rising
> from the cups, the veiled tremor of lights
> behind closed panes,
> and gray feminine forms amidst
> the flash of gems and shot silk—

> Natale nel tepidario
> lustrante, truccato dai fumi
> che svolgono tazze, velato
> tremore di lumi oltre i chiusi
> cristalli, profili di femmine
> nel grigio, tra lampi di gemme
> e screzi di sete. . . .

Contrasting with this is the dream world which the poet evokes when he sees a band of children marching by, and from which he feels himself excluded because of his age:

> And it was lost in the pasture
> that no longer greens for us.

> L'accolse la pastura
> che per noi più non verdeggia.

This dream world is in turn portrayed in realistic detail, when the poet mentions those carnival objects which are a familiar part of a child's world, "the generals with cocked paper-hats [i Generali / con le faluche di cartone]" and "the Privates with candles and lamps [i gregari / con moccoli e lampioni]."

In "Epigramma," another poem for Sbarbaro, the poetic situation or "occasion" (Sbarbaro, a "whimsical child [estroso fanciullo]," putting out the colored paper-boats into a muddy stream) is sketched with a vivid simplicity of detail; and then in the last three lines a touchingly human and symbolic element is introduced:

> You passerby, be kind
> and reach him the delicate flotilla
> with your stick that it may not get lost,
> and guide it to the tiny rocky harbor.

> Sii preveggente per lui, tu galantuomo che passi:
> col tuo bastone raggiungi la delicata flottiglia,
> che non si perda; guidala a un porticello di sassi.

The group of four poems collectively called *Sarcofaghi* was inspired by sculptured sarcophaguses and suggests obvious comparisons with Keats ("Ode on a Grecian Urn") and Leopardi ("Sopra un basso rilievo antico sepolcrale," "Sopra il ritratto di una bella donna," and "La ginestra").[9] Through an intensely realized evocation of the carvings on the sarcophaguses the poet gives life to what is lifeless and captures the living grace of forms and gestures in their immobility. In the first lyric ("Dove se ne vanno") he describes some girls "who bear on their shoulders brimming pitchers / and whose steps are light but firm [che recano le colme anfore su le spalle / ed hanno il fermo passo sì leggero]"—the word *colme* may, at least to an English-speaking reader, suggest by means of phonic association the word *calme,* and the two meanings interact with one another as cause and effect—; in the second ("Ora sia il tuo passo"), it is "the corroded door of a temple / (that) is closed for ever [La porta corrosa d'un tempietto / è rinchiusa per sempre]"; in the third ("Il fuoco che scoppietta"), the image of an old weary man who "sleeps near an andiron / the sleep of the abandoned [dorme accanto a un alare / il sonno dell'abbandonato]"; and lastly (in "Ma dove cercare la tomba"), the image of "a sunflower that opens / and rabbits dancing around [un girasole che si schiude / ed intorno una danza di conigli]". In other words, what is carved in stone is poetically transcribed not only by the vivid realization with which it is represented but also by the symbolic or allegorical kinship that the poet feels between the carvings and life itself, as, for instance, in lines like "in this valley / there is no succession of light and darkness [in questa valle / non è vicenda di buio e di luce]" ("Dove se ne vanno"), "in this abysmal light which seems / to be bronze, don't awaken / you who are asleep [In questa luce abissale / che finge il bronzo, non ti svegliare / addormentato!]" ("Il fuoco che scoppietta") or "the sad artisan who goes to work / and a blind will already beats / at his pulse [il triste artiere che al lavoro si reca / e già gli batte ai polsi una volontà cieca]" ("Ma dove cercare la tomba"). But underlying this poetic evocation is the sense of the unbridgeable gulf between what is dead, even though eternalized by art, and what is living. However, in spite of some extremely felicitous images and expressions in these poems, they are rather too consciously artistic to achieve the quality of effortless originality possessed by a great many poems in *Ossi di seppia.*

It is, however, in "Vento e bandiere" that some of the most characteristic Montalian themes—recollection of the past against the Ligurian landscape, pictorial detail, and philosophical affirmation—are closely interwoven. The memory of the woman loved in the past presents itself with the suddenness and impetuosity of a gust of wind:

9. Keats as well as Leopardi is among the poets Montale studied in his youth.

The squall that lifted the bitter
scent of the sea to the valleys'
winding rims and overwhelmed you,
ruffled your hair, a brief
tangle against the pale sky.

La folata che alzò l'amaro aroma
del mare alle spirali delle valli,
e t'investì, ti scompigliò la chioma,
groviglio breve contro il cielo pallido.

The impassioned vividness with which the poet describes such intense
moments of recollection dramatizes the realization that the past cannot be
altogether recaptured, nor can it be reenacted except in those brief moments
of vision and recollection which constitute what Ungaretti calls the "ferocious
charity of remembrance [la carità feroce del ricordo]": [10]

Alas, time never shapes
the grains in the same way twice!
And there's no escape . . .

Ahimè, non mai due volte configura
il tempo in egual modo i grani! E scampo
n'è: . . .

In "Fuscello teso dal muro" the sea again serves as a background for the
theme of metaphysical immobility and tedium depicted both in general and
particular terms. The twig stretching toward the sea is like the hand of a sun
dial that scans "the sun's career / and mine, so brief [la carriera / del sole e
la mia, breve]":

           . . . Down there
where the sea plain can be seen,
a three-masted boat with its crew
and booty leans to the wind
and glides away. Whoever
watches from above can see
that the deck shines and the helm
leaves no trace in the water.

            . . . Laggiù,
dove la piana si scopre
del mare, un trealberi carico

---

10. In "Ultimi cori per la terra promessa," *Il Taccuino del Vecchio*.

> di ciurma e di preda reclina
> il bordo a uno spiro, e via scivola.
> Chi è in alto e s'affaccia s'avvede
> che brilla la tolda e il timone
> nell'acqua non scava una traccia.

The naturalness of the scene, described as it is with a wealth of realistic detail, has itself a certain metaphysical air about it. And yet it can stand by itself as a vividly outlined vignette of a particular aspect or movement of the sea.

It is, however, those poems specifically grouped under the title *Ossi di seppia* that reveal Montale's art at its best. Here that continual extinction of personality which Eliot regarded as an essential prerequisite to the progress of an artist is achieved not so much by an escape from emotion as by a process of elimination and organization operating both at the conscious and the unconscious level. This makes for the kind of concentration that is both verbal and moral, the one in fact being a corollary of the other. Perceptions, impressions, and emotions are woven into a pattern of images. Montale's diction—with its "stony" ruggedness—is itself the result of that concentration. No doubt his knowledge of Shakespeare's plays (some of which he translated) and of the poetry of Donne, Keats, Hopkins, Browning, Pound, and Eliot (not to mention the Italian poets like Dante, Leopardi, Pascoli, Gozzano, and D'Annunzio) also influenced the development of his poetic diction. But it is chiefly through this concentration that Montale achieves the rich synthesis of realistic and symbolic meaning which characterizes his poetry. Immediacy or closeness (Montale's own word is *adherence*) [11] to his own thought, experience, or intuition is his overriding concern in his use of the language and in his "wrestle with words." [12] Moreover, his lifelong interest in music enabled him to achieve a perfect balance between sound and sense and architectonic unity in a given poem. This group of poems thus forms the earliest and most representative body of poetry wherein all the essential qualities and characteristics of Montale's art are impressively present—a positive and creative form of countereloquence, a delicate balance between concentration and diffusion ("I was aware," says Montale, "that poetry cannot function in a vacuum and that one cannot achieve concentration except in the wake of diffusion"). [13] They also exhibit the metallic timbre of the language and the evocative and symbolic richness of imagery, both words "that might mold our formless soul" [che squadri da ogni lato / l'animo nostro informe] ("Non chiederci la

11. "Intenzioni: intervista immaginaria," p. 344.
12. The phrase is T. S. Eliot's: "the intolerable wrestle / with words and meanings" ("East Coker," *Four Quartets*).
13. "Intenzioni: intervista immaginaria," p. 343.

parola") and "just a few maimed syllables / dry as a twig [sì qualche storta sillaba e secca come un ramo]," [14] as well as a robust matter-of-factness of impressionistic detail in all its allusive complexity. Sergio Solmi describes these poems as being "integrally interwoven into that context of rapid 'correspondences' buried in the intuitive zone, where logical and oratorical passages no longer exist." [15] The intuitive depth and richness of Montale's poetry are expressed through his strikingly original images no less than through gnomic aphorisms. Take, for instance, the first poem "Non chiederci la parola":

> Don't ask for words that might mold
> our formless soul,
> blaze it out in fiery letters
> like a crocus lost in a dusty meadow.
>
> Ah! the man who walks self-assured,
> a friend to himself and to others,
> heedless of how the dog-days
> stamp his shadow on the unplastered wall.
>
> Don't ask for a formula that might
> open worlds; just a few maimed syllables
> dry as a twig. All we can say today
> is what we are *not,* what we *do not* want.

> Non chiederci la parola che squadri da ogni lato
> l'animo nostro informe, e a lettere di fuoco
> lo dichiari e risplenda come un croco
> perduto in mezzo a un polveroso prato.
>
> Ah l'uomo che se ne va sicuro,
> agli altri ed a se stesso amico,
> e l'ombra sua non cura che la canicola
> stampa sopra uno scalcinato muro!
>
> Non domandarci la formula che mondi possa aprirti,
> sì qualche storta sillaba e secca come un ramo.
> Codesto solo oggi possiamo dirti,
> ciò che *non* siamo, ciò che *non* vogliamo.

Here the attention claimed by such a vivid and forceful image as a crocus lost in a dusty meadow, or a man's shadow which the dog-days stamp on the unplastered wall, relates not only to its striking appropriateness and originality

14. "Non chiederci la parola."
15. *Scrittori negli anni,* p. 292.

or to its logical and intuitive link with the meaning and structure of the poem as a whole, but also to the way it serves as an objective correlative for the poet's feeling of moral and metaphysical perplexity. This feeling is further clinched by the way in which the poet distinguishes himself from "the man who walks self-assured," as well as by the explicit formulation of the last couplet, which sums up his own predicament as well as that of his contemporaries in the perplexing age of the early 1920s that saw the rise of fascism in Italy. It is, however, characteristic of Montale's poetry that, although the various images, allusions, or affirmations merge together harmoniously within the structural and stylistic unity and complexity of a given poem, they nevertheless succeed in retaining a certain degree of personal autonomy.

That a good many of Montale's poems bear no titles has a certain significance. Of all the important twentieth-century Italian poets Montale is the one in whose case it is most difficult to proceed by explicating, through definite formulations and statements, what a particular poem is about. In other words, what comes out through the reading of the poem and what was in the poet's mind when he wrote it, seldom lend themselves to a condensed summary. And the kind of artistic, verbal, and technical maturity that each poem displays is itself either too generally diffused in the whole poem, or too concentrated in some parts to enable the poet to give it a suitable title. Hence the charge of obscurity that has sometimes been leveled against Montale.[16] But the fact is that not only the nature of the technique—to which the alleged obscurity is largely attributed—but also the very nature of what the poet wants to convey in all its depth and complexity is such that a title, far from doing justice to the poem, might only mislead the reader.

In other words, the absence of a title is indicative not so much of the absence of thematic unity as of the structural complexity of a given poem. For instance, in the first stanza of "Non chiederci la parola," which is addressed to an imaginary interlocutor, the impossibility of what words can do is conveyed by means of such images as "fiery letters" or "a crocus lost in a dusty meadow." In the second stanza we pass from the sense of contrast between what words are incapable of doing and what they actually do, or what the poet makes them do, to the contrast on a moral plane—that between the poet and the practical man, "the man who walks self-assured" and for whom, by implication, the problem of communicating and defining "our formless soul" has either been easily resolved, or has never even arisen. It is, however, not the man of action but the poet who alone can understand the moral and philosophical dilemmas of a destiny that cannot be defined except nega-

16. Above all by Alfredo Gargiulo in his review of *Le occasioni*, now included in the enlarged edition of *Letteratura italiana del Novecento*, 1958.

tively. The element of conscious or unconscious self-deception in such a man is implicitly present in the first two lines of the second stanza, and comes out explicitly in the last two lines. In the second stanza the poet refers to the contrast between what a "formula" or a "syllable" should ideally be able to do, and what in reality it cannot. The conceptual climax comes in the last two lines when we are presented with the other extreme—what words or formulas or syllables *can* do; that is to say, state "what we are *not,* what we *do not* want." Thus the sense of a limited or negative communication as the only alternative to words, syllables, or formulas pervades the whole poem and determines its structural and organic form and complexity.

The second poem in the group, "Meriggiare pallido e assorto," is one of the earliest and best known to be found in this volume. It was written when the poet was only twenty, and yet it already shows a remarkable degree of maturity and self-control in achieving the kind of organic and structural unity and complexity referred to above. It also signals a decisive departure from the kind of poetry represented by Carducci, Pascoli, and D'Annunzio. Against the rich mosaic of objects described—objects selected and grouped together in an apparently casual way—the poet sums up his reading of what "all life and its travail [tutta la vita e il suo travaglio]" means. And what it means is rendered with metaphorical concreteness in the last stanza. Even the use of rhyme, assonance, and onomatopoeia serves to emphasize the modernity of the poem, in that they express, not a sense of harmony, but of discord.

Thus, this poem both exemplifies and anticipates some of the salient characteristics of Montale's later style, technique, and diction, as well as of his poetic temperament—a temperament that is instinctively drawn to watch

> through leafy branches.
> the distant throbbing of the sea-scales,
> while the tremulous note of the cicada
> rises from the bare hill tops——
>
> Osservare tra frondi il palpitare
> lontano di scaglie di mare
> mentre si levano tremuli scricchi
> di cicale dai calvi picchi——

and to feel

> . . . with sad bewilderment how
> all life and its travail
> is like following a wall with pieces
> of broken bottle stuck to its rim.

> . . . con triste meraviglia
> com'è tutta la vita e il suo travaglio
> in questo seguitare una muraglia
> che ha in cima cocci aguzzi di bottiglia.

The wall with pieces of broken bottle stuck to its rim is a typically Montalian image, representing as it does the world of objects both animate and inanmiate and configurating, whether in the form of an objective correlative or in an overtly or implicitly metaphorical or symbolical form, the poet's inner world of thoughts and feelings. Hence, what Wordsworth called "the mighty world of eye and ear" [17] is something at once vaster and more varied in Montale's poetry. The sight of the sea palpitating through leafy branches is another Montalian symbol of life in its moral and metaphysical essence.

In "Non rifugiarti nell'ombra" the physical and metaphysical, the moral and naturalistic elements are fused together in the poet's contemplation of "the forms of life that are crumbling [le forme della vita che si sgretola]" and the "play of the arid waves/that languishes in this restless hour [gioco d'aride onde / che impigra in quest'ora di disagio]." The poet tells the woman or the imaginary companion he is talking to not to take refuge in the shadow of "that dense verdure [quel fòlto di verdura]" and to leave behind "the stunted reed-thicket that seems to drowse [il canneto stento che pare s'addorma]." He then proceeds to describe, by means of a set of images and analogies at once realistic and metaphorical, the nature of the predicament in which both he and the woman are caught:

> We move in pearl-colored dust
> vibrating in a glitter
> that catches our eyes and tires us.
> Yet you hear it in the play
> of the arid waves that languishes
> in this restless hour: let's not cast
> our wandering life into a bottomless pit.
>
> Like that rocky boundary that seems
> to unwind into a web of clouds;
> so our parched souls
> in which illusion burns—a fire
> full of ashes—are lost in the calm
> of a certainty: the light.

17. "Lines Written a Few Miles Above Tintern Abbey."

Ci muoviamo in un pulviscolo
madreperlaceo che vibra,
in un barbaglio che invischia
gli occhi e un poco ci sfibra.

Pure, lo senti, nel gioco d'aride onde
che impigra in quest'ora di disagio
non buttiamo già in un gorgo senza fondo
le nostre vite randage.

Come quella chiostra di rupi
che sembra sfilacciarsi
in ragnatele di nubi;
tali i nostri animi arsi

in cui l'illusione brucia
un fuoco pieno di cenere
si perdono nel sereno
di una certezza: la luce.

Concept-images like "our parched souls in which illusion burns," "our wandering life," or "the calm of a certainty: the light," with their vitally abstract quality are juxtaposed with object-images, with their lapidary firmness and explicitness, like "that rocky boundary" or the "play of the arid waves." If Montale's poetry is metaphysical, it is so not because it has recourse to abstract concepts not already implicit in the situation or occasion concretely presented, but because it subjects the moral and emotional aspects of personal experience to a closely knit artistic and technical pattern. Few modern poets in Italy have succeeded, as Montale has, in drawing their poetic inspiration and strength almost exclusively from a personal or autobiographical source, without becoming imprisoned within the bounds of subjectivism in the narrow sense of the term.

When interpreting a poem by Montale it is possible to separate the central idea, concept, or theme. For instance, one may say that "Non rifiugiarti nell'-ombra" deals with the theme of rejecting or discouraging any recourse to false consolation, superstition, or make-believe, and pleads for the acceptance of the unpleasant facts and situations of life; but this would be to restrict the scope of what the poem really represents in its verbal, stylistic, and conceptual unity and complexity.

Even an apparently personal poem like "Ripenso il tuo sorriso" goes beyond the scope of purely personal lyricism in its use of objects and images which are at once realistic and symbolically evocative. If the recollection of the friend's smile is described as "limpid water [acqua limpida]" forming a "little mirror in which an ivy might look at its corymbs [esiguo specchio in cui guardi un'ellera i suoi corimbi]," the idyllic charm of these metaphors and images is finely counterbalanced by the rugged quality of "the stones of a dry river-bed [le petraie d'un greto]." Similarly, in the last stanza, the images of "a wave of calm [un'ondata di calma]" and "the top of a young palm [la cima d'una giovinetta palma]" offset the notion of "capricious vexations [i crucci estrosi]." One of the poetic devices most frequently used by Montale is that of presenting an abstract thought, feeling, or emotion, not so much through the objective correlative in the Eliotian sense as through an objective transfiguration or extension. For instance, he talks of the wanderers who "bear their suffering like a talisman [recano il loro soffrire con sé come un talismano]," thus enriching and heightening the significance of the concept of suffering by the comparison.

In "Portami il girasole," too, "the sunflower gone crazy with light [il girasole impazzito di luce]"—the sunflower is a favorite flower in Montale's poetry, embodying as it does the legend of Clizia's falling in love with Apollo, her transformation into a sunflower, and continuing love for him [18]—serves as an emblem of the poet's own metaphysical anxiety as well as a symbol of personal identity when everything around him melts in "a flow of tints [un fluire di tinte]" or "blond transparencies [bionde transparenze]." The image of the "soil burnt by the briny sea [terreno bruciato dal salino]" serves as a starting-point for the poet's quest after "the chance of chances [la ventura delle venture]" when "dark things tend toward the light [tendono alla chiarità le cose oscure]" and "bodies dissolve in a flow of tints [si esauriscono i corpi in un fluire / di tinte]."

There are various levels at which the personal and impersonal, the autobiographical and philosophical elements merge together in Montale's poetry. In "Mia vita, a te non chiedo lineamenti" one can see the various levels acting upon each other in a subtle way:

> My life, I don't ask for set features,
> plausible faces or possessions.
> In your restless round by now
> honey and absinth have the same taste.
>
> The heart that disdains each movement
> is rarely overwhelmed by emotion.
> Thus sometimes the peace of a countryside
> is broken by a gunshot.

18. See Montale's poem "La primavera hitleriana" (*La bufera e altro*).

Mia vita, a te non chiedo lineamenti
fissi, volti plausibili o possessi.
Nel tuo giro inquieto ormai lo stesso
sapore han miele e assenzio.

Il cuore che ogni moto tiene a vile
rare è squassato da trasalimenti.
Così suona talvolta nel silenzio
della campagna un colpo di fucile.

The poem offers a succinct portrayal of Montale's personality in its moral and metaphysical essence. It also suggests—in fact stresses—that stage in the development of the poet's soul, that level of moral and philosophical maturity, where one ceases to care for set features, plausible faces, or possessions, and where honey and absinth have the same taste. The sense of self-possession and stoic acceptance of what the vicissitudes of life may bring in their restless round, conveyed in the first stanza, is clinched in the second by means of a simile at once startling and homely.

Belonging to the same class as "Mia vita, a te non chiedo lineamenti" are poems like "Spesso il male di vivere ho incontrato" and "Ciò che di me sapeste." If the "critical corrosion of existence" entails an awareness of the dilemmas and predicaments of life as well as of the humdrum and prosaic aspects of everyday experience, such an awareness is depicted in a nutshell in "Spesso il male di vivere":

I have often come across the evil of living:
the choked stream gurgling,
the parched leaf curling up,
the horse collapsing on the ground.

No other good did I know
than the portent of divine Indifference;
the statue in a drowsy noon,
the cloud and the hawk soaring.

Spesso il male di vivere ho incontrato:
era il rivo strozzato che gorgoglia,
era l'incartocciarsi della foglia
riarsa, era il cavallo stramazzato.

Bene non seppi, fuori del prodigio
che schiude la divina Indifferenza:
era la statua nella sonnolenza
del meriggio, e la nuvola, e il falco alto levato.

Here each image, sharply chiseled and autonomous though it is, symbolically enacts what the poets calls "the evil of living" and "divine Indifference." Montale's concept of the evil of living is basically similar to Leopardi's, although expressed in a different way, rather than to Baudelaire's. "Life," says Leopardi, "is in itself an evil . . . and nonliving, or extenuated living, both by way of extension and by way of intensity, simply a good or a lesser evil." [19] In fact, because of the simplicity, concision, and evocative potency of the language, imagery, and metaphors through which this quintessential philosophical truth is conveyed, this poem, more than any other, may be regarded as the Montalian counterpart of Leopardi's "L'Infinito." On the musical and rhythmical level, too, it has a subtly orchestrated pattern of inner rhymes, assonance and cadences. The onomatopoetic value of such words as *strozzato* ("choked") and *gorgoglia* ("gurgles"), or *incartocciarsi* ("curling up"), is linked to the efficacy with which they enact the objective correlative or metaphorical expression of the concept of "the evil of living." The symbolic richness and intensity of these images—"the choked stream" conveying the force and violence of evil, "the parched leaf" the spasm of pain, the horse's collapsing, the fatal and irresistible impact of the blow—is counterbalanced by the simplicity and almost prosaic starkness of the diction. On the other hand, the concept of "divine Indifference," denoting the subjugation of passion and the renunciation of self as the only alternative to "the evil of living" is pictorially translated into such images of what Montale elsewhere calls "clinical imperturbability" as "the statue in a drowsy noon" and "the cloud and the hawk soaring." The marked lengthening of the last line itself contributes to the sense of lull, passivity, and indifference.

In "Ciò che di me sapeste" the poet turns from the contemplation of the evil of living to a searching analysis of his own identity. He distinguishes what is extraneous to him ("this rind [questa scorza]") from "my true self [la mia vera sostanza]," only to find that the two are one and the same thing and that what looks like a shadow is not a shadow at all, but himself:

> What you knew of me
> was only an exterior,
> a garment that clothes
> our human destiny.
>
> And perhaps behind the camouflage
> was the blue serene;
> only a seal prevented us
> from seeing the limpid sky.

19. *Zibaldone,* ed. Francesco Flora (Milan: Mondadori), 2 : 874–75.

Or indeed there was the bizarre
change in my life,
the opening of a fiery clod
that I will never see again.

Hence only this rind has been
my true substance;
ignorance was for me
a fire that never dies.

If you notice a shadow by chance,
it's not a shadow, but me.
I wish I could pluck it from me
and offer it to you as a gift.

Ciò che di me sapeste
non fu che la scialbatura,
la tonaca che riveste
la nostra umana ventura.

Ed era forse oltre il telo
l'azzurro tranquillo;
vietava il limpido cielo
solo un sigillo.

O vero c'era il falòtico
mutarsi della mia vita,
lo schiudersi d'un'ignita
zolla che mai vedrò.

Restò così questa scorza
la vera mia sostanza;
il fuoco che non si smorza
per me si chiamò: l'ignoranza.

Se un'ombra scorgete, non è
un'ombra —— ma quella io sono.
Potessi spiccarla da me,
offrirvela in dono.

The theme of self-exploration continues in the following two poems, "Porto-venere" and "So l'ora in cui la faccia più impassibile." In the first, it is in the context of mythological and Christian antiquity ("There the Triton gushes out / from the waves which lap the threshold / of a Christian temple [Là fuoresce il Tritone / dai flutti che lambiscono / le soglie d'un cristiano / tempio]," and "every approaching hour is ancient [ed ogni ora prossima / è antica])" that the poet discovers his identity by acquiring the sense of his origins. It is only after having momentarily merged his identity with the sense of the cosmic and the primordial that he goes on "to assume a face [assumere un volto]." In the second poem it is "a cruel grimace [una cruda smorfia]" on a habitually impassive face that reveals, however briefly, the poet's inner pain, "the secret bite, the wind / that blows in the heart [il morso / secreto, il vento che nel cuore soffia]" more than words can ever do. But even when so revealed, the poet's real identity remains unknown to "the people on a crowded highway [la gente nell'affollato corso]," and he concludes that the best way to preserve one's identity is not to reveal it: "He who remains mute / is most right [La più vera ragione è di chi tace]." [20]

And yet this realization acts both as a moral and a creative incentive to the poet, enabling him to wring from words a peculiar force and beauty which does ample justice to what he himself theoretically postulates as being by its very nature incommunicable and inexpressible. In his poetic and psychological exploration of reality as well as in his analytical insight into the meaning of what is explored, he thus works on the principle of opposites. For instance, if he says (as in one of the *Xenia* poems) [21] that his identity was doubtful from the very outset, he then proceeds to demonstrate with great poetic effect what constitutes the essence of that identity and how it distinguishes him from "the people on a crowded highway."

To some extent this principle is also evident in "Gloria del disteso mezzogiorno." What is seen in the blinding "glory of the outstretched noon / when the trees give no shade / and the forms of things around / show up more and more yellow / in the light [Gloria del disteso mezzogiorno / quand' ombra non rendono gli alberi, / e più e più si mostrano d'attorno / per troppa luce, le parvenze, falbe]" makes the poet realize that "the most beautiful hour / is beyond the wall [l'ora più bella è di là dal muretto]" and "the greatest joy is in waiting [ma in attendere è gioia più compita]." Just as for the 'crepuscular' poets the twilight hour held a particular fascination, the midday hour of a hot Mediterranean summer holds one for Montale. On the one hand it serves, as it were, as an objective correlative of the poet's clairvoyance and on the other it symbolizes his sense of the dissolution of things

---

20. Cf. Hardy's poem "Mute Opinion" (*Poems of the Past and the Present*) where, while contrasting "a large-eyed few, and dumb" with those who speak out strongly "Their purpose and opinion / Through pulpit, press and song," the poet tells us that when, after his death, he returned to the earth, "grown a shade," he found the earth's history "outwrought / Not as the loud had spoken, / But as the mute had thought."

21. Cf. "Anch'io sono incrostato fino al collo se il mio / stato civile fu dubbio fin dall'inizio" ("L'alluvione ha sommerso il pack dei mobili," *Xenia*).

and of life itself. The more vividly defined the physical contours of objects
are, the more conscious he is of the sense of dissolution underlying them,
which makes the act of waiting fundamentally creative, like Wordsworth's
"wise passiveness." [22]

Again in "Felicità raggiunta" Montale translates into words the psychological validity as well as poetic efficacy of that very thing which he conceptually denies. He succeeds in portraying through concrete imagery the tone,
color, and sensation of happiness attained. The more evanescent the nature
of happiness, the more concrete is the pattern of metaphorical images and
analogies he employs:

> Happiness, for your sake
> one walks on the edge of a blade;
> you are a flickering gleam for the eye,
> for the foot, ice that cracks;
> hence let him not touch you who most loves you.
>
> If you reach hearts
> in the grip of sadness and brighten them,
> your morning's both sweet and disturbing,
> like nests in the eaves;
> but nothing can console the child
> whose balloon disappears behind the houses.

> Felicità raggiunta, si cammina
> per te su fil di lama.
> Agli occhi sei barlume che vacilla,
> al piede, teso ghiaccio che s'incrina;
> e dunque non ti tocchi chi più t'ama.
>
> Se giungi sulle anime invase
> di tristezza e le schiari, il tuo mattino
> è dolce e turbatore come i nidi delle cimase.
> Ma nulla paga il pianto del bambino
> a cui fugge il pallone tra le case.

The three images—the edge of a blade, the flickering gleam and the ice that
cracks—are interlinked through the progressive logic of the words—*eyes*
(needed to see what one is pursuing), *foot* (one proceeds to reach or attain
happiness), and *touch* (when one has reached the object, one wishes to
touch it). The link between the various steps involved in the pursuit of

22. "Expostulation and Reply."

happiness enhances the poetic relevance of the pictorial and visual images. The two images in the second stanza further characterize the nature of happiness which, when it finally reaches "hearts in the grip of sadness," is both "sweet and disturbing, like nests in the eaves," yet as elusive as the balloon behind the houses. The idyllic sweetness of the first image prepares the ground for the wistful tenderness of the second, so that the last stanza may be regarded as the emotional gloss and counterpart of the concrete image pattern of the first.

"Il canneto rispunta i suoi cimelli" has all the characteristics of a typically Montalian lyric: the sense of immobility and "impenetrable sultriness [afa stagna]" looming upon the scene and landscape, the hour of waiting and metaphysical suspense ("An hour of waiting soars to the sky, empty [Sale un'ora d'attesa in cielo, vacua]"), and everything melting into nostalgia for the absent person. This poem also anticipates the spirit, ethos, and technique of the subsequent poems in this volume (for instance, "Delta," "Casa sul mare," "Incontro"), as well as the poems in *Le occasioni*—poems in which the poetic inspiration, as Sergio Solmi points out, centers round the contrast between two basic attitudes: "on the one hand, a fundamentally negative sense of indifference and atony or immobile sorrow . . . and on the other the sudden sentimental rupture of the initial 'petrification,' the 'message' from the hidden depths of the poem. A figure, a landscape, a color, a sign, quite incommensurable with the objects of everyday reality, all bring about this rupture, kindling the 'light of the lamp' that changes them into 'something rich and strange.' " [23] The present poem aptly exemplifies this. In the first two stanzas the sense of the immobility and suspension of life is evocatively described together with the sense of something to come, accentuated as it is by "a tree of clouds grows on the water / then crumbles like ashes [un albero di nuvole sull'acqua / cresce, poi crolla come di cinigia]." Finally, in the last stanza, the poet turns with an impulsive wistfulness to the woman who is absent and whose presence-absence is so poignantly evoked:

> O absent one how I miss you
> in this region that's haunted by you
> and wasted without you;
> you are far away and yet everything
> leaves its path, cracks, dissolves
> into mist.

23. *Scrittori negli anni*, pp. 193–94. Cf. also Gargiulo's penetrating comments on the "vita non vissuta" and the "occasioni che ne concentrano come in un punto l'attonito vuoto." The latter phrase was to serve Montale as the title of his second book of poems. See *Letteratura italiana del Novecento*, p. 456.

Assente, come manchi in questa plaga
che ti presente e senza te consuma:
sei lontana e però tutto divaga
dal suo solco, dirupa, spare in bruma.

In "Forse un mattino andando" Montale's artistic power and maturity
reach a high watermark that he was seldom to surpass. The lyric has an
effortless poise, concentration, and directness of approach as well as a technical sureness and command which give it a classic finish, philosophical depth,
a sense of inevitability, and a structural rigor and compactness that his more
complex and elaborate poems do not always achieve. The theme is provided
by a casual and clairvoyant glimpse of the dissolution and annulment of
all forms of life—trees, houses, hills (alberi case colli)—and a void opening
up behind the poet as he turns around. But when this vision is gone, all
these things return to their proper places "by a customary trick [per l'inganno
consueto]":

Perhaps one morning while walking in crisp
glassy air as I turn round I'll see
the miracle happen: nothingness at my back
and a void behind me, with the terror of a drunk man.

Then suddenly, as on a screen, hills, houses,
trees will all assemble as though
by a customary trick; but 'twill be
too late, and I'll go away quietly
with my secret among men who don't turn.

Forse un mattino andando in un'aria di vetro,
arida, rivolgendomi, vedrò compirsi il miracolo:
il nulla alle mie spalle, il vuoto dietro
di me, con un terrore di ubriaco.

Poi come s'uno schermo, s'accamperanno di gitto
alberi case colli per l'inganno consueto.
Ma sarà troppo tardi; ed io me n'andrò zitto
tra gli uomini che non si voltano, col mio segreto.

The word *perhaps* prepares us for the fortuitous nature of the experience,
just as the word *glassy,* referring to the brittle quality of the air, reminds us
of its transitoriness. The dry glassy air also enacts the working of an invisible
power of determinism that brings about the miracle and makes the poet
turn around. Even if the realization of the essential emptiness of things and

the terror it inspires are short-lived, it is like the tearing of the veil, "an ex-
plosion, the end of the illusion as representation," [24] and it leaves a permanent mark on the poet's mind and consciousness. In the end the trees, houses,
and hills all return and resume their places. For not only can mankind not
bear "very much reality," [25] it cannot bear it for any length of time. Most
men don't even turn around but keep walking, like the man in "Non chiederci la parola," the man "who walks self-assured / . . . heedless of how the
dog-days / stamp his shadow on the unplastered wall." But for the poet who
is one of those men who do turn around, the vision of what he has seen will
last forever. He cannot, to use a phrase of Hardy's, "unsight the seen." [26]

In "Valmorbia, discorrevano il tuo fondo" Montale recollects his experiences of World War I. The idyllic charm of Valmorbia in Trentino, where
he was stationed, contrasts with the tragedy and hopelessness of war. With
the passage of time the recollected atmosphere of Valmorbia ("the clear
nights were all one dawn [le notte chiare erano tutte un'alba]" and "in the
womb of solitude one heard / no other sound than that / of the hoarse Leno
[nel grembo solitario / non dava suono, che il Leno roco]") acquires a dreamlike quality and becomes "a land where it doesn't get dark [terra dove non
annotta]." In "Tentava la vostra mano" and "La farandola dei fanciulli," on
the other hand, it is through the juxtaposition of the real and the illusory
that the significance of a given moment or scene from the past is poetically
realized. In the first poem the woman playing the piano finds that she cannot
play the piece: "your eyes / read the unintelligible marks on the page, / and
each chord was broken like a voice / broken with grief [i vostri occhi legge-
vano sul foglio / gl'impossibili segni; e franto era / ogni accordo come una
voce di cordoglio]." There is an embarrassing silence: "Nothing around
found words [Nessuna cosa prossima trovava le sue parole]". Then "a fleeting dance of butterflies [una fugace danza di farfalle]" and "a leafy bough
[that] stirred / in the sunshine [una fronda si scrollò nel sole]" break the
suspense. However, the poet and the pianist are drawn together by this
predicament: "your sweet ignorance was mine, was *ours* [era mia, era *nostra*
la vostra dolce ignoranza]."

In "La farandola dei fanciulli," the world of Ligurian objects and landscapes such as the "gravel-bed [greto]," the "drought [arsura]" and the
"sparse reeds [rare canne]," forms a canvas on which the poet depicts his
view of life. Between the poet and what he contemplates there emerges, how-

---

24. "Intenzioni: intervista immaginaria," p. 345.
25. T. S. Eliot, "Burnt Norton," *Four Quartets.*
26. See Hardy's poem "To Meet, or Otherwise," *Satires of Circumstance:* "Nor God nor
Demon can undo the done, / Unsight the seen."

ever, a sense of estrangement that amounts to a "torment [supplizio]." But this itself leads to the realization of life in its primordial plethora, gaiety, and spontaneity as symbolized by "the farandole of the children on the gravel-bed [La farandola dei fanciulli sul greto]." Similarly their innocence and purity symbolize the "golden age flourishing on happy shores [età d'oro florida sulle sponde felici]" where "even a name and a garment were vices [anche un nome, una veste, erano un vizio]."

In "Debole sistro al vento" the poet succeeds in capturing evocatively, and with an almost uncanny subtlety of perception, the fleeting and sporadic nature of "a lost cicada's / faint sistrum in the wind [Debole sistro al vento / d'una persa cicala]" and using it as a symbolic counterpart of the fragile and ephemeral nature of man's world—his words, actions, and gestures—or of what Leopardi in "Canto notturno" calls "my frail being" [l'esser mio frale]:

> If you make a sign, the decayed
> remains would tremble in the gray
> air, for the void doesn't swallow them.
>
> Hence the gesture is annulled,
> and every voice is hushed,
> and barren life descends to its mouth.
>
> Se tu l'accenni, all'aria
> bigia treman corrotte
> le vestigia
> che il vuoto non ringhiotte.
>
> Il gesto indi s'annulla,
> tace ogni voce,
> discende alla sua foce
> la vita brulla.

The implicitly symbolic evocativeness of such lines as "our world can hardly stand [il nostro mondo / si regge appena]" or "the gesture is annulled, / and every voice is hushed [il gesto indi s'annulla, / tace ogni voce]" is itself as thin and ethereal as a lost cicada's faint sistrum. In "Cigola la carrucola del pozzo" the delicacy of feeling and diction as well as of conceit and imagery is so finely balanced as to charge the impressionistic precision and concreteness of detail with a subtle symbolism. The poem centers around what Montale himself was to call "the sudden leap of memory [lo scatto di ricordo]" ("Voce giunta con le folaghe," *La bufera*), in this case the memory of a woman loved coming to life and reflected on the surface of the water drawn from a well. The reflection is poignantly short-lived, for as the poet approaches "the melting lips [evanescenti labbri]," the pail returns to the well. Thus, not only are the memory and the vision lost in the dark depths of the water, but the past is also deformed and seems to belong to someone else:

> The pulley creaks in the well,
> the water comes up and merges
> with the light. A memory trembles
> in the pail full to the brim,
> and an image laughs in the pure circle.
> I bend my face to the melting
> lips; the past is deformed,
> becomes old; it belongs to someone else . . .
> But already the pulley creaks again,
> returns you to the dark depths,
> and a distance divides us.

> Cigola la carrucola del pozzo,
> l'acqua sale alla luce e vi si fonde.
> Trema un ricordo nel ricolmo secchio,
> nel puro cerchio un'immagine ride.
> Accosto il volto a evanescenti labbri:
> si deforma il passato, si fa vecchio,
> appartiene ad un altro....
>   Ah che già stride
> la ruota, ti ridona all'atro fondo,
> visione, una distanza ci divide.

This poem offers an impressive degree of emotional, thematic and architectonic coherence, which, together with the firmly controlled pathos and intensity implicit in the theme, makes it one of the most accomplished lyrics in *Ossi di seppia*. The harsh, mechanical character of the first line serves as a foil to the evocative image of the water rising from the well and merging with the light, thus preparing the ground for the still happier image of a memory trembling in the pail and laughing in the "pure circle." Tempted by the image in the water, which is both illusory and short-lived, the poet approaches "the melting lips," only to find the illusion shattered and "the past . . . deformed" to such an extent that it can't even be recognized or seems to belong to someone else. And as if to clinch the end of such a reverie, "the pulley creaks again," life resumes its normal course, and as the image is consigned to the dark depths of the water, distance (measuring both time and space) and division resume their sway.

In "Arremba su la strinata proda" both symbolism and the objective correlative device enrich the impressionistic setting. A child is playing with his
paper boats; the poet asks him to pull them ashore and sleep in peace without being afraid of the evil spirits who sail in fleets. He wishes for the child
that sense of peace and tranquility which he himself lacks and which he
cannot possess because of his feeling and awareness of impending doom, so
that only a second suffices to destroy "the slow work of months [l'opera lenta
di mesi]." That there is something mysterious about this doom emerges from
the description of the atmosphere—the owl flying about in the garden and
the trails of smoke lingering heavily on the roofs. Hence what the poet tells
the child in the last line acquires an ominous poignancy:

> The owl flies about in the garden
> and trails of smoke are heavy
> on the roofs. Then comes the second
> that destroys the slow work of months,
> now cracking in secret, now uprooting in a gust.
>
> The split comes perhaps without a din.[27]
> He who'd built senses his own doom.
> In this hour only a hove-to boat is saved.
> Moor your fleet among the hedges.

> Nel chiuso dell'ortino svolacchia il gufo
> e i fumacchi dei tetti sono pesi.
> L'attimo che rovina l'opera lenta di mesi
> giunge: ora incrina segreto, ore divelge in un buffo.
>
> Viene lo spacco; forse senza strepito.
> Chi ha edificato sente la sua condanna.
> È l'ora che si salva solo la barca in panna.
> Amarra la tua flotta tra le siepi.

Of the last two poems in the *Ossi di seppia* group, "Upupa, ilare uccello
calunniato" is the weaker—weaker not only than "Sul muro grafito" but also
than any other poem in the group. It is sustained not so much by a genuinely
creative interest as by literary echoes and associations, especially from Foscolo
and Parini. Added to this is the apparent lack of moral or psychological
tension, so that when the poet does strike a deeper note as, for instance, when
he talks about time having stopped and February not dying for the bird, it
somehow seems to be forced. But in "Sul muro grafito" some of the calm

27. Cf. T. S. Eliot: "This is the way the world ends / Not with a bang but a whimper"
("The Hollow Men").

self-assurance and maturity of "Spesso il male di vivere" returns. There is a touch of classic neatness and perfection about the arch of the sky representing both what is finite and what, by inference, is infinite, or about the opaque forms lying scattered "in a cold repose [in un riposo freddo]." As the poet contemplates these forms his mind turns to the past fire "which burnt impetuously / in the veins of the world [ch'arse / impetuoso / nelle vene del mondo]" and to the future:

> Tomorrow I'll see the docks again,
> the wall and the familiar road.
>
> Rivedrò domani le banchine
> e la muraglia e l'usata strada.

Here the adjective *familiar* bears the whole weight and force of what is old and immutable. The only change afforded is the momentary suspense which lays bare not only the present in its static "cold repose," but also the future symbolized by mornings "anchored like boats in a roadstead." The feeling of what is static is, however, conveyed not so much by the word *anchored* as by the image of a cold repose.

The *Ossi di seppia* group is followed by another group called *Mediterraneo*, consisting of nine poems which offer the most impassioned lyrical celebration of the sea that Italian poetry has ever known—not the sea in general, but the Mediterranean sea which laps the Cinque Terre and the Ligurian coast with its distinctively rocky and rugged contours. Critics have been at variance in their assessment of *Mediterraneo*. Gargiulo regarded it as "the most beautiful series" of lyrics in the book. It is the sea, he said, and the sea alone which "can renew in him [Montale] the feeling of an enchanted nirvana and move him with the infinite aspects of its marvelous ferment." [28] Sergio Solmi, on the other hand, while giving this series a very high place in contemporary poetry, nevertheless had certain reservations about the element of rhetoric in it as well as about the use of "approximate" images and themes that are not fully developed.[29] For Contini the series may have been "the most interesting from the documentary point of view," but it was not "the most fruitful in poetic results." [30] As for Solmi, he seems to have changed his view over the years. In a recent letter to me, he admitted that when he reviewed *Ossi di seppia* in 1926 he was still under the influence of post-Crocean aesthetics, which led him to advance the reservations he did

28. *Letteratura italiana del Novecento*, p. 457.
29. *Scrittori negli anni*, p. 23.
30. "Introduzione a *Ossi di seppia*," in *Esercizi di lettura* (Florence: Le Monnier, 1947), p. 75.

concerning *Mediterraneo*. Today he considers it "one of the highest achieve-
ments, perhaps the highest achievement of Montale's poetry." [31] Be that as it
may, there can be no doubt that *Mediterraneo* represents the most ambitious
and most impassioned poetic evocation of and dialogue with the sea. It is
seen as a symbol of cosmic and eternal life as well as a source and inspiration
of the poet's moral and poetic thinking. It has, one might say, the same importance for Montale as Nature had for Wordsworth (The anchor of my
purest thoughts, the nurse, / The guide, the guardian of my heart and soul /
Of all my moral being——) [32] or as Egdon Heath had for Thomas Hardy.
It is both something to contemplate and something that helps the poet in
the task of self-exploration and self-realization, both a guide and a task-
master, a challenge and a consolation. There is no other aspect of nature that
Montale seems to be so instinctively and passionately in sympathy with as the
sea. The tone of lyric abandonment and fervor that characterizes his diction
in these poems is evidence of his familiarity with and insight into the laws
and mystery of the sea. What the suggestive world of the Mediterranean, and
even more specifically of the Ligurian coast, signifies for him is sensuously
wedded to the task of self-exploration and self-realization. The act of per-
ceiving and interpreting what the sea has to offer thus goes hand in hand
with the poet's analysis of his moral and psychological self and of his position vis-à-vis the sea:

When the louder or less loud
din of waters choked by a long
stretch of shallows reaches me;
or sometimes it's the roar
of foam showering again on the rocks.
And as I raise my face
there's a lull above me; two jays,
like azure-white arrows, dart
toward the thundering waves.

Quando più sordo o meno il ribollio dell'acque
che s'ingorgano
accanto a lunghe secche mi raggiunge:
o è un bombo talvolta ed un ripiovere
di schiume sulle rocce.

31. "Recensendo nel '26 gli *Ossi di seppia*," Solmi wrote, "facevo qualche riserva su *Mediterraneo*. Si è che ero ancora influenzato dall'estetica 'frammentista' post-crociana. . . . Poco più tardi mi ricredetti, e ritengo tuttora *Mediterraneo* uno dei più alti esiti, forse il più alto, della poesia montaliana" (Letter to G. Singh, November 24, 1970).
32. "Lines Written a Few Miles Above Tintern Abbey."

> Come rialzo il viso, ecco cessare
> i ragli sul mio capo; e scoccare
> verso le strepeanti acque,
> frecciate biancazzurre, due ghiandaie.

Montale's sense of being inebriated by the voice of the sea helps him to find his spiritual bearings and to translate them into poetic terms and concepts, which are expressed through a vigorous realism of detail that prevents the nostalgic and romantic motifs implicit in the theme or "occasion" of the poem from giving way to a facile sentimentality:

> The house of my far-off summers
> was by your side, you know,
> in the country where the sun beats down
> and the air is thick with mosquitoes.

> La casa delle mie estati lontane,
> t'era accanto, lo sai,
> là nel paese dove il sole cuoce
> e annuvolano l'aria le zanzare.

From this idyllic note the poet proceeds to a moral and analytical comment on what the sea and "the solemn admonition of your breath ([solenne ammonimento / del tuo respiro]" ("Antico, sono ubriacato dalla voce") once meant to him and what it means now:

> You were the first to tell me
> that the tiny ferment of my heart
> was only a motion of yours;
> that your perilous law was at
> the very core of my being:
> to be vast and different, yet fixed.

> . . . Tu m'hai detto primo
> che il piccino fermento
> del mio cuore non era che un momento
> del tuo; che mi era in fondo
> la tua legge rischiosa: esser vasto e diverso
> e insieme fisso:

Thus the sea performs much the same office in Montale's moral and poetic development as the rainbow does in Wordsworth's—namely, that of binding his days "each to each by natural piety."[33] In "Scendendo qualche volta" the

33. "My Heart Leaps up."

moral and metaphysical observations—"the cycle of the seasons and the drip-ping / of inexorable time [la ruota delle stagioni e il gocciare / del tempo inesorabile]," for example—are so closely interwoven in the poetry of the seascape that almost each and every detail seems to be charged, even though not always intentionally, with a symbolism of its own. In other words, the sense of attachment to the sea so imbues the poet's heart and mind that each object around fills him with rapture and at the same time heightens his metaphysical awareness. The very panting "of the hitherto motionless air / on the rocks that bordered the path [dell'aria, prima immota, / sulle rocce che orlavano il cammino]" seems to reflect his state of mind as well as the spirit of what is before him:

> . . . the stone
> wanted to be torn off, stretched out
> in an invisible embrace;
> the hard material sensed
> the coming vortex, and throbbed;
> and the tufts of the eager reeds
> gave to the hidden waters
> their trembling consent.

> . . . la pietra
> voleva strapparsi, protesa
> a un invisibile abbraccio;
> la dura materia sentiva
> il prossimo gorgo, e pulsava;
> e i ciuffi delle avide canne
> dicevano all'acque nascoste,
> scrollando, un assentimento.

Here the vastness and dynamism of the sea are personalized as an almost tyrannical force subduing everything large and small (the stone as well as the clump of reeds), which lie prostrate before it, as if in a fit of passionate surrender. The "suffering of the stones [il patire dei sassi]" is a measure not only of the sea's physical might, but also of its moral and emotional hold over the poet: "I bent among the pebbles, / and the salty breezes entered my heart [Chinavo tra le petraie, / giungevano buffi salmastri / al cuore]."

The sea's capacity to inspire the poet with moral awe is dependent on its phantasmagorically rich and varied moods and aspects—its grottos "vast or narrow, / shady and bitter [vaste / o anguste, ombrose e amare]," its "power-ful architectures filled / with the sky [architetture / possenti campite di cielo]," and its "airy temples, spires, and shooting lights [aerei templi, / guglie scoccanti luci]," as they are brought out in "Ho sostato talvolta." They form a canvas on which he paints his "dream country [patria sognata]," his "uncorrupted land [paese incorotto]." The fusion of the moral and the descriptive, the physical and the metaphysical in what the sea means to the poet is cogently effected in the following passage:

> Thus, father, your unbridled fury
> proclaims a severe law
> to whoever watches you. It's impossible
> to escape it: if I try even a corroded
> pebble on my path condemns me
> —petrified suffering without a name—
> or the shapeless rubbish which the river
> of life cast aside in a tangle
> of branches and straw.

> Così, padre, dal tuo disfrenamento
> si afferma, chi ti guardi, una legge severa.
> Ed è vano sfuggirla: mi condanna
> s'io lo tento anche un ciottolo
> ròso sul mio cammino,
> impietrato soffrire senza nome,
> o l'informe rottame
> che gittò fuor del corso la fiumara
> del vivere in un fitto di ramure e di strame.

Thus the sea's is a presence in Montale's moral and poetic universe "which is not to be put by."[34] It enacts what it inculcates, namely, the sense of the moral law, as well as the concept of evolution allegorized by the image of the river of life casting aside what cannot contribute to the fulfillment of nature's plan or what is too weak to fend for itself in the struggle for survival: "shapeless rubbish which the river / of life cast aside in a tangle / of branches and straw." Such a spectacle induces the poet to assess what destiny may have in store for him: "In the destiny that is in store for me / there's perhaps some respite, / which nothing can threaten [Nel destino che si prepara / c'è forse per me sosta, / niun'altra mai minaccia]." This, with its characteristic "perhaps," is also the message of the sea, both in its wild fury and in its "brief spell of calm [filo della bonaccia]."

However, as in "Giunge a volte," the fury of the sea sometimes frightens the poet, marring the sense of harmony between them, as a result of which

34. The phrase occurs in Wordsworth's "Ode on Intimations of Immortality."

he falls back on himself "devoid of force [vuota di forza]," the thread of communication is well-nigh broken and "your voice seems hollow [la tua voce pare sorda]." This leads him to delve deeper into the question of his personal identity, both in terms of its dependence on and its alienation from the sea conceived as a father figure. For his feeling of disquiet—"silence is still missing from my life [manca ancora il silenzio nella mia vita]"—is part of "the rancor / that every son, sea, feels toward his father [la rancura / che ogni figliuolo, mare, ha per il padre]."

Exploration into the nature and meaning of destiny continues to engage the poet in the poem "Noi non sappiamo quale sortiremo," with its note of uncertainty and doubt as to the future, both in the personal as well as impersonal sense: "We don't know what sort of fate / will befall us tomorrow, bleak or cheerful [Noi non sappiamo quale sortiremo / domani, oscuro o lieto]." Whatever the future may hold, the poet wishes that something of the gift of the sea "might pass forever into the syllables / that we carry about with us, humming bees [sia passato per sempre nelle sillabe / che rechiamo con noi, api ronzanti]." And he hopes that the memory of what the sea once meant to him will continue to haunt and help him in life:

> We shall go far and cherish
> an echo of your voice, as the gray grass
> remembers the sun in the dark
> courtyards among the houses.
> And one day these words without sound
> which we nurtured with you
> on weariness and silence will seem
> to a fraternal heart
> to savour of the salt of Greece.

> Lontani andremo e serberemo un'eco
> della tua voce, come si ricorda
> del sole l'erba grigia
> nelle corti scurite, tra le case.
> E un giorno queste parole senza rumore
> che teco educammo nutrite
> di stanchezze e di silenzi,
> parranno a un fraterno cuore
> sapide di sale greco.

By virtue of its moral and emotional hold on him, the sea thus provides the poet with a measuring-rod or criterion, so to speak. And this makes him

probe into the depths of his moral and philosophical nature and portray its
various facets in terms of poetic concepts and imagery:

> I would have liked to feel myself rugged and essential,
> like the salt-eaten pebbles that you keep
> turning over—a splinter cast
> outside of time—testimony
> of a cold unfaltering will.
> But I was different: a man intent
> on watching in himself and others
> the seething of a transient life,
> and slow to the act which none
> destroys.
>
> . . . .
>
> Having followed a beaten path,
> I soon found my heart lured
> by an opposite one; perhaps
> I needed the knife that severs,
> the mind that decides and resolves;
> other books did I need than your roaring
> page. But I regret nothing:
> you still loosen inner knots with your song
> and your frenzy now soars to the stars.

> Avrei voluto sentirmi scabro ed essenziale
> siccome i ciottoli che tu volvi,
> mangiati dalla salsedine;
> scheggia fuori del tempo, testimone
> di una volontà fredda che non passa.
> Altro fui: uomo intento che riguarda
> in sè, in altrui, il bollore
> della vita fugace —— uomo che tarda
> all'atto, che nessuno, poi, distrugge.
>
> . . . .
>
> Seguìto il solco d'un sentiero m'ebbi
> l'opposto in cuore, col suo invito; e forse
> m'occorreva il coltello che recide,
> la mente che decide e si determina.
> Altri libri occorrevano
> a me, non la tua pagina rombante.
> Ma nulla so rimpiangere: tu sciogli

> ancora i groppi interni col tuo canto.
> Il tuo delirio sale agli astri ormai.

This passage has not only an autobiographical significance, but also a stylistic
and technical one, adumbrating, as it does, some of the qualities of Montale's
later and philosophically and symbolically more complex verse (for instance,
"Dora Markus," some of the Motets, "La casa dei doganieri," "Voce giunta
con le folaghe," "Il sogno del prigioniero," and "Piccolo testamento"). The
phrase "rugged and essential" defines the characteristic amalgam in Montale's
poetry between the neo-Petrarchan vein and caustic self-appraisal entailed by
the "critical corrosion of existence." The discursive flow and subtlety, and the
rhythmic suppleness in this poem are an index of his firm grasp on what he
wants to convey and what is firmly rooted in personal experience. For instance,
the line "the act which none / destroys" is broken in such a way in the
original as to reflect the degree of cool deliberation and decisiveness behind
the act as well as the lasting nature of the impact it makes. Thus while
analyzing such an experience, he transforms it into a moral and philosophical
concept, which enables him to contemplate it with a certain degree of detachment and objectivity. As a result, his diction attains a "rugged and essential"
character and at the same time maintains a certain degree of the warmth and
intimacy of a personal confession, without creating any hiatus or incongruity.
The crystalline hardness and gnomic succinctness of such impersonal phrases
as a man "slow to the act," "the knife that severs," or "the mind that decides
and resolves" confer an inexorable finality on what he has perceived both in
and around himself. For instance, in the lines,

> other books did I need than your roaring
> page. But I regret nothing:
> you still loosen inner knots with your song
> and your frenzy now soars to the stars—

the impact of the concept—which is essentially a moral one—is conveyed
through the sea's frenzy, which in its turn finds a rhythmic and rhetorical
counterpart. In other words, these lines fulfill, to a certain extent, the poet's
desire to match the frenzy of the sea with the lyric power of words—"compel /
into this labored rhythm of mine / some wild raving of yours [costringere /
in questo mio ritmo stento / qualche poco del tuo vaneggiamento]" and "accord my stammering speech / with your voice [accordare alle tue voci il mio
balbo parlare]," as he says in "Potessi almeno costringere." In order to voice
his "melancholy of a child grown old / who should not have thought [la mia
malinconia / di fanciullo invecchiato che non doveva pensare]," the poet has

recourse to the sea, with its "salty words / in which nature and art are fused [salmastre parole / in cui natura ed arte si confondono]." However, though it can help him express this melancholy, it cannot enable him to overcome it, since it is the sea itself, with its "roaring page [pagina rombante]" ("Avrei voluto sentirmi"), which has to some extent inspired the thoughts and feelings, the dreams and desires, which are the very essence of that melancholy. The poet realizes, too, that in order to communicate his experience as a mature adult—an experience which alone can help him to reassess what his early communion with the sea really meant—he needs a more subtle and more complex medium than the sea's "salty words" can furnish him. He is thus confronted with the problem of language; for the "child grown old / who should not have thought" has now not only to take leave of the dreams and illusions of childhood, but also to find a language that can adequately express his more mature feelings and experience. And he doesn't always succeed in this task, for the language that he finds himself using often becomes "mournful literature":

> I have only the worn-out letters of dictionaries,
> and the obscure voice that love
> dictates grows weaker,
> becomes mournful literature. I have
> only these words which like
> women of the street
> offer themselves to all who want them;
> only these tired phrases
> which student rabbles of true verse might
> steal from me even tomorrow.

> Ed invece non ho che le lettere fruste
> dei dizionari, e l'oscura
> voce che amore detta s'affioca,
> si fa lamentosa letteratura.
> Non ho che queste parole
> che come donne pubblicate
> s'offrono a chi le richiede;
> non ho che queste frasi stancate
> che potranno rubarmi anche domani
> gli studenti canaglie in versi veri.

On the one hand the linguistic dilemma that cannot be easily resolved, and on the other the spell that the sea still exercises over the poet, constitute a moral as well as a poetic challenge. For a moment he seems to be lost in the contemplation of the might, vastness, and mystery of the sea and even to become one with it:

> My thoughts abandon me in a rush:
> I have neither sense nor senses. I am limitless.

> M'abbandonano a prova i miei pensieri.
> Sensi non ho; nè senso. Non ho limite.

"Dissipa tu se lo vuoi," the last poem in the group, recapitulates the themes and motifs that have been dealt with in the previous poems as well as the various links between past and present, between what the sea meant to the poet in his childhood and what it means now in his mature experience. Thus to the "order" or the "event" which the sea once represented for the poet is now added the sense of "the heavy and the weary weight / Of all this unintelligible world," [35] which mature age and experience have brought. In fact, as a result of this and in the course of living the poet seems to have forgotten that event or order to which he once instinctively swore allegiance. However, even now, whenever he is reminded of it by the surf on the shore, he feels like returning and surrendering himself to its charm:

> My coming was a testimony to an order
> that I forgot along the way,
> these words of mine swear faith
> to an impossible event, and don't know it.
> But whenever I heard
> your sweet surf on the shore,
> consternation overtook me as it does
> a man who, having lost his memory,
> recalls his country.

> La mia venuta era testimonianza
> di un ordine che in viaggio mi scordai,
> giurano fede queste mie parole
> a un evento impossibile, e lo ignorano.
> Ma sempre che traudii
> la tua dolce risacca su le prode
> sbigottimento mi prese
> quale d'uno scemato di memoria
> quando si risovviene del suo paese.

35. Wordsworth, "Lines Written a Few Miles above Tintern Abbey."

But of all the roles that Montale attributes to the sea—a father figure, a source of the moral law and poetic inspiration, custodian of an order and a secret—it is as an ultimate point of reference in his quest for personal identity that it is most important. Inspired by "some desolate noon of yours [qualche tuo meriggio desolato]," the poet tells the sea, he is not only spellbound by its charm, but he also recognizes (self-realization and self-identification proceeding in close collaboration with each other) that he is "only a spark from a beacon [favilla d'un tirso]":

> Having taken my lesson
> not from your open glory,
> but from the hardly audible panting
> of some desolate noon of yours,
> I surrender myself to you in humility.
> I'm only a spark from a beacon.
> I know it: to burn,
> this—nothing else—is my significance.

> Presa la mia lezione
> più che dalla tua gloria
> aperta, dall'ansar
> che quasi non dà suono
> di qualche tuo meriggio desolato,
> a te mi rendo in umiltà. Non sono
> che favilla d'un tirso. Bene lo so: bruciare,
> questo, non altro, è il mio significato.

Thus, together with the poems in the *Ossi di seppia* group, *Mediterraneo* represents an important stage in Montale's career as a poet and a craftsman. The lyric-cum-rhapsodic elements of *Mediterraneo* were not to be repeated in Montale's subsequent verse, and the youthful élan and passion that characterize it were to be kept increasingly under technical as well as moral control—if not altogether sacrificed—in the interest of a more complex and more elaborately organized pattern of symbolic and allusive detail in *Le occasioni* and *La bufera*. From the dual process of abandonment to the spell of the sea and nostalgic recollection of what it meant in the past, the poet was to retire within himself, or at least to shift his angle of vision to other aspects of nature, as for instance to "the classical architecture of the Tuscan hills." [36] Thus, if there is one group of poems in *Ossi di seppia* that represents

36. "Le classiche architetture dei colli toscani," "Intenzioni: intervista immaginaria," p. 346.

"the first fine careless rapture" of Montale's creative life, it is *Mediterraneo*. The carelessness of the rapture, however, doesn't mean lack of artistic or technical discipline. It is in fact the outcome of a very high degree of discipline—verbal, technical, and stylistic. In his later poetry the sea was not, of course, to be altogether shelved but to serve more as a background for past recollections than as a personalized force.

In the following group of poems, *Meriggi e ombre,* for instance, there is more or less the same thematic and stylistic unity as in *Mediterraneo,* and yet the sea is distanced so as to become merely an object of recollection. In other words, it is not a principal source of poetic inspiration to be reckoned with. In "Fine dell'infanzia," there is no direct communion or dialogue with the sea such as we find in *Mediterraneo;* nevertheless, the dynamic aspects of the sea— "a pulsating furrowed sea [un mare pulsante, sbarrato da solchi]"—both reflect the music of the restless soul of a mature man, "which can't decide," and serve as a background to the idyllic scenes of childhood that are so tenderly evoked:

> Pure hills nestled round
> the houses and the sea; olive trees
> clothed them, scattered here and there
> like herds, or tenuous as smoke
> from a farmhouse, floating
> across the bright face of the sky.

> Pure colline chiudevano d'intorno
> marina e case; ulivi le vestivano
> qua e là disseminati come greggi,
> o tenui come il fumo di un casale
> che veleggi
> la faccia candente del cielo.

Montale turns to these scenes as Wordsworth turned to the sylvan Wye "in darkness, and amid the many shapes / Of joyless daylight" ("Tintern Abbey"), scenes which are recaptured with a vivid and poignant wistfulness and which contain certain conscious Leopardian echoes.[37] Living is recalled as having been "too novel an adventure / hour by hour and the heart / was thrilled

---

37. Cf. "quei monti; varcarli pur non osa / la memoria stancata" and Leopardi:

> . . . la vista
> Di quel lontano mar, quei monti azzurri,
> Che di qua scopro, e che varcare un giorno
> Io mi pensava . . .
>
>   "Le ricordanze"

[ventura troppo nuova / ora per ora, e ne batteva il cuore]." A suggestively
Utopian pen-portrait, this, of the world of childhood, with its specific topographical and geographical contours that now seem to have irredeemably
dissolved:

> Years flew by brief as days
> and a strong and voracious sea
> devoured each certainty . . .

> Volarono anni corti come giorni,
> sommerse ogni certezza un mare florido
> e vorace . . .

The sea represented an order, a point of reference, and gave both a meaning
and definition to the world of the poet's childhood, ensuring a complete
harmony between what he felt within and what he saw around him: "every
movement of the spirit / found a quick response / in the world outside, and
each / thing had a name, and our world / a center [rapido rispondeva / a
ogni moto dell'anima un consenso / esterno, si vestivano di nomi / le cose, il
nostro mondo aveva un centro]." All this, however, comes to an end; and
"heavy clouds [pesanti nubi]," the "perturbed sea [turbato mare]," and "a
stormy event [procelloso evento]" externalize the state of perplexity and bewilderment that followed:

> No doubt we watched mutely,
> waiting for the violent moment;
> then in the false calm above
> the hollowed waters a wind
> started up.

> Certo guardammo muti nell'attesa
> del minuto violento;
> poi nella finta calma
> sopra l'acque scavate
> dovè mettersi un vento.

The imagery in this poem—for instance, "stunted creatures / lost in a horror
of visions [stente creature / perdute in un orrore di visioni]" or "the mold's
damp recesses / covered with shadows and silence [recessi madidi di muffe, /
d'ombre coperti e di silenzi]"—as well as in the following poems, depicts the
disintegration of the golden age of childhood both in realistic and metaphorical
terms. In "Scirocco," "Tramontana," and "Maestrale," a greater degree of
organic compactness is achieved by means of the fusion of such diverse

elements as reflection and evocation, analytical description and comment, than
is the case with "Fine dell'infanzia." Moreover, the sense of the dissolution of
time is at once sharper and more anguished in a poem like "Scirocco":

> Perplexed hours,
> shuddering of a life that escapes
> like water through the fingers.

> Ore perplesse, brividi
> d'una vita che fugge
> come acqua tra le dita.

And preying upon this sense is the knowledge of "events not realized, lights–
shadows, / commotion of the earth's unsteady / things [inafferrati eventi, /
luci-ombre, commovimenti / delle cose malferme della terra]," which contributes to a sense of metaphysical immobility and which the poet feels "like
a torment [come un tormento]." His identifying himself with the agave "that
takes root in the cleft of the reef [l'agave che s'abbarbica al crepaccio / dello
scoglio]" and "runs out from the clutches / of the seaweed into the sea /
which devours the rocks / in its wide-open throat [sfugge al mare da le
braccia d'alghe / che spalanca ampie gole e abbranca rocce]" brings about
a subtle combination of pathetic fallacy and objective correlative. For while
offering the objective correlative for the poet's desire to escape from the imprisonment of immobility, it at the same time enacts that desire. And the
concept of immobility is itself conveyed through the image of "my closed
buds / no longer capable of exploding [i miei racchiusi bocci / che non sanno
più esplodere]." In "Tramontana," however, the poet reacts against this
immobility; leaves behind "the circles of anxiety / that formed on the lake of
the heart [li circoli d'ansia / che discorrevano il lago del cuore]", and identifies
himself with the north wind which, with its iron will,

> . . . sweeps through the air, uprooting
> shrubs, and belaboring the palm-trees
> as it carves in the hard-pressed sea
> deep furrows crested with foam.

> . . . spazza l'aria,
> divelle gli arbusti, strapazza i palmizi
> e nel mare compresso scava
> grandi solchi crestati di bava.

"The turmoil of the elements [subbuglio degli elementi]," too, serves as an
incentive for the poet to react against the torment of immobility and at the

same time as a symbol both of the torment and of the reaction. The firm resolve with which he pursues his goal of self-realization is subject to the law of time that crushes everything in the fury of its march. However, such is the commotion of the elements (the "unbridled winds [venti disfrenati]"), that he is driven to cling to his roots. "My frail life," he says (echoing Leopardi's "esser mio frale"),[38] "how you cling to your roots today [mia vita sottile . . . come ami / oggi le tue radici]." In "Maestrale," which may be regarded as the Montalian counterpart of Leopardi's "La quiete dopo la tempesta," the calm that follows the northwest wind and the smooth sea under the blue and cloudless sky reflect "this poor restless life of mine [codesta povera mia vita turbata]," whereas the image of the seabird conveys a sense of liberation from the imprisonment of immobility.

In "Vasca," one of the earlier poems, the sense of metaphysical suspense, suggested by "the bright surface [la tesa lucente]" of the pool, is abruptly broken by a single casual act:

> The smile of a flowering belladonna
> passed over the tremulous glass,
> clouds kept pressing upon the branches
> and their dim soft reflection
> rose to the surface from the depths.
> One of us threw a stone,
> breaking the bright surface
> and shattering the delicate forms.
>
> Passò sul tremulo vetro
> un riso di belladonna fiorita,
> di tra le rame urgevano le nuvole,
> dal fondo ne riassommava
> la vista fioccosa e sbiadita.
> Alcuno di noi tirò un ciottolo
> che ruppe la tesa lucente:
> le molli parvenze s'infransero.

However, when the water is calm again, another image rises to the surface. But it also disappears before acquiring a definite form or identity, which is

38. Cf. Leopardi:

> Questo io conosco e sento,
> Che degli eterni giri,
> Che dell'esser mio frale,
> Qualche bene o contento
> Avrà fors'altri; a me la vita è male
>
> "Canto notturno di un pastore errante dell'Asia"

Montale's allegorical mode of interpreting the pathos and tragedy, not so much of unfulfilled ambitions, as of something nipped in the bud:

> But look, something else is creeping
> to the surface of the pond that's smooth
> again; it doesn't know how
> to come forth, wants to live
> but doesn't know how;
> if you look at it, it turns away,
> goes down. It was born and now
> it's dead and it didn't even have a name.

> Ma ecco, c'è altro che striscia
> a fior della spera rifatta liscia:
> di erompere non ha virtù,
> vuol vivere e non sa come;
> se lo guardi si stacca, torna in giù:
> è nato e morto, e non ha avuto un nome.

The last three poems in this section "Egloga," "Flussi," and "Clivo" are thematically (and not merely thematically) linked with "Fine dell'infanzia," insofar as they recapture the world of the past through an interplay of specifically focused objects, associations, and landmarks like those on which some of the stories of *Farfalla di Dinard* are based. The nostalgic tenderness suffusing each object or circumstance does not, however, make it appear any less sharply defined:

> To be lost in the undulating gray
> of my olive trees—trees alive
> with turbulent birds and singing
> streams was once a pleasure.

> Perdersi nel bigio ondoso
> dei miei ulivi era buono
> nel tempo andato—loquaci
> di riottanti uccelli
> e di cantanti rivi.

Memories from the past are woven into a rich pattern of realistic impressions and details on the one hand and philosophical fancies and reflections on the other. Against such a background emerges "a female apparition [una parvenza di donna]," which has a more important role in Montale's later poetry. Moreover, these impressions also form a canvas on which the poet can depict his philosophical ideas, as in "Flussi"—

An arrow shines in the air,
fixes in a fence, quivers.
Life is but this show of trite facts,
more vain than cruel—

Brilla in aria una freccia,
si configge s'un palo, oscilla tremula.
La vita è questo scialo
di triti fatti, vano
più che crudele—

bringing out Montale's sense of reality and his firm hold on "the mighty
world / Of eye and ear." [39] Like other such poems where the theme of love is
either not present at all or remains in the background, this poem effects a
poetic union between past and present and between what is observed and what
is intuited. This makes the context both poetically charged and philosophically
rich: "the known fruit no longer hangs / from its branch [dalla sua rama
non dipende / il frutto conosciuto]," "only the statue knows / that time pre-
cipitates and hides / even more amidst the bright ivy [soltanto la statua / sa
che il tempo precipita e s'infrasca / vie più nell'accesa edera]," or "life is more
vain than cruel [la vita è (vana) più che crudele]."

That the poetic efficacy of such ideas or concepts does not depend on their
philosophical validity, and that whatever validity they may have derives
largely from the context in which they are collocated, is illustrated by the
last poem of *Meriggi e ombre*. In "Clivo" the image of the earth that "dis-
solves on the breakers [dissolve sui frangenti]" allegorically represents the
world's renewal, just as "the barks at dawn [le barche all'alba]" suggest the
way the light displays "its great veils [le sue grandi vele]" and hope finds its
way into the human heart. However, when this reverie comes to an end,
"even though the wind is still / you hear the file assiduously / sawing the
chain that binds us [e s'anche il vento tace / senti la lima che sega / assidua
la catena che ci lega]." And what this assiduous process achieves is described
by means of images that are at once vividly pictorial and concrete:

The sound descends, a musical
landslide, then fades away
and so do the gathered voices
from the arid spirals of the cleft,
the groaning of slopes among vines
held tight by the roots.
The hillock paths are no longer

39. Wordsworth, "Lines Written a Few Miles above Tintern Abbey."

there; hands clasp the branches
of dwarf pines; then the day's splendor
trembles and wanes.

Come una musicale frana
divalla il suono, s'allontana.
Con questo si disperdono le accolte
voci dalle volute
aride dei crepacci;
il gemito delle pendìe,
là tra le viti che i lacci
delle radici stringono.
Il clivo non ha più vie,
le mani s'afferrano ai rami
dei pini nani; poi trema
e scema il bagliore del giorno . . .

In the end the commotion subsides,

and an order descends
freeing from their bonds
things that now ask nothing more
than to endure, to persist,
content with the infinite toil
—a heap of stones falling from the sky,
and sinking near the shore.

And in the early evening one hears
the hooting of cornets, dissolving.

e un ordine discende che districa
dai confini
le cose che non chiedono
ormai che di durare, di persistere
contente dell'infinita fatica;
un crollo di pietrame che dal cielo
s'inabissa alle prode....

Nella sera distesa appena, s'ode
un ululo di corni, uno sfacelo.

This is an impressive example of the subtle and concrete rendering of the sense of metaphysical determinism that underlies much of Montale's poetry.

The second section of *Meriggi e ombre* consists of one poem only, "Arsenio," one of Montale's most characteristic poems, in which the deterministic nature of the order binding both man and objects asserts itself in a more explicitly personalized form. It was written, as Montale points out in his succinct note, between 1926 and 1927, and is one of those poems (along with "Vento e bandiere," "Fuscello teso dal muro," "I morti," "Delta," and "Incontro") that were added to the second edition of *Ossi di seppia,* published in 1928 with Alfredo Gargiulo's preface. It may be regarded as a self-portrait in the form of a dramatic and philosophic dialogue with one's alter ego, representing through a series of various images and impressionistic details the poet's attempt to probe into the meaning and essence of his own destiny. Both the seascape and the storm, with their turmoil and frenzy, seem, like Arsenio, to be held in the grip of a mysterious deterministic power. Such images as "eddies of dust on the roof-tops [I turbini sollevano la polvere / sui tetti, a mulinelli]," "hooded horses sniffing the ground, / motionless, in front of the glistening / panes of the hotels [i cavalli incappucciati / annusano la terra, fermi innanzi / ai vetri luccicanti degli alberghi]," or "a refrain of castanets [un ritornello / di castagnette]" form a suggestive framework within which the poet expresses his mood of moral and philosophical uncertainty.

Everything he sees around him—familiar sights and sounds as well as natural phenomena—becomes a means of self-discovery for him and represents a milestone in the exploration of reality. He feels himself to be like a "link in a chain [anello d'una / catena]," caught up in "an all too familiar delirium / of immobility [troppo noto / delirio d'immobilità]." In such a mood of metaphysical contemplation, he finds the distinction between the real and the illusory, the near and the far, the personal and the impersonal, momentarily annulled: "The evening that's near seems far / away [lunge par la sera / ch'è prossima]," "the midday's turned into a night / of lighted globes swinging on the shore [muta il mezzogiorno in una notte / di globi accesi, dondolanti a riva]," or "One shadow only / holds both sea and sky [un'ombra sola tiene / mare e cielo]." Arsenio's profound and perspicuous awareness of himself as well as of the world outside him brings him in touch with the embryonic forces of life and with the "icy multitudes of the dead [ghiacciata moltitudine di morti]." The feeling of remorse for something blighted even before it could bloom heightens his sense of doom and imbues even the words and gestures of everyday life:

> and if a gesture brushes you
> or a word falls by your side
> in the melting hour, Arsenio,
> it's perhaps the token of a strangled

life that had risen for you
and that the wind carries with the ashes of the stars.

e se un gesto ti sfiora, una parola
ti cade accanto, quello è forse, Arsenio,
nell'ora che si scioglie, il cenno d'una
vita strozzata per te sorta, e il vento
la porta con la cenere degli astri.

The third section of *Meriggi e ombre,* also in some respects the most important, starts with "Crisalide." In this poem a subtle and complex type of pathetic fallacy is at work, which enables the poet to identify himself with the chrysalis on aesthetic, symbolic, and philosophical planes and to pinpoint the most characteristic traits and facets of his own personality. Moreover, he attributes to the chrysalis feelings and emotions, memories and reflections, as though it were the embodiment of the woman loved. Thus, here, as in some other poems in this group, a new factor emerges that gives an emotional coloring to Montale's philosophical reflections and questionings and at the same time adds an impetus to his quest for identity and self-realization. Even the notation of natural phenomena and the multiple aspects of the landscape have a certain pathos and delicacy as well as an illuminating vividness of detail about them. While "the air / vibrates with pity for the avid / roots, the tumid bark [Vibra nell'aria una pietà per l'avide / radici, per le tumide cortecce]," the poet plunges into a contemplation of the landscape around him.

In "Intenzioni: intervista immaginaria," Montale observes that the landscape is his prey, but in this poem his prey is the chrysalis. And what emerges from the encounter between him and his prey is an impassioned dramatic colloquy with the nascent forces of life and nature, symbolized by the plants on the one hand and the chrysalis on the other. "For me, as I watch you from this shadow," the poet tells the chrysalis, "another bush greens again / and you are there [Per me che vi contemplo da quest'ombra, / altro cespo riverdica, e voi siete]." The poet's participation in the life of nature is richly sensitive and imaginative, registering, as it does, the minutest changes and movements: "Each second brings you new leaves [Ogni attimo vi porta nuove fronde]," and "life reaches this remote corner / of the orchard in impetuous waves [viene a impetuose onde / la vita a questo estremo angolo d'orto]." But it is when his eye falls on the turf that, as if prompted by the contrast between the flourishing life of the plants and trees and the frustration of human hopes and aspirations,

memories surge up, and almost
overwhelm your heart. A cry

echoes in the distance; time plunges
and disappears with rapid
eddies among the rocks;
each memory is erased;
and from my dark corner I reach out
toward that solar event.

una risacca di memorie giunge
al vostro cuore e quasi lo sommerge.
Lunge risuona un grido: ecco precipita
il tempo, spare con risucchi rapidi
tra i sassi, ogni ricordo è spento; ed io
dall'oscuro mio canto mi protendo
a codesto solare avvenimento.

But if the chrysalis, representing both the object of love and the forces of animate as well as inanimate nature, makes the poet experience what he calls "a brief hour of human tremor [un'ora breve di tremore umano]," it also makes him realize how sterile each growth and renewal is by conjuring up in his mind the image of "the squalid limbo of maimed existences [limbo squallido delle monche esistenze]," which signifies something both unfulfilled and unrealizable, or "a prodigy that failed / like all those flowering beside us [un prodigio fallito come tutti / quelli che ci fioriscono d'accanto]." In other words, not only human endeavor, but even the renewal of nature comes to nothing. The setting sun and the clouds bring "the feverish, tremulous hour [l'ora di febbre, trepida]" to an end, and the image of the "boat of salvation [la barca di salvezza]" represents the desire to escape from this barren futility, "this nameless torture [questa tortura senza nome]." In describing this, Montale sounds the depths of Leopardian pessimism and at the same time achieves a philosophical lyricism comparable to that of "Canto notturno" and "La ginestra." An unblinking appraisal of what human life and destiny ultimately signify, and a full and frank recognition of the power of fate and chance in an amoral universe, form the philosophical core of the penultimate passage in "Crisalide," with its unaffected lyric simplicity:

Ah chrysalis how bitter is this nameless
torture that envelops us
and carries us far away;
not even our footprints are left in the dust
and we shall go forward without
even moving a single stone
of this great wall; perhaps

all is fixed, all's written,
and we won't see rising up on the way
liberty, the miracle, the fact
that wasn't necessary!

Ah crisalide, com'è amara questa
tortura senza nome che ci volve
e ci porta lontani—e poi non restano
neppure le nostre orme sulla polvere;
e noi andremo innanzi senza smuovere
un sasso solo della gran muraglia;
e forse tutto è fisso, tutto è scritto,
e non vedremo sorgere per via
la libertà, il miracolo,
il fatto che non era necessario!

From the admirably controlled lyricism and philosophical depth and impersonality of this passage the poet proceeds, in the final stanza, to something
personal and intimate based on the theme of love. But even the theme of
love has closely interwoven ethical and philosophical undertones, so that the
intensity of personal feeling and sentiment is transformed into moral and
philosophical depth:

Silence wraps us in its band
and lips don't open to announce
the pact I'd like to make
with destiny, to atone
for your joy with my condemnation.
This prayer still rises in my heart,
then every movement will cease.

Il silenzio ci chiude nel suo lembo
e le labbra non s'aprono per dire
il patto ch'io vorrei
stringere col destino: di scontare
la vostra gioia con la mia condanna.
È il voto che mi nasce ancora in petto,
poi finirà ogni moto.

The theme of love, with its characteristic concomitants, memory and moral
and metaphysical questionings, culminates in "Marezzo" and "Casa sul mare."
In the first poem, the poet and his female companion are out rowing on a
calm, bright day. As they emerge from a cave, he tells her to look at "the

world of the sea-bottom outlined / as if deformed by a lens [il mondo del fondo che si profila / come sformato da una lente]." The air around them is like "a smooth wing [un'ala morbida]," while the "slopes of lower vineyards [pendici di basse vigne]" stretch out toward them and gleaners sing "ditties with inhuman voices [stornellano spigolatrici / con voci disumane]." All this constitutes a momentary enchantment for the poet. He tells his friend to take care that "memory doesn't prick you / and disturb these calm noons [che ricordo non ti rimorda / che torbi questi meriggi calmi]." She should come out of her reverie, for "thoughts when too solitary / destroy themselves [Si struggono i pensieri troppo soli]." Then a great wave comes and subverts "forms and confines / and makes them abstract [forme confini resi astratti]," while "already each determined strength / deviates from its path [ogni forza decisa già diverte / dal cammino]." It is during such moments of rapt contemplation of the various forms and processes underlying what is before him that the poet realizes the nature and meaning of life. However, he also knows that "life grows by fits and starts [La vita cresce a scatti]," and that once such moments are gone, the anticlimax inevitably follows, and one is thrown back on the world of everyday experience and reality:

> Unburden your laden heart
> in the wave as it opens;
> like a ballast stone your name
> sinks in the water with a splash.
>
> . . . .
>
> You talk and don't recognize your
> own voice, your memory seems
> washed away; you have passed,
> yet you feel your life consumed.
>
> Now what happens? You feel your weight
> again, and things that were oscillating
> suddenly settle down on their hinges
> and the spell is broken.
>
> Disciogli il cuore gonfio
> nell'aprirsi dell'onda;
> come una pietra di zavorra affonda
> il tuo nome nell'acque con un tonfo.!
>
> . . . .
>
> Parli e non riconosci i tuoi accenti.
> La memoria ti appare dilavata.

> Sei passata e pur senti
> la tua vita consumata.
>
> Ora, che avviene?, tu riprovi il peso
> di te, improvvise gravano
> sui cardini le cose che oscillavano,
> e l'incanto è sospeso.

No wonder the poet and his companion wish the enchantment could go on forever:

> Ah let's stay here, let's not
> be different. Thus immobile.
>
> Ah qui restiamo, non siamo diversi.
> Immobili così. . . .

"Casa sul mare" is one of the best poems Montale ever wrote. Of all the poems in *Ossi di seppia* it is the one most closely linked with Montale's later poetry, while at the same time fully exploiting what *Ossi di seppia* stands for. The poised subtlety and accomplishment of tone and rhythm, as well as the spontaneous ease and self-assurance, both technical and artistic, come out most impressively in the poet's treatment of a deeply moving, yet complex and elusive event. Both the diction and the style, however, are dictated by the inherent nature of the theme and situation and the intensely personal emotion behind them. The very title of the poem, which is reminiscent of a line from Sbarbaro ("la casa sul mare di Loano"), has a romantic aura about it, but what is romantic about the poem emerges from, as in turn it leads to, the poet's mature awareness of the moral and philosophical aspects of his and his beloved's destiny and experience.

> The journey ends here: in the wretched
> cares that divide the soul
> which can no longer utter
> a cry. Now the minutes are equal
> and fixed like the rotations of a pump wheel.
> One rotation: the water rumbles up.
> Another, more water, and an occasional
> creak.
>
> Il viaggio finisce qui:
> nelle cure meschine che dividono
> l'anima che non sa più dare un grido.
> Ora i minuti sono eguali e fissi

come i giri di ruota della pompa.
Un giro: un salir d'acqua che rimbomba.
Un altro, altr'acqua; a tratti un cigolìo.

There is something completely natural and convincing about the way the conceptual and imagistic elements blend together in these lines to achieve a moral, emotional, and psychological synthesis that is the very opposite of what is meant by "the dissociation of sensibility." [40] The journey that ends on the shore, "plied by the slow and assiduous / tides [che tentano gli assidui e lenti flussi]," symbolizes the journey of life. The poet's taking note of the assiduousness with which the tide corrodes the shore as well as of the rarity with which, "in the dead calm / among the vagrant isles of the air / ridged Corsica or Capraia [nella bonaccia muta / tra l'isole dell'aria migrabonde / la Corsica dorsuta o la Capraia]" appears, is indicative of a frame of mind in which each and every object and event seems to be an inseparable part of a symbolically charged context. In such a context the woman's asking the poet if "everything ends thus / in this thin mist of memories [tutto vanisce / in questa poca nebbia di memorie]," acquires a peculiarly lyric tone and depth. And so does the poet's answer, with its doubts, fears, and hopes. "I think that for most there is no salvation [Penso che per i più non sia salvezza]," the poet observes. However, this makes him yearn all the more for the woman's salvation and hope that she may escape the impending doom and destruction that threatens others:

You ask if thus everything ends
in this thin mist of memories,
if in this dull hour or in the sighing
of the breakers each destiny is fulfilled.
I wish I could say no, and that
the hour approaches when you'd pass beyond time;
perhaps only he who wants to becomes infinite,
and you might do so, who knows, not I.
I think that for most there is no salvation,
but then someone may subvert each design,
force his way and find himself
again as he wanted to be.
Before I give in I would like
to show you the path of escape,
transient as foam or a furrow

40. The phrase is Eliot's; it occurs in his essay on Dryden and is further discussed in his second essay on Milton in *On Poets and Poetry*, p. 152 et seq.

in the turbulent fields of the sea.
I give you also my frail hope, since
I'm too tired to feed it in the future;
I offer it as a pledge to fate
that you might escape.

The journey ends here on these shores
which the tide corrodes in its alternate movement.
Perhaps your heart close by doesn't hear me
and has already set sail for the eternal.

Tu chiedi se così tutto vanisce
in questa poca nebbia di memorie;
se nell'ora che torpe o nel sospiro
del frangente si compie ogni destino.
Vorrei dirti che no, che ti s'appressa
l'ora che passerai di là dal tempo;
forse solo chi vuole s'infinita,
e questo tu potrai, chissà, non io.
Penso che per i più non sia salvezza,
ma taluno sovverta ogni disegno,
passi il varco, qual volle si ritrovi.
Vorrei prima di cedere segnarti
codesta via di fuga
labile come nei sommossi campi
del mare spuma o ruga.
Ti dono anche l'avara mia speranza.
A' nuovi giorni, stanco, non so crescerla:
l'offro in pegno al tuo fato, che ti scampi.

Il cammino finisce a queste prode
che rode la marea col moto alterno.
Il tuo cuore vicino che non m'ode
salpa già forse per l'eterno.

In "I morti" Montale deals with a theme to which he was to return in his later poetry and in *Farfalla di Dinard*—the theme of the dead revisiting places known to them when alive:

The sea breaking on the opposite shore
raises a cloud that foams
until the plain absorbs it.
Here on the gray coast we

once threw our hope, more panting
than the sea, and the barren vortex
greens as in the days
which saw us among the living.

Il mare che si frange sull'opposta
riva vi leva un nembo che spumeggia
finchè la piana lo riassorbe. Quivi
gettammo un dì su la ferrigna costa,
ansante più del pelago la nostra
speranza!—e il gorgo sterile verdeggia
come ai dì che ci videro fra i vivi.

Each and every detail of what the dead observe or recall is fraught with a
significance which can be interpreted only in terms of the life they actually
lived. Thus the coast on which they hurled their hope suggests the desperate
futility of that hope. However, the business of living, with its inexorable
round, its existential fever and fret (aptly suggested by the image of the "arc
of the lashed horizon [arco d'orizzonte flagellato]") goes on as usual. Even
the sea and the shore are affected by that fever. And so are the dead themselves "wandering and immobile [immobili e vaganti]," as they are, and
caught up in "a gelid fixity [una fissità gelida]," since they are still attached
to what they once knew and what knew them:

Thus perhaps rest is denied
even to the dead in the earth,
and a force more ruthless than that
of life drags them back to these shores
—ghosts pricked by human memories,
breath without substance, voice
betrayed by the dark—and even now,
barely divided from us,
they brush by us in their brief
flights before sinking
in the sieve of the sea —

Così
forse anche ai morti è tolto ogni riposo
nelle zolle: una forza indi li tragge
spietata più del vivere, ed attorno,
larve rimorse dai ricordi umani,
li volge fino a queste spiagge, fiati

senza materia o voce
traditi dalla tenebra; ed i mozzi
loro voli ci sfiorano pur ora
da noi divisi appena e nel crivello
del mare si sommergono....

Thus Montale goes further than Leopardi, who believed that death at least offered one a liberation from the "flame of life" or the "ancient pain" and a refuge for "our naked nature." [41]

"Delta," too, anticipates the tone and ethos of Montale's later poetry. It is addressed to a woman with whom the poet has, or had, deeper emotional ties than he can possibly define or analyze except by evoking her as a "suffocated presence [presenza suffocata]." Just as in a delta the tributaries flow into the sea, so the poet's passions and "secret effusions [travasi secreti]," or what Coleridge calls "All thoughts, all passions, all delights / Whatever stirs this mortal frame," [42] flow into and merge with her. The pathos and poignancy implicit in his recollection of the past and of his tie with her are a measure of his moral and spiritual dependence on her even in the present. It is a "silent message that sustains me / on the way [messaggio / muto che mi sostenta sulla via]." Linked with the image of the delta, representing the ties by which the poet is bound to the woman loved, is the image of water symbolizing time. For it is when time "is choked at its dykes [s'ingorga alle sue dighe]" that this woman's memory is most vivid and her hold on him most powerful. And yet, the poet tells her:

I know nothing about you except
the silent message that sustains me
on the way: if you exist
as a form or a whim in the smoke
of a dream fed by
a torbid feverish river
that roars against the tide.

Nothing about you in the wavering
hours whether gray or rent
by a flash of sulfur—except

41. Cf. "Coro di morti":

In te, morte, si posa
Nostra ignuda natura;
Lieta no, ma sicura
Dall'antico dolor.

42. See his poem "Love."

the whistle of the tugboat that
comes ashore out of the mist.

Tutto ignoro di te fuor del messaggio
muto che mi sostenta sulla via:
se forma esisti o ubbia nella fumea
d'un sogno t'alimenta
la riviera che infebbra, torba, e scroscia
incontro alla marea.

Nulla di te nel vacillar dell'ore
bige o squarciate da un vampo di solfo
fuori che il fischio del rimorchiatore
che dalle brume approda al golfo.

Just as "Felicità raggiunta" deals with the nature and concept of happiness,
which is presented with a poetic concreteness, so "Incontro" deals with the
concept of sadness as an aid to the poet's exploration of reality and human
destiny. In his development as a poet, Montale finds sadness "the only living
portent in this cloud [solo presagio vivo in questo nembo]" that has helped
him to explore the nature of reality around him as well as within, by incul-
cating in him the awareness of "human acts consumed, / pallid lives that set /
beyond the boundary encircling us [umani atti consunti, / d'impallidite vite
tramontanti / oltre il confine / che a cerchio ci rinchuide]." The realization
of the waste and futility both in the life of man and in nature, and the resultant feeling of sadness, are thus important factors in the poet's artistic
as well as moral development, as they emerge from the following lines, with
their personal as well as impersonal symbolism:

Perhaps I'll again have a face:
in the grazing light a movement
brings me to a withered branch
in a vase above the tavern door.
I stretch my hand toward it and feel
another life merging with mine,
encumbered by a form that was
snatched from me, and hair,
not leaves, twists around me, almost
like rings on the fingers.

Then nothing more . . .

Forse riavrò un aspetto: nella luce
radente un moto mi conduce accanto

a una misera fronda che in un vaso
s'alleva s'una porta di osteria.
A lei tendo la mano, e farsi mia
un'altra vita sento, ingombro d'una
forma che mi fu tolta; e quasi anelli
alle dita non foglie mi si attorcono
ma capelli.
Poi più nulla.

When at his touch the plant sheds its dry, withered leaves, the sense of life
as well as of death and dissolution overwhelms him, assuming the form of
a female companion who personifies love and salvation. In the concluding
passage, with its dexterous admixture of Dantesque and Leopardian echoes,[43]
the poet asks the woman to pray for him:

. . . that I may descend
through another path than the city street,
in the dark air before the swarm
of the living, that I may feel
your presence beside me,
that I may go down without cowardice.

. . . ch'io discenda altro cammino
che una via di città,
nell'aria persa, innanzi al brulichio
dei vivi; ch'io ti senta accanto; ch'io
scenda senza viltà.

Ossi di seppia closes with "Riviere," one of Montale's earliest poems. It is
not clear why it should have been put at the end of the volume. In theme
and ethos it belongs to the group of poems called *Movimenti* and, to some
extent, also to *Mediterraneo*. Insofar as it depicts the poet's moral, emotional,
and artistic involvement with the sea and the world of childhood, it may be
regarded as a prologue that is at the same time also an epilogue or a leave-
taking. Artistically, however, it is less impressive than most other poems in
Ossi di seppia. There is an emotional exuberance about it which makes for
poetical diffuseness as against lyric tautness, as the poet recollects the period
of "sweet captivity [dolce cattività]" during which the sea cast a powerful

43. Cf. Dante's use of the word *perso* in the line "che visitando vai per l'aere perso"
(*Inferno*, Canto 5, line 89) and in the line "L'acqua era buia assai più che persa" (*Inferno*,
canto 7, line 103). Or cf. Leopardi: "Com'usa / Per antica viltà l'umana gente," "Amore e
morte").

spell over him. However, recalling that past now is like "replaying an ancient game / that was never forgotten [rivivere un antico giuoco / non mai dimenticato]."

Maturity is the word to be emphasized in closing. It characterizes, in an impressively compact way, a substantial part of *Ossi di seppia,* and makes it in more than one respect a unique book. For one thing, it is not only Montale's most original book but also the most original and influential book of lyrics to have appeared in Italy after D'Annunzio's *Alcyone* (1903–04) and Ungaretti's *L'Allegria* (1919). When considering the whole of Montale's poetic output, it is necessary to bear in mind that, although his subsequent poetry grew away from *Ossi di seppia,* in a significant way it also grew out of it. No doubt new themes and new pressures, both of a personal and historical nature, dominate *Le occasioni, La bufera,* and *Satura* and entail a new technique and a new diction. But the verbal, stylistic, and metrical innovations through which the development of Montale's art first revealed itself were cogently exemplified in his treatment of themes and occasions that are distinctly peculiar to *Ossi di seppia.*

The impressive and fertile union in Montale's poetry between "the critical corrosion of existence" on the one hand and the passion and effervescence of youth on the other, against the feelingly captured background of the Ligurian landscape, was not to be repeated. Montale's departure from Genoa for Florence soon after the publication of *Ossi di seppia* and his exchange of the Ligurian sea for "the classical architecture of the Tuscan hills" coincided with his growing preoccupation with his inner emotional life, which registers a notable shift of emphasis and perspective in his later poetry. In other words, the cosmic setting and metaphysical bent of *Ossi di seppia* gives way to a world of personal emotions and preoccupations. Hence *Le occasioni* and *La bufera* as well as *Xenia* revolve, for the most part, around the theme of personal love, however symbolically rich and universally appealing Montale's technique of dealing with such a theme may be. The prevalent tone and ethos of *Ossi di seppia,* on the other hand, are based on intuitions, perceptions, and observations of a creatively philosophical and impersonal nature such as Italian poetry hasn't known since Leopardi's "Canto notturno" and "La ginestra."

3: *Le occasioni*

In 1939 Montale brought out his second volume of verse, *Le occasioni*. While it represents the same degree of maturity and accomplishment as *Ossi di seppia*, it does so through a new technique which changes the tone and inflection of the verse. Moreover, the sensibility it expresses has itself been molded by different pressures and preoccupations, and tends to be formulated in more personal and autobiographical terms than was the case with *Ossi di seppia*. But the more personal the nature of experience and circumstance in Montale, the more allusive and symbolically dense the language he uses. Thus, he generally transforms what is rooted in personal life and experience into something unique—something that has the unmistakable impersonality of art. "The farther we go," Sergio Solmi quotes Rilke as saying, "the more personal and more unique life becomes. The work of art is a necessary, irrefutable, and definitive expression of this experience . . . precisely because it is unique, because it is what nobody would be able to understand or would have the right to understand."[1] It is this awareness of personal destiny and of unique experience that determines the particular texture and ethos of *Le occasioni*. But, generally speaking, the nature of a personal experience is such that however much a poet may try to reveal its deepest, most subtle, and most hidden aspects, there is always something about it that cannot be revealed: it can only be adumbrated allusively or symbolically. Hence the frequent use of symbolic or allusive language in this book and in *La bufera e altro*.

1. *Scrittori negli anni*, p. 295. Another German poet who comes to mind in connection with this volume is Goethe. In the fourth of his *Römische Elegien* (1788–90), Occasion, or "Gelegenheit," is personified as a goddess: "Diese Göttin, sie heisst *Gelegenheit;* lernet sie Kennen! / Sie erscheinet euch oft, immer in andrer Gestalt." Goethe himself wrote "occasional poems" ("Gelegenheitsgedichte"); his concept of "Gelegenheit," like Montale's, has more to do with an inner experience than with the outer "occasion" according to the Baroque tradition.

However, too personal a symbolism or allusiveness can sometimes lead to obscurity, as happened with some of the poems in *Le occasioni* that Gargiulo was the first to criticize. Whereas in *Ossi di seppia*, he thought, the feeling or emotion that inspired a particular poem was either directly expressed or figuratively represented, in *Le occasioni* what we have is "exterior figurations which have not been animated by any sentiment." This, together with the presence of "too personal a datum," accounts for the lack of that element of inevitability in *Le occasioni* which we find so impressively present in the best lyrics of *Ossi di seppia*. And some poems in the former merely tend to be "prosa d'arte." [2]

More than one Italian critic has come out in defense of *Le occasioni*, among them Sergio Solmi and Gianfranco Contini. For Contini it is the closely integrated link between "poetry" and "nonpoetry"—to use the Crocean terminology—which characterizes Montale's verse in general and *Le occasioni* in particular. What Gargiulo considers to be the "atony" of *Le occasioni* is not the same thing as the absence of sentiment. And if he cannot do justice to the kind of art and technique displayed in *Le occasioni* it is because of his inability to appreciate "the crisis of another culture in respect of a sensibility that is averse to eloquence concerning its own limits." [3] For Solmi, on the other hand, the difference between *Ossi di seppia* and *Le occasioni* is that, while the former expresses "the immediacy of an elementary situation in the world," the latter brings out "the dimension of a personal destiny which, in the jealous consciousness of a modern artist, is presented with the charged intensity of a secret, with the shades and reticences of a confidence which is at once precious and difficult to express, with its stratifications of reality." [4]

Be that as it may, some of Montale's most intense and best-known poems are to be found in *Le occasioni*—poems like "Dora Markus," some of the Motets ("La speranza di pure rivederti," "Il saliscendi bianco e nero," "Infuria sale o grandine," and "Non recidere"), "La casa dei doganieri," "Eastbourne," and "Notizie dall'Amiata." Moreover, *Le occasioni* represents an important stage in Montale's poetic career, paving the way for the kind of artistic achievement and originality that *La bufera e altro* and *Xenia* offer. With the exception of "Lontano, ero con te," "Ti libero la fronte," and "Al primo chiaro, quando," all the poems in *Le occasioni* are dated though not chronologically arranged. "Vecchi versi" and the first part of "Dora Markus" were written in 1926, and "Alla maniera di Filippo De Pisis" and "Il rit-

2. *Letteratura italiana del Novecento*, pp. 634, 638, et seq.
3. See Contini's "Di Gargiulo su Montale," in *Un anno di letteratura* (Florence: Le Monnier, 1942).
4. *Scrittori negli anni*, p. 295.

orno," in 1940. All the other poems were written between 1928 and 1939.

Like *Ossi di seppia, Le occasioni* also starts with a dedicatory poem, "Il balcone," which is representative of the whole volume. It is dedicatory in the sense that it is addressed to or inspired by the woman loved, whom the poet calls Clizia and who is at the center of most of the poems in this volume. Her presence in fact is as pervasive and impelling here as in *La bufera*. She is depicted both as an individual and in her symbolic role as an angel or savior. "Il balcone" thus epitomizes the thematic and stylistic qualities and characteristics of most of the poems in *Le occasioni*. With the exception of poems like "Vento e bandiere," "Casa sul mare," "Delta," and "Marezzo," *Ossi di seppia* had represented the preponderance of impressionistic, naturalistic, and metaphysical details and motifs, almost to the exclusion of personal sentiments, especially that of love. As he tells us in "Il balcone," Montale does not so much abandon that vein as enrich it by interweaving it with others: "It seemed an easy game / to change the space that had opened up / before me into nothing, your certain / fire into uncertain boredom [Pareva facile giuoco /mutare in nulla lo spazio / che m'era aperto, in un tedio / malcerto il certo tuo fuoco]." And it is the vein of personal as well as symbolic love represented by a real or ideal woman addressed as "tu"[5] that takes pride of place in *Le occasioni*. It constitutes the source of life as well as of poetic inspiration: "the life that glimmers is the life / which you alone discern. / You lean out toward it from this window / that doesn't light up [La vita che dà barlumi / è quella che sola tu scorgi. / A lei ti sporgi da questa / finestra che non s'illumina]." "Il balcone," therefore, illustrates the new ethos and technique that Montale was to use throughout this volume.

Poem after poem in *Le occasioni* illustrates this technique in one form or another, whether through the transformation of the abstract into the concrete, or the metaphysical into the metaphorical, and vice versa. It was this aspect of Montale's poetry that Pietro Pancrazi had in mind when he referred to him as a "physical and metaphysical" poet.[6]

After "Il balcone," the first poem in the volume is "Vecchi versi," which serves as a bridge between *Ossi di seppia* and *Le occasioni*. Both in theme and ethos it is one with the world of *Ossi di seppia*—the world of Montale's childhood with its Ligurian background and memories. But by virtue of the density of particular and concrete detail of a personal or autobiographical nature and the way in which it is subtly impregnated with a symbolic and impersonal significance, it is equally representative of the general technical and stylistic characteristics of *Le occasioni*. For instance, such details as

5. See Montale's poem "Il tu," in *Satura* (1971).
6. See Bibliography.

The lights of the port of Vernazza
were blotted out at intervals
by the surging waves
invisible in the depth of the night . . .

Dal porto
di Vernazza le luci erano a tratti
scancellate dal crescere dell'onde
invisibili al fondo della notte . . .

merge with the metaphysical transfiguration of a domestic scene in a seaside
place. The poet is sitting with his mother at the table and watching a moth
attracted by the light flying round the lamp until it falls exhausted on the
playing cards on the table. In memory the moth becomes one with

. . . things that come to a safe
end like the day,
and memory nourishes them,
the only living remnant of a life
gone underground, together
with the familiar faces no longer
dispersed by sleep, but by
another kind of boredom,
near the ancient wall, or the shore
where the tartan received each month
its cargo of pine logs
or near the point where the torrent still descends
carving its way to the sea.

. . . le cose che chiudono in un giro
sicuro come il giorno, e la memoria
in sè le cresce, sole vive d'una
vita che disparì sotterra: insieme
coi volti familiari che oggi sperde
non più il sonno ma un'altra noia; accanto
ai muri antichi, ai lidi, alla tartana
che imbarcava
tronchi di pino a riva ad ogni mese,
al segno del torrente che discende
ancora al mare e la sua via si scava.

Use of real place-names such as the Rock of Tino, Corniglia, and Vernazza
help to fix memories and sentiments in a particular time and place. But far

from limiting the scope of the poem, they enrich its symbolic as well as artistic appeal. Montale's comments on the poet's need for a particular rather than a general truth are especially relevant here. "The poet's need," he tells us, "is the search for a particular truth, not a general one," and a poet should sing of "what unites man to other men," but at the same time "he should not ignore what divides him from others and makes him unique and unrepeatable." [7]

"In "Buffalo," an "occasional" poem inspired by the particular circumstance of a cycle race in Paris, and in "Keepsake," which lists the characters of various operettas that Montale saw in his early life and that continue to haunt him in memory, there is an overconcentration of the specifically personal or circumstantial, resulting in disparate intuitions, images, and symbols that are not creatively enough fused. According to Pancrazi, the most serious defect of such poems in *Le occasioni* is that "sometimes too many and too diverse elements concur in [the poet's] vein, which instead of resolving them, become turgid with them." [8] Gargiulo, too, while criticizing "Buffalo," referred to the discrepancy between a rich and powerful "external figuration" and the lack of "a truly emotional response." [9]

However, from "Lindau" onward we find the lyric triumph of the new technique and style most convincingly displayed. This technique transforms personal emotion or feeling into a concrete image which is at the same time rich in evocative intensity:

> The swallow comes back with the grass blades,
> doesn't want life to pass;
> but the dead water corrodes the pebbles
> between the banks by night.
> Under the smoking torches shadows
> disperse on the empty shore.
> And in the middle of the square
> a saraband beats out to the roar
> of the paddle-boats' wheels.

> La rondine vi porta
> fili d'erba, non vuole che la vita passi.
> Ma tra gli argini, a notte, l'acqua morta
> logora i sassi.
> Sotto le torce fumicose sbanda
> sempre qualche ombra sulle prode vuote.

7. "Intenzioni: intervista immaginaria," p. 344.
8. In *"Le occasioni* di Eugenio Montale," *Scrittori d'oggi,* 4th ser. (Bari: Laterza, 1946).
9. *Letteratura italiana del Novecento,* p. 635.

Nel cerchio della piazza una sarabanda
s'agita al mugghio dei battelli a ruote.

The title of the poem suggests its "occasional" nature insofar as it is inspired
by the poet's being at Lindau, a German town on the Lake of Constance.
The neatness and precision of the impressionistic details—the swallow coming back with the grass blades, the water corroding the pebbles, the smoking
torches, etc.—does not interfere with a thin layer of evocative symbolism in
the poem. Thus, the swallow's coming back with the grass blades is a token
of the life-impulse, while the dead water corroding the pebbles represents
the deterministic force behind the laws of nature. These two concepts are
juxtaposed in such a way that they reinforce each other's poetic and moral
relevance in the structural unity of the poem.

The same interplay of visual, realistic, and surrealistic images and impressions sustains the four minor poems that precede "Carnevale di Gerti." In
"Bagni di Lucca" the poet strikes a happy balance between the movement of
a hesitant heart and the thud of chestnuts. In "Cave d'autunno" the picture
of a frozen spring landscape serves as a foil to the note of love and hope
symbolized by a bounteous hand. In "Altro effetto di luna" the image of the
silver fingers is an apt illustration of the surrealistic character of the poem.
And in "Verso Vienna," too, both the landscape—"the baroque convent of
foam and biscuit [Il convento barocco / di schiuma e di biscotto]," "a glimpse
of slow waters and tables / laid, scattered here and there / with leaves and
ginger [uno scorcio d'acque lente / e tavole imbandite, qua e là sparse / di
foglie e zenzero]"—and the protagonists—the swimmer "dripping under a
cloud of gnats [sgrondò sotto / une nube di moscerini]" and the outrider
leaping out of a garage, with a gaily barking dachshund, "the only fraternal
voice / in the sultriness [fraterna unica voce dentro l'afa]"—add up to an
evocative framework within which another "occasion," the poet's and his
female companion's journey to Vienna, is commemorated.

With "Carnevale di Gerti," "Dora Markus," and "La casa dei doganieri"
we touch the core of Montale's lyricism at its most mature and accomplished.
In the first poem (written in 1928) the poet is talking to a woman from
Austria, whom he came to know in Florence where her husband was a
military officer. The poem is enveloped in an atmosphere of metaphysical
suspense. Both Gerti and the poet are thinking of a Christmas or New Year's
Eve in the past and see in their minds' eye the Christmas presents laid out
in her room. They seem to be laboring under the weight of a mysterious
doom, as a result of which even time seems to be spellbound and can be
reversed the moment Gerti moves the hand of her wristwatch:

(Oh your carnival will be even sadder
tonight than mine, locked up
with your presents for those absent;
rosolio-colored carts, puppets, guns,
rubber balls, utensils from a Lilliputian
kitchen; the ballot assigned them to
each of your distant friends,
when January came to a close
and in the silence the magic game was played.
Is it the carnival or December
lingering still? I think
if you move the hand of your little wristwatch,
everything will return
into a shattered prism of chaotic
forms and colors.)

(Oh il tuo Carnevale sarà più triste
stanotte anche del mio, chiusa fra i doni
tu per gli assenti: carri dalle tinte
di rosolio, fantocci ed archibugi,
palle di gomma, arnesi da cucina
lillipuziani: l'urna li segnava
a ognuno dei lontani amici l'ora
che il Gennaio si schiuse e nel silenzio
si compì il sortilegio. È Carnevale
o il Dicembre s'indugia ancora? Penso
che se tu muovi la lancetta al piccolo
orologio che rechi al polso, tutto
arretrerà dentro un disfatto prisma
babelico di forme e di colori....)

Few passages in Montale's poetry are at once so richly phantasmagorical
and so morally charged. They represent, as it were, an intersection of movement with stasis, timelessness with time, anxiety to live out one's life with
the desire to arrest or reverse its course. The memories of the past mingle
with the carnival atmosphere and surroundings to create a fanciful world into
which Gerti as well as the poet can take refuge from the oppressive reality of
the present—"a world / blown up inside a tremulous / bubble of air and
light / where the sun salutes your grace [un mondo soffiato entro una tremula / bolla d'aria e di luce dove il sole / saluta la tua grazia]." As a result
the past merges into the present and the present into the future. It is not so
much that time seems to be dissolving, which is often the case in Montale's

poetry, as that it seems to be unrecognizable and unidentifiable: "Is it the carnival or December / lingering still? [E' Carnevale / o il Dicembre s'indugia ancora?]" Even the sense of physical reality is blurred, so that the world appears to be "a shattered prism / of chaotic forms and colors [un disfatto prisma / babelico di forme e di colori]." However, events unfold as if completely governed by some deterministic power, as shown through the image of the blades of the mill that "rotate / fixed on the noisy wells [rotano fisse sulle pozze garrule]." Any escape from or radical change in the situation as it is in its metaphysical essence and predetermined character is as much an impossibility as trying to stop "time above the countryside / that spreads all around [tempo sul paese / che attorno si dilata]," or to retain the sound of "silver bells / or the hoarse sound of doves / above the village [le campane / d'argento sopra il borgo e il suono rauco / delle colombe]." In the end, however, the sense of everyday reality reasserts itself, and the poet realizes that the past is irrevocable and that the future, in spite of Gerti's fond illusion that she can read it, is inscrutable: "nothing / comes back except perhaps / through these ambiguities of the possible [nulla torna se non forse in questi / disguidi del possibile]." And this enhances the pathos and poignancy of the situation:

> How everything seems strange and difficult,
> how everything's impossible, you say.

> Come tutto si fa strano e difficile,
> come tutto è impossibile, tu dici.

"Carnevale di Gerti" is followed by three minor poems, "Verso Capua," "A Liuba che parte" and "Bibe a Ponte all'Asse." Like "Verso Vienna", "Verso Capua" commemorates a certain occasion or stage in the poet's journey toward Capua. The commemoration itself acquires its lyric impetus and *raison d'être* from the image of the woman that comes up at the end of the poem and toward which the whole poem seems to be converging. The more casual the assortment of realistic detail, the more sharply particularized the picture of the woman that emerges: "You who kept waving down there / a scarf, the starry flag! [e tu in fondo che agitavi / lungamente una sciarpa, la bandiera stellata!]"

In "A Liuba che parte" the theme has a certain kinship with that of "Dora Markus" and "Carnevale di Gerti." Liuba, an Austrian Jewess, is leaving her country to escape the racial sanctions and takes with her what little she can, including a cat that represents her household god. The very paucity of her belongings eloquently represents her own plight as well as the inhumanity of "the blind times [i ciechi tempi)."

"Dora Markus" (part 1 written in 1926, part 2 in 1939) is not only one of Montale's best-known poems, but, together with "La primavera hitleriana," "Il sogno del prigioniero," and "Piccolo testamento," also the most impassioned and lyrical testimony to the poet's involvement in the historical and political dilemmas and tragedies of his times. Love and war are in fact the two themes which, together with the technical and stylistic qualities that their treatment entails, link *Le occasioni* with *La bufera*. And although *Le occasioni* came out at the outset of World War II, whereas *La bufera* was published some fifteen years later, the ethos behind the poet's moral and emotional involvement with contemporary problems and predicaments, as well as his mode of translating that involvement in terms of art, is basically the same. "Dora Markus" is about a Jewish woman and her vicissitudes. Like Arsenio, Dora embodies the poet's own metaphysical anguish. In the first part of the poem he recalls a moment from the past when they were together and she pointed out to him her "true land [patria vera]," namely, Carinthia, on "the other invisible shore [altra sponda invisibile]," which she had to leave. Her exile's plight, coupled with her attachment to her own country, confers upon her stoicism and resilience in the face of such tragic odds a heroic dignity, which makes her the most moving and evocative character in Montale's poetry and which the poet brings out with admirably controlled intensity of feeling and a firm and masterly selectivity of detail. Apart from its pictorial vividness and concreteness, the poem is also rich in symbolic and evocative power. In spite of the absence of any narrative or rational thread to link the various intensities and emotions underlying it, it has a remarkable architectonic unity, and the various levels of thematic and emotional complexity merge together coherently.

> It was at Porto Corsini
> where the wooden bridge puts out into
> the high sea and a few men,
> almost motionless, cast
> or pull in the nets, that with
> a wave of your hand you pointed
> to the other shore,
> the invisible shore of your true land.
> We followed the canal as far
> as the docks, shiny with soot,
> in that low-lying part, where spring
> sinks inert, and leaves no memory.
>
> Fu dove il ponte di legno
> mette a Porto Corsini sul mare alto

e rari uomini, quasi immoti, affondano
o salpano le reti. Con un segno
della mano additavi all'altra sponda
invisibile la tua patria vera.
Poi seguimmo il canale fino alla darsena
della città, lucida di fuliggine,
nella bassura dove s'affondava
una primavera inerte, senza memoria.

A psychological as well as structural unity underlies the emotional complexity
of the poem and gives life to a rich pattern of images and impressions, both
in their diversity and in their interdependence. The topographical precision
of detail in the first two lines, for instance, not only counterbalances, but also
contributes to the haunting vagueness and distancing charm of the phrase
"the invisible shore of your true land." Similarly, the concrete specificity of
detail—"we followed the canal as far / as the docks, shiny with soot"—leads
on to and stresses the evocative pathos of the last line, "where spring / sinks
inert, and leaves no memory." What the poet himself feels about Dora Markus and her destiny is conveyed through language and imagery that display
a happy blend of the general and the particular, the concrete and the symbolic:

Your restlessness makes me think
of the birds of passage that dash
against the lights on stormy evenings,
even your sweetness is a storm
that rages, but remains unseen
and whose lulls are even rarer.
I do not know how, though exhausted,
you can survive in this lake of indifference—
your heart. Perhaps it's an amulet
that you keep with your lipstick,
powder-puff, and nail-file, which saves you:
a white ivory mouse! And thus
you exist.

La tua irrequietudine mi fa pensare
agli uccelli di passo che urtano ai fari
nelle sere tempestose:
è una tempesta anche la tua dolcezza,
turbina e non appare,

> e i suoi riposi sono anche più rari.
> Non so come stremata tu resisti
> in questo lago
> d'indifferenza ch'è il tuo cuore; forse
> ti salva un amuleto che tu tieni
> vicino alla matita della labbra,
> al piumino, alla lima: un topo bianco,
> d'avorio; e così esisti!

The fortuitous choice of such matter-of-fact and inherently unpoetic objects as lipstick, powder-puff, and nail-file emphasizes the extreme precariousness of the objects, circumstances, and conditions on which one's salvation or perdition might well depend in these "blind times."

The second part of "Dora Markus" finds Dora at home in Carinthia, her true land on the invisible shore and in the relaxed atmosphere of "the myrtles in bloom [mirti fioriti]" and "the awnings of quays and boarding-houses [tende da scali e pensioni]." The landscape and the environment teem with objects, sights, and impressions that suggest a recovery from the past, with its errors, oppressions, and sad memories. However, Dora's destiny and legend remain embodied, with ominous precision and clarity, in the ancestral portraits in her room, reminding her that the past may yet repeat itself. But whatever else time may sweep away in its inexorable march, it cannot take away one's pride in being rooted in a particular tradition and in having a particular destiny or spiritual home, which the poet transmutes into the delicately symbolic image of "the evergreen laurel for the kitchen":

> The evergreen laurel for the kitchen
> resists, the voice doesn't change,
> Ravenna's far, a terrible
> faith distills poison.
> What does it want from you?
> Voice, legend, fate
> is not something one can yield.
> But it is late, always too late.

> . . . Il sempreverde
> alloro per la cucina
> resiste, la voce non muta,
> Ravenna è lontana, distilla
> veleno una fede feroce.
> Che vuole da te? Non si cede

> voce, leggenda o destino....
> Ma è tardi, sempre più tardi.

"Dora Markus" is followed by two poems, "Alla maniera di Filippo De Pisis" and "Nel Parco di Caserta." The former merely serves the external need of giving expression in poetry to what the poet would have liked to reproduce in color, rather than obeying any creative or moral impulse. "Nel Parco di Caserta," on the other hand, offers a subtly interwoven pattern of images and impressions which has no need of any moral or philosophical gloss:

> Where the cruel swan preens
> and contorts itself, a sphere,
> ten spheres are formed
> on the surface of the pond, among the foliage,
> and a torch gleams from the bottom,
> ten torches.

> Dove il cigno crudele
> si liscia e si contorce,
> sul pelo dello stagno, tra il fogliame,
> si risveglia una sfera, dieci sfere,
> una torcia dal fondo, dieci torce.

In "Accelerato" the poet is recalling—or reminding his interlocutor of—an occasion in the past the emotional core of which is conveyed through a series of rhetorical questions:

> Was it thus, like the cold shudder
> that runs through the suburbs and raises
> the ashes of the day
> to the poles of the towers?

> Fu così, com'è il brivido
> pungente che trascorre
> i sobborghi e solleva
> alle aste delle torri
> la cenere del giorno,

or like

> the rainy squall that repeats
> through the bars its onslaught against
> the drooping willows

. . . il soffio
piovorno che ripete
tra le sbarre l'assalto
ai salici reclini ——

These questions reveal indirectly but unequivocally the intimate relationship
between the poet and the woman. The cold shudder and the rainly squall suggest the moral and emotional turmoil within the poet. And when the turmoil
subsides "a glimpse of the azure [foro d'azzurro]" conjures up the idyllic
picture of childhood represented by "the nymphal Entella [la ninfale En-
tella]" flowing back "from the sky of childhood / beyond the future [dai cieli
dell'infanzia / oltre il futuro]." In the last lines the feeling of calm after
the storm assumes a more humane aspect, and the tempo of the verse slackens
accordingly:

Then other shores came, the wind
changed, more washing appeared
on the lines, men came out again
and new nests disturbed the eaves —

poi vennero altri liti, mutò il vento,
crebbe il bucato ai fili, uomini ancora
uscirono all'aperto, nuovi nidi
turbarono le gronde ——

All this leads on to and has a bearing upon the question that has by now
almost acquired, by virtue of incantatory repetitiveness, the force of an affir-
mative answer.

The twenty lyrics grouped under the title *Mottetti* were all written between
1934 and 1938, with the exception of "Lontano, ero con te," "Ti libero la
fronte," and "Al primo chiaro" whose dates of composition are not known.
They constitute a body of poetry of extraordinary lyric force and originality—
poetry in which all the facets of Montale's art and personality are impressively
present: his stylistic and spiritual maturity, inventive resourcefulness, technical
ingenuity, and psychological as well as poetic realism and perceptiveness. Most
of these poems would be called love poems were it not for the fact that they
represent a much more complex experience, entailing a more subtle use of
language and a more symbolic pattern of images, analogies, and impressions
than is the case with love poetry in the ordinary sense of the term. Moreover,
the allusive and symbolic character of the technique adopted in these poems
served Montale to some extent as a device by which he could both hide or
express what suited him during the Fascist regime. The so-called hermetic

nature of Montale's verse was therefore at least partly a matter of political
expediency.

Hence if the *Motets* represent something more complex than what is generally known as love poetry, it is because Montale succeeded in blending his
experience of love with the moral pressures and dilemmas of his age, thereby
widening the scope and impact of his lyricism. So that on the one hand his
art traces, through the various occasions and emotional vicissitudes, the stages
of his moral and poetic development, and on the other it reflects and offers
a penetrating commentary on the *Zeitgeist*. The focal point of these lyrics is
represented by the figure of the woman whom the poet calls Clizia, and
who actually combines several female presences. At times she is a real woman,
at times an angel or a spirit. She calls forth in the poet the deepest passions
and sentiments and at the same time acts as his guide and his inspiration
in the exploration of reality and of himself. The poems are thus based on
and inspired by sudden flashes of recollection of the woman loved, the apparently casual incidents and episodes relating to her and the poet's everyday
life together, all interwoven into a closely knit pattern with allusive and evocative undertones. They have both the warmth and the intensity of a personal experience and the objectivity and impersonality of something larger
and more complex. Places, landscapes, and objects are described so as to
render what is familiar metaphysically rich and strange, and what is metaphysical, familiar. In other words, the poet's inner world is both minutely
depicted and seen in a wider perspective, so that these *Motets* acquire a tone,
a timbre, and a quality which is at once moving and impressively symbolic.

The *Motets,* then, may be regarded as being what Browning called "incidents in the development of a soul,"[10] except that these incidents, "occasions," or "flashes" are presented in such a quintessential way that all we
have is the poetic upshot of a given situation, not the emotional turmoil that
caused it. However, in spite of the underlying unity of theme and spirit, each
poem more or less represents an independent unit, a fragment of reality lived
and suffered, and a particular aspect or episode of love in its specifically
realized concreteness of ethos and realistic detail.

The first motet (1934) interweaves the motif of love with that of the
Ligurian landscape, whose hold on the poet seems to belong to the same
order of moral and emotional itensity as his love for the woman:

> You know I must lose you again and I cannot.
> Like a well-aimed shot, each action,

10. In his dedicatory letter to J. Misland of Dijon, with which he prefaces *Sordello:* "my
stress lay on the incidents in the development of a soul: little else is worth study."

each cry excites me, even
the salty breeze that comes
from the pier and makes a dark
spring of Sottoripa.

A forest of iron and masts
in the evening dust. A long drone
comes from the open and tears
against the panes like nails.
I look for the lost sign—the only
pledge you had graced me with.
And hell is certain.

Lo sai: debbo riperderti e non posso.
Come un tiro aggiustato mi sommuove
ogni opera, ogni grido e anche lo spiro
salino che straripa
dai moli e fa l'oscura primavera
di Sottoripa.

Paese di ferrame e alberature
a selva nella polvere del vespro.
Un ronzìo lungo viene dall'aperto,
strazia com'unghia ai vetri. Cerco il segno
smarrito, il pegno solo ch'ebbi in grazia
da te.
        E l'inferno è certo.

The sense of being snatched away from the world of one's childhood is conveyed by sharp and bristling images such as a forest of iron and masts or
the humming sound tearing against the panes like nails. These two images
serve as a foil to the morally and spiritually pregnant symbol of the lost sign
or the pledge with which the poet was graced in the past. And the fear of
hell is connected with the loss of memory—the memory of the world of childhood—as well as with uncertainty about the future.

Motet 2 (1934) connects the memory of a particularly difficult year spent
"on a foreign lake ablaze / with sunsets [sopra il lago / straniero su cui ar-
dono i tramonti]," while the woman loved was lying ill in a sanatorium in
Switzerland (also the theme of Motet 3), with the memories of childhood
(St. George and the Dragon is the emblem of the city of Genoa). In such
an emotionally and symbolically charged context, the poet pledges his eternal
loyalty to the woman loved. In the third motet (1934) the same theme and

atmosphere of a foreign sanatorium is juxtaposed, or rather interwoven, with
memories of the war:

> Brine on the windows, the sick
> always united and always
> apart and at the tables
> the long soliloquies over the cards.
>
> That was your exile. I think
> of mine too, of the morning
> when I heard among the rocks
> the explosion of the bomb.

> Brina sui vetri; uniti
> sempre e sempre in disparte
> gl'infermi; e sopra i tavoli
> i lunghi soliloqui sulle carte.
>
> Fu il tuo esilio. Ripenso
> anche al mio, alla mattina
> quando udii tra gli scogli crepitare
> la bomba ballerina.

In the last two lines of the first stanza the poet gives a characteristic touch
to the card games played by the sick, investing them with a symbolic significance. The wings of death brush past, but then only indicate the wrong
card; for it is not yet the woman's turn to die. In the fourth motet the sense
of solitude and uncertainty makes the poet suffer all the more from the
absence of the woman loved and makes him desire to unite his own life and
destiny with hers. In the first two lines, "Though far, I was with you when /
your father died and bid you farewell [Lontano, ero con te quando tuo
padre / entrò nell'ombra e ti lasciò il suo addio]," he recalls his sense of
waste before he met her as well as his experience of war—another kind of
waste.

Motet 5 (1939) is one of the most "hermetically" quintessential. Its theme
is a parting at the railway station. The sound of farewells, whistles in the
dark, coughing, lowered windows, and the staccato movement of the verse
enact the drama of separation from the woman loved through a poignant
sequence of events which precede the actual parting. The last three lines—

> Do you also add
> this horrid, faithful carioca
> to the faint litany of the train?

——Presti anche tu alla fioca
litania del tuo rapido quest'orrida
e fedele cadenza di carioca?——

concern the sound of the train as it moves, which acquires in the poet's mind the rhythm of a carioca, and he wonders if it also produces the same effect on the woman. In motet 6 (1939), the hope of seeing the woman loved again, seems to be ebbing away, and the poet's vision is clouded by a screen of images which may betoken death and oblivion or merely a fleeting and distorted glimpse of her former dazzle:

The hope of even seeing you again
abandoned me;

and I asked if that which blots out
in me all knowledge of you
—a screen of images—has about it
the signs of death, or of
your past dazzle, now fleeting
and distorted . . .

La speranza di pure rivederti
m'abbandonava;

e mi chiesi se questo che mi chiude
ogni senso di te, schermo d'immagini,
ha i segni della morte o dal passato
è in esso, ma distorto e fatto labile,
un *tuo* barbaglio . . .

The uncertainty is resolved by the recollection of a particular incident from the past—the liveried servant leading two jackals on a leash—which reminds the poet that Clizia used to be fond of such animals:

At Modena, among the porches
a liveried servant was dragging
two jackals on a leash.

(a Modena, tra i portici,
un servo gallonato trascinava
du sciacalli al guinzaglio).

Motet 7 (1938) also deals with the theme of the poet's revisiting a certain scene from the past that has many associations with the absent Clizia. The vividness and delicacy of the image of the black and white line of swallows contrasts with the verbal starkness and conceptual explicitness of the lines describing his sense of desolation in her absence:

> The black and white line of the swallows
> undulating from the telegraph pole
> to the sea doesn't soothe your sorrow
> at the quay nor does it bring you back
> to where you no longer are.

> Il saliscendi bianco e nero dei
> balestrucci dal palo
> del telegrafo al mare
> non conforta i tuoi crucci su lo scalo
> nè ti riporta dove più non sei.

In spite of the feeling of moral and emotional perturbation, the poet's eye for the landscape does not fail to cull such details as the elder tree casting its perfume on the upturned earth in the brightness that follows the storm. This detail in a way symbolizes the poet's sense of uneasy calm menaced, as it is, by the possibility of her memory coming back to upset it:

> Already the thick elder perfumes
> the upturned earth; the squall dies away.
> And if the brightness is a truce,
> your dear threat consumes it.

> Già profuma il sambuco fitto su
> lo sterrato; il piovasco si dilegua.
> Se il chiarore è una tregua,
> la tua cara minaccia la consuma.

In Motet 8 (1938) casual images and impressions bring out the haunting yet elusive character of the loved woman's presence-absence, suggested by such phenomena as a palm tree "burnt by the dazzle of the dawn [bruciato dai barbagli dell'aurora]" or the almost inaudible sound of an approaching step in the snow:

> The step that comes lightly from the greenhouse
> isn't muffled by the snow, it's still
> your life, your blood in my veins.

> Il passo che proviene
> dalla serra sì lieve,
> non è felpato dalla neve, è ancora
> tua vita, sangue tuo nelle mie vene.

Or, as in Motet 9 (1937), the four concentrated, sharply defined, and incongruous images present, in a syncoptic way, certain glimpses and aspects of the absent woman loved:

> The green lizard, if it darts out
> from the stubble under the great whip—
>
> the sail, when it flaps and is engulfed
> where the fortress leaps up—
>
> the cannon at midday fainter
> than your heart and the chronometer if
> it goes off without a sound —

> Il ramarro, se scocca
> sotto la grande fersa
> dalle stoppie ——
>
> la vela, quando fiotta
> e s'inabissa al salto
> della rocca——
>
> il cannone di mezzodì
> più fioco del tuo cuore
> e il cronometro se
> scatta senza rumore ——

But even if the woman reveals herself through such imagistic and impressionistic flashes, there is always something about her that cannot be recaptured or pinpointed; for, as the poet tells her, "yours was a different mold [Altro era il tuo stampo]."

In Motet 10 (1939) the existential hope and anxiety of waiting for his belovèd's apparition is concentrated in the first two words—"Why linger? [Perché tardi?]"—and the rest of the poem is a metaphorical as well as impressionistic elaboration of it:

> In the pine the squirrel beats its tail
> like a torch against the bark.
> The half-moon descends with its horn
> in the sun which makes it pale.
> And the day is done.

> . . . Nel pino lo scoiattolo
> batte la coda a torcia sulla scorza.
> La mezzaluna scende col suo picco
> nel sole che la smorza. È giorno fatto.

Whether the hoped-for apparition appears or not, the poetic eye can still focus that point in the cloud of smoke which contains her; in fact the more tenuous and intangible the signs of her presence, the firmer and more tenacious the poet's imaginative hold on it:

> The slow smoke is startled by a breeze,
> defends itself at a point
> which contains you. Nothing ends,
> or everything,
> if you, lightning, leave the cloud.

> A un soffio il pigro fumo trasalisce,
> si difende nel punto che ti chiude.
> Nulla finisce, o tutto, se tu fòlgore
> lasci la nube.

The apparently casual mode of collocating objects or situations through which the woman's pervasive presence is summed up can be seen in Motet 11 (1938):

> The soul that scatters polka
> and rigadoon at each new season
> of the road feeds on a secret
> passion and finds it more
> intense at every corner.

> Your voice is this diffuse spirit.
> On wires, on wings, in the breeze,
> by chance, with the muse's help
> or that of a mechanical device,
> it returns happy or sad.
> I talk of other things to others
> who do not know you, and your voice
> is outlined there, insisting
> *do re la sol sol* . . .

> L'anima che dispensa
> furlana e rigodone ad ogni nuova
> stagione della strada, s'alimenta
> della chiusa passione, la ritrova
> a ogni angolo più intensa.

> La tua voce è quest'anima diffusa.
> Su fili, su ali, al vento, a caso, col

favore della musa o d'un ordegno,
ritorna lieta o triste. Parlo d'altro,
ad altri che t'ignora e il suo disegno
è là che insiste *do re la sol sol*....

Any pretext, circumstance, or impression is enough to make the poet feel her presence and unbare a quality or aspect of her multiform and multifaceted personality. Motet 12 depicts this presence in terms of qualities that are at once earthly and celestial, romantic and realistic. The very first sentence establishes a tone of personal intimacy that runs through the whole poem:

> I free your forehead from the icicles
> which you gathered while crossing the lofty
> nebulae; your feathers are torn
> by a cyclone and you awake with a start.

> Ti libero la fronte dai ghiaccioli
> che raccogliesti traversando l'alte
> nebulose; hai le penne lacerate
> dai cicloni, ti desti a soprassalti.

In the next stanza there is a transition to a more sharply defined feeling of time and place that gives a touch of intimacy to the poet's sense of recognition which nobody else can share:

> Midday: the medlar prolongs
> its black shadow in the square; a cold sun
> endures in the sky; and the other
> shadows turning round the lane
> don't know that you are here.

> Mezzodì: allunga nel riquadro il nespolo
> l'ombra nera, s'ostina in cielo un sole
> freddoloso; e l'altre ombre che scantonano
> nel vicolo non sanno che sei qui.

And underlying the sense of a specific time, place, and circumstance is a poetic feeling which enables the poet to transmute what he recalls into something at once real and symbolic, as for instance in Motet 13 (1938). The scene is set in Venice. The gondola "gliding forward / in a dazzle of tar and poppies" evokes "one evening among many" in the poet's past;[11] and the more

11. The setting and atmosphere of this lyric may be compared with those of the story "Sera difficile," in *Farfalla di Dinard*.

vividly particularized the recollection, the sharper the sense of desolation he
feels in the absence of the woman. Indeed, he is so immersed in his recollection of the past that only the writhing catch of a solitary fisherman can bring
his mind back to the present:

> The gondola gliding forward
> in a dazzle of tar and poppies,
> the secret song arising
> from the masses of rigging, the tall
> doors closing on you and the laughter
> of the masked escaping in hordes.
>
> One evening among many
> and my night is most profound!
> Down there a pale mass writhes
> by fits and starts and makes me
> one with that intent fisher
> of eels on the bank.
>
> La gondola che scivola in un forte
> bagliore di catrame e di papaveri,
> la subdola canzone che s'alzava
> da masse di cordame, l'alte porte
> rinchiuse su di te e risa di maschere
> che fuggivano a frotte ——
>
> una sera tra mille e la mia notte
> è più profonda! S'agita laggiù
> uno smorto groviglio che m'avviva
> a stratti e mi fa eguale a quell'assorto
> pescatore d'anguille dalla riva.

Helped by the storm and the analogical possibilities it offers, the poet celebrates another moment of recollection-cum-recognition in Motet 14 (1938).
The coming and going of the woman loved and the commotion they cause
find a dramatic externalization in the fury of the elements and the turmoil
among plants and flowers, as well as in the icy spheres:

> Is it salt or hail that rages?
> Making havoc of the bell-flowers, uprooting
> the cedars. An underwater peal
> approaches and fades away
> like the one you used to awaken.

The pianola of the infernal zone
gains volume and rises to the icy
spheres — glitters like you as when,
playing the part of Lakmé, you would trill
Aria delle Campanelle.

Infuria sale o grandine? Fa strage
di campanule, svelle la cedrina.
Un rintocco subacqueo s'avvicina,
quale tu lo destavi, e s'allontana.

La pianola degl'inferi da sè
accelera i registri, sale nelle
sfere del gelo.... —— brilla come te
quando fingevi col tuo trillo d'aria
Lakmé nell'Aria delle Campanelle.

The poet isolates one particular aspect of the cataclysm—the pianola's gaining volume and glittering in the icy spheres like the woman loved—which serves to fuse what is human with the nonhuman and impersonal aspects of nature. At the end of the poem the detail of her playing the part of Lakmé epitomizes the way the emotional drama and the turmoil and combustion of the elements merge. And the transition from the personal to the impersonal and vice versa is achieved with a characteristic subtlety and suppleness both verbal and rhythmic.

In Motet 15 the various glimpses of everyday life in its familiar and monotonous routine are made more humane and tolerable, the poet tells his beloved, "if you insist on interweaving them with your thread." The link as well as the contrast between what is dull and monotonous in life and the inner life of feelings, sentiments, and memories is implicitly present throughout the poem:

At dawn when the sudden noise of trains
tells me of men closed in,
coursing through a mountain tunnel,
lit up at intervals by glimpses
of sky and water,

at dusk when the woodworm eating
the table redoubles its efforts
and the watchman's footsteps draw near;
at dawn and dusk, still human pauses these
if you insist on interweaving them with your thread.

Al primo chiaro, quando
subitaneo un rumore
di ferrovia mi parla
di chiusi uomini in corsa
nel traforo del sasso
illuminato a tagli
da cieli ed acque misti;

al primo buio, quando
il bulino che tarla
la scrivanìa rafforza
il suo fervore e il passo
del guardiano s'accosta:
al chiaro e al buio, soste ancora umane
se tu a intrecciarle col tuo refe insisti.

In Motet 16 (1937) the drama of the separation between the poet and Clizia is metaphorically reenacted in terms of the physical distance between two funicular stations:

The flower that repeats
from the edge of the cliff
"forget me not" has neither
lighter nor gayer tints
than the space thrown between you and me.

A creaking starts up, throws us apart,
the stubborn blue doesn't reappear.
In the almost visible sultriness
the funicular brings me back
to the opposite stage, already dark.

Il fiore che ripete
dall'orlo del burrato
non scordarti di me,
non ha tinte più liete nè più chiare
dello spazio gettato tra me e te.

Un cigolìo si sferra, ci discosta,
l'azzurro pervicace non ricompare.
Nell'afa quasi visibile mi riporta all'opposta
tappa, già buia, la funicolare.

The sense of desolation and division finds its conceptual as well as pictorial counterpart in the creaking of the funicular, the blue disappearing behind "the almost visible sultriness," and the darkness enveloping the funicular station at which the poet arrives. Similarly, the tints marking "the space thrown between me and you" symbolize the hope and desire for a reunion.

In Motet 17 (1938) there is—at least in the revised version—no explicit reference to the woman. We are presented with a densely rich and compact pattern of vivid and concrete images forming a country landscape:

> The frog, first to attempt
> a chord from the pond which engulfs
> reeds and clouds, the rustle
> of interwoven carobs, where a cold
> sun extinguishes its rays, a late
> sluggish hum of the coleoptera round
> the flowers still sucking the sap,
> last sounds, sparse life of the country.
>
> With a breath the hour comes to an end,
> the slate sky prepares for the bursting
> of the three lean horses, to the sparking
> of hooves.

> La rana, prima a ritentar la corda
> dallo stagno che affossa
> giunchi e nubi, stormire dei carrubi
> conserti dove spenge le sue fiaccole
> un sole senza caldo, tardo ai fiori
> ronzìo di coleotteri che suggono
> ancora linfe, ultimi suoni, avara
> vita della campagna. Con un soffio
>
> l'ora s'estingue: un cielo di lavagna
> si prepara a un irrompere di scarni
> cavalli, alle scintille degli zoccoli.

The landscape, and particularly the skyscape, may be interpreted as reflecting the poet's spiritual lethargy and dejection, which only a reunion with the woman loved can help him overcome. In earlier editions of *Le occasioni* the last three lines ran as follows:

> . . . the slate sky prepares for the bursting
> of the three horsemen! Greet them
> with me.

> . . . un cielo di lavagna
> si prepara all'irrompere dei tre
> cavalieri! Salutali con me.

This apostrophe, apparently addressed to the woman loved, is replaced in the present edition by the overtly impersonal image of "the sparking of hooves," which suggests the springs of life and love gushing out against the background of the slate sky.

Motet 18 (1937), with its Dantesque clarity, precision, and concreteness of diction on the one hand and—something rare in Montale—its direct emotional effusiveness on the other, is one of the best known. The verbal economy and compression it displays are an indication of the poet's grasp over the emotional and conceptual possibilities implicit in the theme. He asks the scissors of time (or forgetfulness) not to disfigure or obliterate that face which he anxiously cherishes in memory:

> Scissors, don't cut that face,
> fading memory's sole possession;
> don't turn her large attentive eyes
> into my perpetual mist.
>
> The cold swoops down —The slash
> is merciless. The wounded acacia
> shakes off the cicada's husk
> into November's early mud.
>
> Non recidere, forbice, quel volto,
> solo nella memoria che si sfolla,
> non far del grande suo viso in ascolto
> la mia nebbia di sempre.
>
> Un freddo cala.... Duro il colpo svetta.
> E l'acacia ferita da sè scrolla
> il guscio di cicala
> nella prima belletta di Novembre.

There is something at once indeterminate and intensely particularized about "that face" which gives the poem its symbolic as well as lyric potency and evocativeness. The imaginative ordering of his feelings and experiences is brought about by the poet chiefly by means of a pattern of concretely realized significances and a rather deliberately ambiguous collocation of certain key words. For instance, the word *solo* in the second line could be interpreted to mean the only face that memory treasures as well as the face that has no existence outside the poet's memory. Similarly, the phrase *large attentive eyes* could refer to the memory of a particular expression the poet once saw on the woman's face and which has remained impressed on his memory ever since, and at the same time to the form the poet has given it in his recollection. Similarly, *attentive* could also suggest, in its literal meaning, anxiety, fear, and uncertainty, not only on the poet's part, but also on the part of the face itself fearing the harm that the scissors of time might do by reducing it to a perpetual mist.

However, what is feared in the first stanza happens—and happens with catastrophic finality and ruthlessness—in the second. As if decreed by some unknown and implacable force, the cold swoops down on the poet's world of sentiments and memories, bringing about precisely what he was afraid of. The effect is conveyed through the concrete yet suggestive image of the acacia shaking off the cicada's husk into November's early mud, a poignant symbol of the poet's frustration as well as the wreck of those remnants of the past which he had shored against the tide of oblivion.[12] The image clinches, in a subtle and conclusive way, the fact of "that face" being reduced to a "perpetual mist."

In the penultimate motet (1938) the poet ceases to look for signs of his belovèd's presence amidst familiar scenes and circumstances on the earth:

> The reed that softly sheds
> its red plume in spring; the gravel
> path by the ditch, the black
> current overflown by dragonflies
> and the panting dog coming home
> with a bundle in its mouth;

> La canna che dispiuma
> mollemente il suo rosso
> flabello a primavera;
> la rèdola nel fosso, su la nera
> correntìa sorvolata di libellule;
> e il cane trafelato che rincasa
> col suo fardello in bocca . . .

Instead, he proceeds to visualize her through a framework of intangible symbols and emblems:

> It is not for me to recognize myself here,
> but there where a glare burns brighter
> and the cloud lowers, beyond

12. Cf. T. S. Eliot: "These fragments I have shored against my ruins" (*The Waste Land,* V. *What the Thunder Said*).

> her now far-off eyes, just two
> crossed beams of light.
> And time passes.

> oggi qui non mi tocca riconoscere;
> ma là dove il riverbero più cuoce
> e il nuvolo s'abbassa, oltre le sue
> pupille ormai remote, solo due
> fasci di luce in croce.
>   E il tempo passa.

Thus he looks for the signs of her presence not only beyond this earth, but also beyond death itself.

In the last motet (1937), however, the poet returns again to the contemplation of familiar sights and objects both outside and inside his room—a shell on which a volcano has been painted and a paperweight of lava with a coin encased in it. These objects, for all their triviality, allegorically sum up what is left of life, which once seemed rich and vast. At the outset the poet strikes a note of acceptance of what has remained, together with a note of nostalgia for what time has taken away:

> — well so be it. The sound of a horn
> converses with the swarms in the oak grove.
> And in the shell which reflects the evening
> a painted volcano smokes happily.

> The coin encased in the lava
> also shines on the table
> and holds down a few papers. Life
> that seemed vast is smaller than your handkerchief.

> . . . ma così sia. Un suono di cornetta
> dialoga con gli sciami del querceto.
> Nella valva che il vespero riflette
> un vulcano dipinto fuma lieto.

> La moneta incassata nella lava
> brilla anch'essa sul tavolo e trattiene
> pochi fogli. La vita che sembrava
> vasta è più breve del tuo fazzoletto.

The *Motets* are followed by a third section consisting of one long poem in three parts and entitled *Tempi di Bellosguardo* (Bellosguardo, as celebrated by Foscolo in *Le Grazie*, is the name of a hill outside Florence). Although it is not dated, it was obviously written during Montale's stay in Florence:

Oh how the hum of evening
fades away in the luminous expanse
that arches toward the hills and how
the trees converse with the trite murmur
of the sand; how this common life
that we no more possess than our breath
is channeled in the dignity of the columns
flanked by the willows and the big
leaping wolves in gardens among
pools that are full to the brim . . .

Oh come là nella corusca
distesa che s'inarca verso i colli,
il brusìo della sera s'assottiglia
e gli alberi discorrono col trito
mormorio della rena; come limpida
s'inalvea là in decoro
di colonne e di salci ai lati e grandi salti
di lupi nei giardini, tra le vasche ricolme
che traboccano,
questa vita di tutti non più posseduta
del nostro respiro.

An impassioned philosophical contemplation of the landscape is the theme as
well as the occasion for the poem. The hill affords Montale both a vantage-
point and a perspective through which he can see both what is in front of
him and what is within him. He is deeply affected by the pervasive sense of
peace in the atmosphere and by the multiple sights and sounds around him—
"the steaming bends [l'anse vaporanti]," "the crossings of chimneys [incroci
di camini]," "shouts from hanging gardens [grida dai giardini pensili]," and
"dismay and long laughter / on the sharp-cut roofs [sgomenti e lunghe risa /
sui tetti ritagliati]," as seen from "the wings of thick foliage [le quinte / dei
frondami ammassati]." The pictorial rendering of the concept of peace as a
light "illumining" the whole landscape "by glints" is a typical example of
Montale's ability to translate his perceptions and intuitions into poetically
concrete terms:

. . . It's too sad that so much peace
should illumine by glints, and that
everything should rotate
with rare flashes on the steaming bends . . .

        . . . è troppo triste
   che tanta pace illumini a spiragli
   e tutto ruoti poi con rari guizzi
   su l'anse vaporanti, . . .

In the second part of the poem, with its nimbler rhythm, an even deeper and
more spontaneous fusion between what the poet perceives and what he feels is
effected. The "desolate . . . foliage / of the green-brown magnolia [derelitte
. . . / fronde della magnolia / verdibrune]" makes him ponder on "the still
more desolate foliage / of the living lost in the prism / of the minute [più
ancora / derelitte le fronde / dei vivi che si smarriscono / nel prisma del
minuto]," the dramatic contrast or the "brief see-saw [fugace altalena]," as
he puts it, "between life that passes / and life that stays [tra vita / che passa e
vita che sta]," and the monotonous round of existence in which both organic
and inorganic nature are caught up:

        feverish limbs caught in the movement
        recurring within a brief circle:
        pulsating sweat, sweat of death,
        acts and minutes mirrored,
        always the same, broken echoes
        of a beating on high that facets
        the sun and the rain.

        le membra di febbre votate
        al moto che si ripete
        in circolo breve: sudore
        che pulsa, sudore di morte,
        atti minuti specchiati,
        sempre gli stessi, rifranti
        echi del batter che in alto
        sfaccetta il sole e la pioggia.

From the plane of analogy between the seen and the unseen, between what is
half perceived and half created, the poet moves on to the moral and philosophical plane in order to sum up the existential dilemma:

        Up here there's no escape:
        one dies knowingly, or chooses
        a life that changes and doesn't know:
        another death.

quassù non c'è scampo: si muore
sapendo o si sceglie la vita
che muta ed ignora: altra morte.

However, this dilemma doesn't invalidate—in fact it enhances—the experience
of love, sacrifice, and fidelity as embodied in the stones, galleries and busts
that have survived through the centuries. There is something at once cogent
and appealing about the image or the gesture representing such virtues. The
gesture

. . . lingers: fathoms the deep
and sounds out its boundaries: the unknown
gesture which expresses itself
and no other . . .

. . . il gesto rimane: misura
il vuoto, ne snoda il confine:
il gesto ignoto che esprime
sè stesso e non altro . . .

The last section of *Tempi di Bellosguardo* starts with a question that takes
up almost two-thirds of the whole poem. The rhythm and cadence acquire a
more vigorous tempo, which reflects both the storm beating down on the
roof-tiles and the particularly fruitful interaction between thought and imagery—a sharp vividness and concreteness of naturalistic detail and a rich
conglomeration of objects, incidents, and concepts. The question leads up to
a climax and ends there. What follows is not a direct answer, but a series
of images depicting the miscellaneous and apparently unconnected aspects
and data of the physical world, accompanied by the prolonged sound of the
clay pots, which may be taken as an objective correlative to the answer and
as having acquired in the last three lines the conclusive force of an ethical summing up. The "hard work" of the "heavenly weavers," we are told, has been
interrupted "on the loom of man." In other words we are to take the objects
and phenomena, the sights and sounds that the poet perceives "from this
height," as well as the ethical and philosophical musings they prompt, as
being the work both of nature, or the heavenly weavers (symbolizing the
three Fates) and of the poet's own creative imagination. The last two words
in the poem, *And tomorrow,* suggest uncertainty about the future in the
philosophical sense as well as the improbability, if not impossibility, of another
such fruitful combination of or collaboration between man's power and that
of nature ever recurring:

A prolonged sound comes from the clay pots,
the fences hardly defend
the ellipses of the convolvulus, and
the locusts fall from the arbors
and hobble on the books;
hard work, heavenly weavers,
interrupted on the loom of man.
And tomorrow —

. . . Un suono lungo
dànno le terrecotte, i pali appena
difendono le ellissi dei convolvoli,
e le locuste arrancano piovute
sui libri dalle pergole; dura opera,
tessitrici celesti, ch'è interrotta
sul telaio degli uomini. E domani....

The fourth and last section of *Le occasioni,* which has almost the same
degree of thematic and emotional unity as *Mottetti,* opens with "La casa dei
doganieri."

You don't remember the coast-guards' house
perched sheer on the edge of the cliff
and waiting desolately for you ever since
your restless thoughts flocked there one evening.

The southwest wind has lashed
its old walls for years, and your laughter
is no longer gay; the compass veers at random
and the score of the dice adds up no longer.
You don't remember; other times
distract your memory; a thread winds.

I still hold an end; but the house
keeps receding and the smoky weathervane
spins relentlessly on the rooftop.
I hold an end; but you are alone
and don't breathe here in the dark.

Oh the receding skyline
where the oil tanker's light rarely appears!
Is this the passage? (The breakers storm the cliff

which descends steeply to the sea—)
You don't remember the house of this my evening,
and I don't know who goes and who stays.

Tu non ricordi la casa dei doganieri
sul rialzo a strapiombo sulla scogliera:
desolata t'attende dalla sera
in cui v'entrò lo sciame dei tuoi pensieri
e vi sostò irrequieto.

Libeccio sferza da anni le vecchie mura
e il suono del tuo riso non è più lieto:
la bussola va impazzita all'avventura
e il calcolo dei dadi più non torna.
Tu non ricordi; altro tempo frastorna
la tua memoria; un filo s'addipana.

Ne tengo ancora un capo; ma s'allontana
la casa e in cima al tetto la banderuola
affumicata gira senza pietà.
Ne tengo un capo; ma tu resti sola
nè qui respiri nell'oscurità.

Oh l'orizzonte in fuga, dove s'accende
rara la luce della petroliera!
Il varco è qui? (Ripullula il frangente
ancora sulla balza che scoscende....)
Tu non ricordi la casa di questa
mia sera. Ed io non so chi va e chi resta.

This poem is one of the best known and most popular in this section and
indeed in the whole corpus of Montale's poetry. It illustrates a high degree
of artistic and technical accomplishment, maturity of thought and feeling, and
a complex balance between the personal and the impersonal, which one invariably associates with a major artist like Montale. What it offers is neither
a "turning loose of emotion" nor an escape from it.[13] While recollecting a
romantic episode from the past—his visit to the coast-guards' house by the
sea in the company of the woman loved—the poet not only relives it, but
sees it both morally and philosophically charged in recollection. Thus what is
recollected acquires a new dimension and a new perspective. But even

13. Cf. Eliot: "Poetry is not a turning loose of emotion, but an escape from emotion; it is
not the expression of personality, but an escape from personality" (*The Sacred Wood,*
"Tradition and Individual Talent").

though circumstances have drastically changed, and the woman is no longer there to share this experience with him, his hold on the characteristic specificity of time, place, and atmosphere is not the less firm, as it comes out from what is evoked. Montale shows himself to be in complete possession of his own feelings, thoughts, and emotions, and thus armed, he sets out to explore the moral, psychological, and emotional implications and challenges with which the scene and the landscape before him, as well as what he was to call in a later poem "the sudden jerk of memory" ("Voce giunta con le folaghe"), confront him. As the poet contemplates the familiar landscape, seascape, and the coast-guards' house in its eloquent desolation, a sense of inevitability and monotony weighs on the recognition of each and every detail, which, while linking the past with the present, at the same time stresses the distance and division between the poet and the woman loved. "Ever since / your restless thoughts flocked there one evening," the landscape seems to have been overhung by a cloud of unmitigated gloom. Even such trivial and prosaic objects as the compass or the weathervane have something mysterious about them: "The compass veers at random / and the score of the dice adds up no longer." The poem starts with a note of directness and familiarity ("You don't remember the coast guards' house"), expands into the concrete and particularized realism of the description of the coast-guards' house ("perched sheer on the edge of the cliff"), gathers weight as the house is poetically personalized ("waiting desolately for you ever since / your restless thoughts flocked there one evening"), and then plunges into the depths of a moral and emotional drama.

What the scene once meant to the poet and to the woman loved is recalled and relived with a dual intensity, as it were—the intensity inherent in the experience as such, and in the realization that the woman is no longer with him. The poet's return to the scene sets in motion the interplay of sentiment and recognition in which even the woman seems to participate as if she were standing by his side. Thus, from the core of what is recollected as well as from the realization of what is no longer there, a poignantly ambiguous situation emerges—a situation in which the woman is both present and absent. The mode of intimate familiarity with which he addresses her contributes to this sense of ambiguity and enriches the implicit symbolism of the desolate house, with its wind-lashed walls. The poet's noting that her laughter is no longer gay lends a pathos and a romantic credibility to the illusion that she is by his side, and at the same time confirms the deep division between them, thereby shattering that illusion. The restlessness of her thoughts, which "flocked there one evening" and which were indicative of her moral and emotional stresses and turmoil when she was with the poet, are seen to be, in retrospect, a prelude to "other times" that distract her memory now. The suggestive indeterminateness of the words *other times* contrasts with the specific "thisness" of "the house of this my evening" and emphasizes the chasm that has opened between the poet and the woman. The mad veering of the compass dramatizes the impossibility of a return to the past and the irreversibility of the course that events have taken, "and the score of the dice adds up no longer."

However, impelled by the will to resuscitate and reenact the past, the poet still grasps his end of the thread, while the woman has let hers drop. But this merely confirms the poignantly illusory nature of the bond between him and the woman loved. Thus, both the house and the skyline are seen receding and his grasp on the thread becomes weaker and weaker. And this means that the moral and emotional impetus—not to mention justification to keep hold of his end—ebbs away too, ebbs away precisely as a result of the woman having let go her end of the thread, thereby severing any possible connection or communication with him. The repetition of the phrase "I still hold an end" and, later, "I'm holding an end" denotes, not only an act of desperate fidelity on the poet's part, but also a moral determination to fight the corroding influence of time and oblivion.

But it is all in vain: "Oh the receding skyline / where the oil-tanker's light rarely appears!" The question the poet asks, "Is this the passage?", might possibly be an unconscious echo of a similar question the woman may have asked in the past and thus may represent the last remnant of the illusion that the past is somehow the present. And the passage the poet inquires about might be interpreted as being that through which he might rejoin the woman loved, or it might signify the poet's search for his moral and spiritual bearings and for a way out from the state of bewilderment in which the past and the present are grappling together for their hold on the poet's mind and imagination. All that he hears by way of an answer is the sound of the breakers "storming the cliff which crashes," and this brings his reverie and his search for the past to an end. He is forced to recognize and accept the stark and unequivocal truth of the phrase with which the poem started and with which it virtually ends: "You don't remember the house."

The fact that the poem ends almost as it began suggests that it may be interpreted as a musical as well as architectonic whole. Its strophic division, its imagery, its allegorical and symbolic layers all being closely interwoven, there is something of a musical progression about the way it proceeds. Starting with the bass tone of "You don't remember the coast-guards' house," it gathers momentum from the woman's "restless thoughts" flocking there and the compass veering madly, and finally reaches a climax with the weathervane spinning relentlessly on the rooftop. The repetition of "you don't remember" and "I still hold an end," together with the metaphysical solemnity of the phrase "and the score of the dice adds up no longer," marks the diminuendo taking us down to "the receding skyline," which signals the melting away of the imaginary fabric the poet has woven. After that there is a pause, followed by the question "Is this the passage?" And then toward the end the first line returns with an added force and assurance: "You don't remember the house." This time, however, it is not the coast-guards' house, but "the house of this my evening" which has become a symbol of the poet's moral and philosophical loneliness.

Although in a relatively minor key, "Bassa marea" is, like "La casa dei doganieri," a love poem with the sea as a background. The dominant thought and sentiment are summed up in the line "That time no more." Coupled with and actually motivated by such a realization is the awareness that everything around is dissolving and disappearing. Memory struggles to preserve and perpetuate itself—especially the memory of a particular person bound to the poet's past by ties of love—by resisting the drift toward "a dismal whirlpool / of sucked in existences."

> That time no more. Now rapid
> oblique flights cross the wall,
> everything descends without a pause,
> even the rock from which you first
> touched the waves
> is lost on the rugged shore.
>
> A dismal whirlpool
> of sucked in existences comes
> with the breath of spring;
> and in the evening only your memory
> —black bindweed—writhes and defends itself.

> Non più quel tempo. Varcano ora il muro
> rapidi voli obliqui, la discesa
> di tutto non s'arresta e si confonde
> sulla proda scoscesa anche lo scoglio
> che ti portò primo sull'onde.
>
> Viene col soffio della primavera
> un lugubre risucchio
> d'assorbite esistenze; e nella sera,
> negro vilucchio, solo il tuo ricordo
> s'attorce e si difende.

"Stanze," on the other hand, has a rich gamut of themes and concepts interwoven into a complex pattern of anatomical and physiological metaphors
and similes by means of which the poet tries to pinpoint the specific traits of
the nature and significance of the woman loved, as well as her genesis. Thus
he has recourse to such images as "the blood which nourishes you," the "sap
which designs / your hands, beats at your wrists / unnoticed," or "the
minute net of your nerves." And the degree of analytical subtlety and minuteness serves as a measure of the richness and complexity of the bond between
her and the poet:

> I search in vain for the point
> whence moved the blood which nourishes you,
> the endless widening out of circles
> beyond the brief span of human
> days and brought you face to face
> with a torment of agonies that
> you don't know, alive in the putrid
> marsh of a submerged star;
> and now it's sap which designs
> your hands, beats at your wrists
> unnoticed, and enflames your face
> or pales it.

> Ricerco invano il punto onde si mosse
> il sangue che ti nutre, interminato
> respingersi di cerchi oltre lo spazio
> breve dei giorni umani,
> che ti rese presente in uno strazio
> d'agonie che non sai, viva in un putre
> padule d'astro inabissato; ed ora
> è linfa che disegna le tue mani,
> ti batte ai polsi inavvertita e il volto
> t'infiamma o discolora.

Verbal echoes from Dante ("the point / whence moved the blood which
nourishes you") [14] coexist with such unmistakably Montalian images as "the
putrid / marsh of a submerged star" and form a lyrically charged pattern
that is rich in psychological and metaphysical allusiveness rendered in terms
of a sensuously particularized experience. Thus the elusive charm and essence
of the woman are figured as a halo of rays or a "corolla of light ashes

14. Cf. Dante: "quando l'amor divino / mosse da prima quelle cose belle" (*Inferno*, canto 1,
lines 39–40) or "da cima del monte, / onde si mosse" (*Inferno*, canto 12, line 7).

[corolla / di cenere leggera]," and the element of suddenness or surprise in
her numerous revelations is conveyed through such images as "a white wing
in flight [candida ala in fuga]," "wandering wraiths [vagabonde larve],"
"the twang of the bow that is sprung [il ronzio / dell'arco ch'è scoccato],"
or the furrow that ploughs the sea and closes in on itself. Such revelations
serve to indicate the moral and emotional hold she has over the poet, so that
when she disappears, it is nothing short of damnation for him:

> I seem to see in you
> a last corolla of light
> ashes that doesn't last, but
> falls away in flakes. Thus your nature
> is both willed and unwilled.
> You touch the sign, pass over. Oh
> the twang of the bow that is sprung,
> the furrow that ploughs the flood
> and closes in on itself.
> And now the last bubble rises
> to the surface. Perhaps damnation
> is this bitter raving darkness
> that descends on whoever stays.

> In te m'appare un'ultima corolla
> di cenere leggera che non dura
> ma sfioccata precipita. Voluta,
> disvoluta è così la tua natura.
> Tocchi il segno, travàlichi. Oh il ronzìo
> dell'arco ch'è scoccato, il solco che ara
> il flutto e si rinchiude! Ed ora sale
> l'ultima bolla in su. La dannazione
> è forse questa vaneggiante amara
> oscurità che scende su chi resta.

"Sotto la pioggia" combines a romantic attitude to one's experience with
a moral and philosophical gloss on its significance. The poet sees a reflection
of his human condition and dilemmas—"the naked hopes and the gnawing /
thoughts [le nude / speranze ed il pensiero che rimorde]"—in the image of
the woman's house fading away "as in the mist of memory [come nella bruma
del ricordo]." His love for the woman itself takes the form of a spiritual
quest, and such impressionistic objects as the "eggshell that ends up in the
mud [guscio d'uovo che va tra la fanghiglia]," "the bright showers [i lucidi

strosci]," or "the smoke trailed by a ship [il fumo strascicato d'una nave]"
represent so many milestones in that quest:

> You are for me
> what the stork dares when having taken
> its flight from the misty peak
> it wings its way toward Cape Town.

> Per te intendo
> ciò che osa la cicogna quando alzato
> il volo dalla cuspide nebbiosa
> rèmiga verso la Città del Capo.

In "Punta del Mesco," another love poem, the recollection of the woman
mingles with that of her childhood—the intensely realized local and topographical detail with which the poem starts bringing out the personal nature
of the experience in an evocatively impersonal way:

> Under the sky of the quarry lined at dawn
> by the partridges' straight flight, the smoke
> from the mines rose slowly and tenderly
> up the steep slopes.

> The water spirits, silent trumpeteers,
> turned over from the pilotboat's prow
> and swiftly plunged into the foam
> that you used to skim over.

> Nel cielo della cava rigato
> all'alba dal volo dritto delle pernici
> il fumo delle mine s'inteneriva,
> saliva lento le pendici a piombo.

> Dal rostro del palabotto si capovolsero
> le ondine trombettiere silenziose
> e affondarono rapide tra le spume
> che il tuo passo sfiorava.

Such a recollection enables the poet to assess the moral and philosophical
depth of the present:

> I see the path I trod
> one day like a restless dog;
> it skirts the wave, climbs among the rocks,

and disappears at times
amidst scattered litter. All's equal.
The roaring waters' echo
rages in the wet gravel, while
the humid sun shines on the bent
stonebreakers' tired limbs as they hammer.

Vedo il sentiero che percorsi un giorno
come un cane inquieto; lambe il fiotto,
s'inerpica tra i massi e rado strame
a tratti lo scancella. E tutto è uguale.
Nella ghiaia bagnata s'arrovella
un'eco degli scrosci. Umido brilla
il sole sulle membra affaticate
dei curvi spaccapietre che martellano.

Against the seething and tormented background of concrete impressionistic
details the poet attempts to forge a link between past and present, while the
woman's rare gestures return in memory:

Figureheads that rise again
and remind me of you. A drill
engraves a heart on the rock
—and louder crashes the thunder.
I grope in the smoke, but see again:
your rare gestures return and so
does your face which dawns at the window,
and your childhood torn by the shots.

Polene che risalgono e mi portano
qualche cosa di te. Un tràpano incide
il cuore sulla roccia —— schianta attorno
più forte un rombo. Brancolo nel fumo,
ma rivedo: ritornano i tuoi rari
gesti e il viso che aggiorna al davanzale, ——
mi torna la tua infanzia dilaniata
dagli spari!

Regarding the following poem, "Costa San Giorgio," Montale tells us in his
note that it is about "a walk by two people on the well-known slope and a
little farther up, and hence the poem could be entitled 'The Walk.' Maritornes,
or someone like her, is from *Don Quixote*. It is well known that El Dorado

was the myth of the golden man, before becoming that of the golden land. Here the poor fetish is now in the hands of men and has nothing to do with 'the secret enemy' that works within. . . . The poem is incomplete: but perhaps it would be inconceivable to complete it." The note doesn't, however, help the reader very much just where he most needs help, that is to say, in those lines or parts of the poem which are obscure and which represent what Solmi calls "the less accomplished zones of Montale's poetry," [15] or what Gargiulo considered to be the raw documentary and psychological residuum.[16] For instance, it is not clear what he means by *El Dorado* being a cause of "mourning among your ancestors [lutto fra i tuoi padri]" or the Idol being barred or dead. Nevertheless, the metaphysical-cum-existential aspects of the imagery, as well as such surrealistic details as the will-o'-the-wisp covering the street with dust and the gas-fitter pedaling down rapidly with the ladder on his shoulder, come off quite effectively, as does the metaphorical presentation of such abstract concepts as the circle not opening and everything rapidly descending or climbing up the arches. All these concepts and images are interwoven in a dramatic and meditative monologue:

15. *Scrittori negli anni,* p. 199. In a letter to me (dated Milan, February 17, 1972) Solmi himself explained the significance of the lines "più / non distacca per noi dall'architrave / della stalla il suo lume, Maritornes." These lines, Solmi points out, "si riferiscono all'episodio narrato nel cap. XVI del romanzo. Don Chisciotte, bastonato a sangue in una precedente avventura, giunge a una *venta* (osteria), che al solito prende per un castello, e l'oste per il castellano. Nell'osteria c'e una serva puttana, Maritornes, che dorme nella stalla, e che ha dato un appuntamento a un *harriero* (carrettiere), il quale dorme nella stessa stanza con don Chisciotte e Sancio Panza. Don Chisciotte, che ha sempre in mente i prediletti libri di cavalleria, crede che la brutta Maritornes sia una principessa bellissima, e che si sia perdutamente innamorata di lui. Perciò, vedendola arrivare all'incerta lume della lampada, le si avvinghia, scusandosi con lei se non può accedere ai suoi desideri, sia perchè mal ridotto dalle bastonature, sia perchè ha giurato fedeltà alla sua dama Dulcinea. Sopravviene il carrettiere, ascolta quelle parole, e, ingelosito, si mette a picchiare l'infelice Chisciotte. E Maritornes, che cerca rifugio sul letto di Sancio, il quale, destato di colpo, la prende a pugni. Arriva l'oste, che prende a pugni tutti e due. Bastonatura generale, finchè arriva la *"Santa Hermandad,"* cioè la polizia.
    I versi di Montale significano: Maritornes, non per noi (il poeta) ma per altri (il carrettiere) tu distacchi il tuo lume dall' architrave della stalla. Cioè, secondo me, adombra sè stesso nella figura di Don Chisciotte. Vuol dire: noi poeti, noi esclusi dalla vita, dall'intensità delle passioni umane, condannati unicamente a pascersi di sogni. Il tema era stato già adombrato da Montale nella Esterina di *Falsetto* (Ti guardiamo noi, della razza / di chi rimane a terra), nel *Carnevale di Gerti* (le primavere che non fioriscono), nel *Balcone* (il poeta che vede soltanto barlumi, illusioni di vita, sempre sull'orlo del nulla)."
16. "In Montale," Gargiulo observes, "non v'è traccia alcuna di residuo letterario: il residuo à appunto tutto documento, vita" (*Letteratura del Novecento,* p. 455). While making this observation, Gargiulo does not seem to take into account the presence of literary echoes and reminiscences in Montale's poetry, not only from Italian poets (Dante, Leopardi, Pascoli, Boine, Sbarbaro, Govoni, Ceccardi, etc.), but also from foreign poets like Keats, Pound, and Eliot.

There's no respite; nothing avails:
Maritornes no longer removes
her light for us
from the architrave of the stable.

Everything's equal; don't laugh:
I know from the very outset
the mournful creaking of the years
on their hinges, the morning a limbo
of senseless descent and in the end
the torch of the silent enemy
who keeps pressing—

           If a pendulum's sound comes out
from the enclosure it brings
the splash of a puppet knocked down.

Non c'è respiro; nulla vale: più
non distacca per noi dall'architrave
della stalla il suo lume, Maritornes.

Tutto è uguale; non ridere: lo so,
lo stridere degli anni fin dal primo,
lamentoso, sui cardini, il mattino
un limbo sulla stupida discesa ———
e in fondo il torchio del nemico muto
che preme....

           Se una pendola rintocca
dal chiuso porta il tonfo del fantoccio
ch'è abbattuto.

In "L'estate," too, the pattern of impressions and images, for all their particularity of detail, is not sufficiently informed or held together by any dominant, vitalizing thought or theme, so that at the end when we come to a philosophically pregnant line like "Too many lives are needed to form one [Occorrono troppe vite per farne una]," we feel as if it has been tacked on to the poem as an afterthought rather than emerging from the moral drift or context of the poem. "Eastbourne," on the other hand, is artistically and technically more accomplished. It is inspired by the poet's visit to Eastbourne on an August bank holiday. Everything he sees and hears around him —"the trumpets from the pavilion [le trombe / da un padiglione]," "the mica whiteness of the cliffs [il candore di mica della rupi]," "the disabled in wheelchairs / accompanied by long-eared dogs, / silent children or old people [vanno su sedie a ruote i mutilati, / li accompagnano cani dagli orecchi / lunghi, bimbi in silenzio o vecchi]"—becomes an integral part of a scene which is real and which, at the same time, seems to be as unreal as a dream. And while he is thus engrossed, the thought of his beloved—"voice of blood, lost and restored / to my evening [voce di sangue, persa e restituita / alla mia sera]"—overtakes him and colors everything around him, so that the holiday gaiety and excitement serve to reflect as well as accentuate his sense of desolation in the absence of the woman loved. And this state of mind leads him to muse on the nature of evil itself as well as on what he calls, in *Ossi di seppia,* "the evil of living [il male di vivere]":

> The holiday has no pity.
> The band roars out again,
> in the dusk unarmed goodness unfolds.
>
> Evil conquers. . . . The wheel doesn't stop.
>
> You too knew it, light-in-darkness.

> . . . La festa
> non ha pietà. Rimanda
> il suo scroscio la banda, si dispiega
> nel primo buio una bontà senz'armi.
>
> Vince il male....La ruota non s'arresta.
>
> Anche tu lo sapevi, luce-in-tenebra.

However, as the holiday festivities come to an end, the woman's image also disappears, leaving the poet still more dejected:

> In the burning quarter where you vanished
> at the first peal of the bells,
> only a bitter ember remains
> of what was bank holiday.

> Nella plaga che brucia, dove sei
> scomparsa al primo tocco delle compane, solo
> rimane l'acre tizzo che già fu
> *Bank Holiday.*

In "Corrispondenze," too, the woman's vision delineates itself through "a mirage of vapors [un miraggio di vapori]" or "nightmares of gold [incubi d'oro]," and hence it is precariously short-lived. Moreover, in spite of the lyric intensity of the interplay of response and recognition, she remains tantalizingly enigmatic and mysterious:

I recognize you; but don't know
what you read beyond the flights
fluttering above the pass.
In vain do I ask the plain
where a mist wavers between flashes and shots
on the scattered roofs,
or ask the hidden fever
of the express trains on the smoking coast.

Ti riconosco; ma non so che leggi
oltre i voli che svariano sul passo.
Lo chiedo invano al piano dove una bruma
èsita tra baleni e spari su sparsi tetti,
alla febbre nascosta dei diretti
nella costa che fuma.

"Barche sulla Marna" is a more satisfyingly complex and better organized poem. Using the river landscape as a canvas for impressionistic images as well as for ethical and philosophical reflections, the poet tends alternately to blend and separate the confines of dream and reality. Thus the flow of the river and the flow of time breed in him a sense of dull monotony and at the same time heighten his moral and metaphysical awareness so that he can see "the veiled tomorrow [il domani velato]" in today, and "great repose [grande riposo]" in "great torment [gran fermento]." At times, while in a state of "wise passiveness," [17] he watches such sights as the cork drifting with the current, the boats on the river, the butterfly catcher with his net, and the full moon shining palely in the light. At times he uses them as a basis for a poetical philosophizing concerning the world outside as well as within himself:

. . . but where's
the slow procession of seasons,
that was an infinite dawn without streets,
where's the long waiting and what's
the name of the void that engulfs us.

The dream is this: a vast,
interminable day which suffuses
with its almost immobile light
the dykes, and at every turn
the good work of man and the veiled
tomorrow without horror.

17. Wordsworth, "Expostulation and Reply."

> . . . ma dov'è
> la lenta processione di stagioni
> che fu un'alba infinita e senza strade,
> dov'è la lunga attesa e qual è il nome
> del vuoto che ci invade.
>
> Il sogno è questo: un vasto,
> interminato giorno che rifonde
> tra gli argini, quasi immobile, il suo bagliore
> e ad ogni svolta il buon lavoro dell'uomo,
> il domani velato che non fa orrore.

While watching another landscape, he describes some of its features in terms at once evocative and paradoxical, such as "the deepest silence / in the concordant noise of the afternoon [silenzio altissimo nel grido / concorde del meriggio]," "evening that was but / a longer morn [un mattino / più lungo era la sera]," or "the great ferment" that is synonymous with "great repose." Such phenomena acquire a dreamlike quality and transform "that nameless void which engulfs us" into an "interminable day" whose light suffuses the good works of man and gives meaning to them. But not everything lends itself to such a process of symbolic transformation—for instance, the color of the mouse that leapt up

> among the rushes or with its dash
> of poisonous metal, the starling
> that disappears in the smoke of the river.
>
> tra i giunchi o col suo spruzzo di metallo
> velenoso, lo storno che sparisce
> tra i fumi della riva.

Such phenomena exemplify in a realistic way and offer a metaphysical gloss, as it were, on the obstinate nature of things, while at the same time creating a sense of irony and paradox.

The same irony informs in varying degrees the remaining five poems in *Le occasioni*. For all their vivid and concrete realization of temporal and topographical data, the impressionistic elements in these poems operate within a framework of unobstrusive symbolism. Take, for instance, "Elegia di Pico Farnese" with its rich conglomeration of detail and imagery:

> Streets and steps that rise
> in pyramids, thick with engravings,
> webs of stone where darkness
> gapes, animated by

the confident eyes of pigs,
archivolts tinged with verdigris,
the singing spreading out slowly
from among the umbels of pines
and lingering faintly amidst
the indigo dripping on gorges,
edges, segments of walls.

Strade e scale che salgono a piramide, fitte
d'intagli, ragnateli di sasso dove s'aprono
oscurità animate dagli occhi confidenti
dei maiali, archivolti tinti di verderame,
si svolge a stento il canto dalle ombrelle dei pini,
e indugia affievolito nell'indaco che stilla
su anfratti, tagli, spicchi di muraglie.

Such a closely interwoven pattern of images, however, merely highlights the
spiritual poverty of the place, which is a village in the province of Frosinone.
Against such a background the poet evokes the figure of the woman loved and
the concept of love itself:

Love is quite different—it flashes
among trees with your sorrow and with
your fringe of wings, gloomy messenger!

. . . Ben altro
è l'Amore e fra gli alberi balena col tuo cruccio
e la tua frangia d'ali, messaggera accigliata!

This vision translates itself into an elaborate texture of emotional and sensory
data as well as of the specific details of time and place which relate that
vision back to the humdrum reality of everyday life. Thus the beholder is no
less spellbound than what he beholds and

The flash of your clothes melts in
the humor of the eye that reflects
other colors in its crystal.

. . . Il lampo delle tue vesti è sciolto
entro l'umore dell'occhio che rifrange nel suo
cristallo altri colori. . .

Perhaps more than any other poem in *Le occasioni*, "Nuove stanze" anticipates the tone and spirit of *La bufera*, especially insofar as the background of
World War II is concerned. In "Intenzioni: intervista immaginaria" Montale

observes: "I projected the Selvaggia, the Mandetta, or the Delia (call her what you like) of the *Mottetti* onto the background of a cosmic and terrestrial war, without scope or reason." Both the technique and the motif outlined here are central to "Nuove stanze," although it was written before the war. A mysterious woman, who shares with the poet a presentiment of this cosmic and terrestrial war, without scope or reason, is intent on a game of chess. The sense of mystery is further deepened as the ivory shapes are terrified by "a spectral light of snow":

> Now that you've extinguished
> the last shreds of tobacco in the crystal
> ashtray, the smoke rings rise
> slowly to the ceiling watched
> in amazement by the knights and bishops
> on the chessboard; while new rings
> follow them, more mobile than
> those on your fingers.

> Poi che gli ultimi fili di tabacco
> al tuo gesto si spengono nel piatto
> di cristallo, al soffitto lenta sale
> la spirale del fumo
> che gli alfieri e i cavalli degli scacchi
> guardano stupefatti; e nuovi anelli
> la seguono, più mobili di quelli
> delle tue dita.

The smoke rings from the woman's cigarette are somehow seen as a presentiment of the war looming on the horizon—a war that is now "a cloud at your door." It seems that the woman alone can construe the sense of the game, which would also enable her to read the omens of war, although at one stage the poet feels unsure about the woman's capacity to understand that game herself.

> It was once my doubt that perhaps
> you yourself didn't know the game
> that is played on the board and that's
> now a cloud at your door.

> Il mio dubbio d'un tempo era se forse
> tu stessa ignori il giuoco che si svolge
> sul quadrato e ora è nembo alle tue porte:

But he is nevertheless convinced about the woman's ability to look un-
flinchingly in the face of the coming tragedy and to "oppose the burning
mirror / that blinds the pawns with your / eyes of steel":

> Today I know what you want;
> the Martinella peals its faint note
> and frightens the ivory shapes
> in a spectral light of snow.
> But he alone wins the prize
> of the solitary vigil, who can
> oppose the burning mirror
> that blinds the pawns with your
> eyes of steel.

> Oggi so ciò che vuoi; batte il suo fioco
> tocco la Martinella ed impaura
> le sagome d'avorio in una luce
> spettrale di nevaio. Ma resiste
> e vince il premio della solitaria
> veglia chi può con te allo specchio ustorio
> che accieca le pedine opporre i tuoi
> occhi d'acciaio.

"Il ritorno," on the other hand, deals with a relatively simple theme. The
poet goes out rowing at Bocca di Magra (La Spezia) and describes this experience and the landscape around him with an intimate knowledge of and
a firm hold upon the actual. Such a mastery and control over the material is
all the more remarkable inasmuch as the poet is recollecting something from
the past:

> . . . see the spice of the pines
> spreading more pungently among
> the poplars and willows, the windmill
> beating its blades, and the path
> which follows the wave into the earthy
> flood, the poisonous mildewing
> of ovules. . . .

> . . . ecco il pimento
> dei pini che più terso
> si dilata tra pioppi e saliceti,
> e pompe a vento battere le pale

e il viottolo che segue l'onde dentro
la fiumana terrosa
funghire velenoso d'ovuli; . .

At the core of and inspiring this wealth of descriptive data is the presence of the woman loved. "Here they are still," the poet tells her in a moment of rapt recognition,

> . . . those chipped steps of the winding
> staircase spinning right up
> and beyond the veranda
> in the multicolored frost of the ogives,
> here they listen to you,
> these old steps of ours

> . . . ecco
> ancora quelle scale
> a chiocciola, slabbrate, che s'avvitano
> fin oltre la veranda
> in un gelo policromo d'ogive,
> eccole che t'ascoltano, le nostre vecchie scale . . .

"Palio" is another "occasional" poem in which the world of perceptions and impressions, realistic details and imagery, is veiled in a symbolic significance. Consequently, by pinpointing the particular and the occasional, the poet manages to probe into the nature and meaning of human destiny as well as of his own drama of love. Both the theme and the object of love are invested with a spiritual significance—another link with *La bufera* as the tragedy of the war that is about to engulf mankind unfolds itself. Hence, on the one hand the poet catches the spirit and atmosphere of the *palio,* and on the other he deals with the drama of love between him and his beloved. Our attention is thus engaged on two levels, the objective and the personal. The poem starts with a personal reference accompanied by a concrete and dynamic image:

> Your flight wasn't then lost
> in the spinning of a top by the roadside:
> in its spirals that thin out as far
> as here, in the purple hole
> where a tumult of souls salute
> the ensigns of Liocorno and Tartuca.

> La tua fuga non s'è dunque perduta
> in un giro di trottola

al margine della strada:
la corsa che dirada
le sue spire fin qui,
nella purpurea buca
dove un tumulto d'anime saluta
le insegne di Liocorno e di Tartuca.

After a temporary separation the woman is united with the poet. But although she is watching the spectacle, her mind is preoccupied with the thought of war, that "imminent storm, that tepid / dripping of clouds rent apart [tempesta / imminente e quel tiepido stillare /delle nubi strappate]." But it is by virtue of the very intensity of her preoccupation and fear regarding the future that makes her an embodiment of hope—the hope of redemption and deliverance. For she holds in her fingers, the poet tells her,

the imperious seal I'd thought
lost and the former light
is diffused on the heads, turning
them white like its lilies.

. . . il sigillo imperioso
ch'io credevo smarrito
e la luce di prima si diffonde
sulle teste e le sbianca dei suoi gigli.

Hence the poet can look hopefully beyond the present and place his trust in the future:

away from the forest of flags,
on the pealing of bells in the limitless
sky, beyond the sight of man . . .

. . . fuor della selva
dei gonfaloni, sullo scampanìo
del cielo irrefrenato, oltre lo sguardo
dell'uomo . . .

Although written before "Palio" (1939), "Il ritorno" (1940), and "Nuove stanze" (1939), "Notizie dall'Amiata" (1938) is placed at the end of the volume, perhaps because it offers a more cogent and more elaborate summing up of the cardinal themes and motifs of Le occasioni. It may be regarded as a love poem in the form of a letter sent to the woman loved from Mount Amiata in Tuscany, where the poet is staying. The sense of remoteness from her—and remoteness in Montale usually means distance both in the physical

and in the moral sense—as well as the peculiar character of the place described in vivid detail, put him in a frame of mind that is at once observant
and creative:

> The fireworks of the bad weather
> will be a murmur of hives in late evening.
> The room has worm-eaten rafters
> and the smell of melons penetrates the floor-boards.
> The soft smoke rises from the valley
> of elves and mushrooms
> to the transparent cone of the summit
> and clouds my window as I write you
> from this remote table, this honey-cell
> of a sphere hurled into space
> and the covered cages, the hearth
> where the chestnuts explode, the veins
> of saltpetre and mold are the scene
> which you will soon break into.
> Life that fables you is still
> too brief if it contains you! Your icon
> is revealed in the luminous depth.
> And outside it's raining.

> Il fuoco d'artifizio del maltempo
> sarà murmure d'arnie a tarda sera.
> La stanza ha travature
> tarlate ed un sentore di meloni
> penetra dall'assito. Le fumate
> morbide che risalgono una valle
> d'elfi e di funghi fino al cono diafano
> della cima m'intorbidano i vetri,
> e ti scrivo di qui, da questo tavolo
> remoto, dalla cellula di miele
> di una sfera lanciata nello spazio ——
> e le gabbie coperte, il focolare
> dove i marroni esplodono, le vene
> di salnitro e di muffa sono il quadro
> dove tra poco romperai. La vita
> che t'affàbula è ancora troppo breve
> se ti contiene! Schiude la tua icona
> il fondo luminoso. Fuori piove.

In a way the very sense of distance and remoteness from the woman loved constitutes an ideal perspective in which the poet can assess his own feeling for her. And seen in such a perspective life seems "too brief if it contains you!" This realization heightens his feeling of being alive, just as her intensely visualized image illumines the dark depth of the room where he is sitting and writing—an image to which the bad weather outside serves as an apt foil.

The intensity of the evocation in the first section gives a moral as well as an emotional weight and credibility, so to speak, to the illusion that she will soon join him. In the second section, therefore, the poet starts tracing the course that her journey through its various stages will take:

> and you would follow the fragile architecture
> blackened by time and coal,
> the square courtyards with deep wells
> in the center and the muffled flight
> of the nocturnal birds and at the end
> of the gully the sparkling Galaxy,
> the balm of every torment.

> E tu seguissi le fragili architetture
> annerite dal tempo e dal carbone,
> i cortili quadrati che hanno nel mezzo
> il pozzo profondissimo; tu seguissi
> il volo infagottato degli uccelli
> notturni e in fondo al borro l'allucciolìo
> della Galassia, la fascia d'ogni tormento.

But the possibility of her joining him is no more than an illusion, as the poet himself recognizes. Hence he descends from the peak of imagination to the plane of reality. The step that has long been echoing in the dark (or in his own mind) is not his beloved's step, but that of one who, like him, has had to come to grips with solitude and with the sense of general dissolution:

> But the step that echoes long
> in the dark is of one who goes
> alone and sees nothing but this
> falling of arches, shadows,
> folds. The stars have stitched
> too fine an embroidery, the bell-tower's
> eye is fixed at two o'clock,

even the creepers are an ascent of darkness
and their perfume a bitter pain.

Ma il passo che risuona a lungo nell'oscuro
è di chi va solitario e altro non vede
che questo cadere di archi, di ombre e di pieghe.
Le stelle hanno trapunti troppo sottili,
l'occhio del campanile è fermo sulle due ore,
i rampicanti anch'essi sono un'ascesa
di tenebre ed il loro profumo duole amaro.

He realizes that, after all, he cannot bring about any change in his moral and metaphysical condition, nor can he come to terms with the "four bare walls" or "the limits of the 'Ugly,'" as he says in one of his earliest poems.[18] In despair he invokes the north wind, hoping that it at least, with its cataclysmic strength and fury, may bring about such a change.

Return tomorrow colder,
north wind, break up the ancient
hands of sandstone, scatter
the books of hours in the attics,
and let everything be a calm lens,
a mastery and imprisonment
of the sense that doesn't despair!
Come back stronger, wind
of the north, wind that makes bonds dear
and seals up the spores of the possible!

Ritorna domani più freddo, vento del nord,
spezza le antiche mani dell'arenaria,
sconvolgi i libri d'ore nei solai,
e tutto sia lente tranquilla, dominio, prigione
del senso che non dispera! Ritorna più forte
vento di settentrione che rendi care
le catene e suggelli le spore del possibile!

But even this, the poet soon realizes, can only be a self-delusion, fruit of the invincible instinct of hoping against hope in the face of the inexorable course of time, oblivion, and death:

The streets are too narrow,
the black donkeys clattering by

18. See Montale's early poem "Contrabbasso" and also Appendix 1.

in single file strike up sparks,
and from the hidden peak magnesium
flares answer. Oh the slow dripping
of time on dark hovels, time turned
into water, the long colloquy
with the poor dead, with the ashes,
the wind, the wind that lingers,
death, death that lives.

Son troppo strette le strade, gli asini neri
che zoccolano in fila dànno scintille,
dal picco nascosto rispondono vampate di magnesio.
Oh il goccìolìo che scende a rilento
dalle casipole buie, il tempo fatto acqua,
il lungo colloquio coi poveri morti, la cenere, il vento,
il vento che tarda, la morte, la morte che vive!

The struggle between hope and despair, illusion and disillusion, life and death, culminates in the third and last section of the poem, in what the poet calls "this Christian dispute" (i.e. the conflict between body and soul), with its unresolved doubts and perplexities and, trickling through their midst, a "thin stream of pity"

This Christian dispute—mere words,
enveloped in sorrow and darkness—
what does it tell you of me?
Less than what the millrace
snatches from you before entering
gently into its dyke of cement.
A grinding-wheel, an old stump,
last boundaries of the world.
A pile of straw is blown off;
and the porcupines, coming out late
to unite my vigil with your
deep sleep which receives them, drink
at a thin stream of pity.

Questa rissa cristiana che non ha
se non parole d'ombra e di lamento
che ti porta di me? Meno di quanto
t'ha rapito la gora che s'interra
dolce nella sua chiusa di cemento.

Una ruota di mola, un vecchio tronco,
confini ultimi al mondo. Si disfà
un cumulo di strame: e tardi usciti
a unire la mia veglia al tuo profondo
sonno che li riceve, i porcospini
s'abbeverano a un filo di pietà.

Le occasioni thus ends on a note that links the volume in more than one respect with *La bufera* rather than with *Ossi di seppia*. It also shows how, after the publication of *Ossi di seppia*, Montale's poetic development has to be traced increasingly in terms of autobiographical data, symbols, and allusions concerning the theme of personal love. However, for all the moral, philosophical, and symbolical aspects and undertones, and for all the rich and complex gamut of intensities and subtleties through which it works, there is a certain shrinking of the range of philosophical interest, perception, and intuition—a certain loss in terms of cosmic and impersonal depth and insight in *Le occasioni* and in Montale's subsequent poetry in general, as compared with *Ossi di seppia*, which remains a unique body of lyric-cum-philosophic poetry in Italian after Leopardi's *Canti*.

4: *La bufera e altro*

La bufera e altro, the third volume of Montale's poetry, came out in 1956. It includes *Finisterre,* a group of poems written between 1940–42 and published in 1943 at Lugano in a semiclandestine way. It was too risky to publish them at that time in Italy because the first poem, "La bufera," contained an epigraph from Agrippa D'Aubigné, which, with its reference to the rulers' blindness and tyranny ("Les princes n'ont point d'yeux pour voir ces grand's merveilles, / Leurs mains ne servent plus qu'à nous persécuter") could hardly have escaped the eye of the censor, still less met with his approval. In this volume Montale's lyricism takes on an even more intimately personal and autobiographical character, and the theme of love on the one hand and that of the tragedy of the war and of political and spiritual salvation on the other become more closely intertwined than was the case with some of the poems on similar topics in *Le occasioni.* There is also a certain loosening of the verbal and rhythmical texture in *La bufera,* although this does not mean that Montale has altogether dispensed with symbolic and allegorical devices, which are used to bring out the intimately personal nature of his poetry.

Montale's own opinion of this book is to be found in his preface to Gösta Andersson's Swedish translation of a selection of his poems. *Finisterre,* he observes,

> concludes *Le occasioni,* while the other poems in *La bufera e altro* turn to a more direct expression and loosen the web of a too rigidly woven texture. The interplay of the images remains unchanged, "profondément incorporées à la texture verbale: elles se présentent à l'intérieur du language un peu comme des noeuds dans le bois ou des noyaux dans la pierre; se sont des centres affectifs, l'émotion se concentre autour d'elles" (A. Pieyre de Mandiargues, *Nouvelle Revue Française,* January 1960).
>
> I consider *La bufera e altro* as my best book, although one cannot penetrate it without going through the whole of the itinerary preceding

it. It vividly reflects my historical as well as my human condition. Poems like "La primavera hitleriana," "Il sogno del prigioniero," "Congedo provvisorio," and "La primavera del '48" are the testimony of a writer who has always rejected the clericalism of the two opposite creeds (the "black" and the "red") which afflict Italy today.[1]

One may or may not agree with Montale in considering *La bufera* his best book, but there is no doubt that in many ways it is his most personal. In spirit, and at times even in form, diction, and imagery, some of the poems in it anticipate *Xenia,* the series of poems Montale wrote after the death of his wife. Hence, while *Finisterre* concludes *Le occasioni, Xenia,* in some respects, continues *La bufera.* However, there are other poems in this volume which are closer in spirit to *Le occasioni*—poems in which the dominant theme and sentiment concern the loss of the person loved and her evocation as a phantom figure, a "cloud or woman, angel / or petrel," [2] a messenger or a savior. There are thus some obvious links between *La bufera* and *Mottetti* too.

However, the intimately subjective nature of the theme and inspiration in these poems does not detract from their universality of appeal. In fact, as we have seen, the more subjective and individual the experience presented in Montale's poetry, the more firmly rooted and concretely realized it is within the framework of objects, images, and symbols. Sometimes the most subtle and delicate feeling for the woman loved is expressed through such objects as birds, fish, or trees, so that what the poet sees around him in everyday life and what he recollects become one. Even his mode of recollecting amounts to a creative act; as Contini points out, "more than remembering, Montale *reacts."* [3] The physical and metaphysical, the subjective and objective are so interfused that the poet's individual experiences acquire a symbolic value and a universal validity. This amalgam is further enriched by the vein of religiosity that becomes more explicit in *La bufera* than in the preceding books. Similarly, while dealing with the theme of his communings with the dead he engages our attention at a deeper and more complex level. All in all, *La bufera* thus stands out as being something conspicuously distinct, not only from *Ossi di seppia,* but to a certain extent also from *Le occasioni;* and the cause and nature of the distinction have to be interpreted at least partly in terms of historical as well as personal and autobiographical pressures and contingencies, and partly in terms of a technical and stylistic development.

1. In his foreword to the Swedish translation of a selection of his poems by Gösta Andersson (Stockholm: Casa editrice Italica, 1960).
2. "Intenzioni: intervista immaginaria," p. 347.
3. *Esercizi di lettura,* p. 108.

The book starts with *Finisterre,* and the first poem is entitled "La bufera."
From the point of view of style, technique, and imagery, it is fairly representative not only of *Finisterre* but also of the rest of the volume. The storm and
the chain of reactions it produces in the world of natural phenomena allego-
rize World War II and at the same time serve as a foil to the poet's feeling
for the woman loved. What he sees in "that eternity of an instant" is a
measure of his insight into the nature of reality, the exploration of which
is tied up with the form and significance of the woman loved thrown into
such dramatic relief by the storm:

> The flash that crystallizes trees
> and walls and surprises them in
> that eternity of an instant
> —marble manna and destruction—
> that you bear carved inside you
> for your condemnation and that binds you
> to me more than love, strange sister—
> and then the rude crash, the rattling,
> and the shaking of tambourines above
> the dark pit, the stamp of the fandango,
> and some groping gesture on high — . . .
>
> As when you turned and clearing
> your forehead of its cloud of hair,
> greeted me with your hand,
> before entering into the dark.

> il lampo che candisce
> alberi e muri e li sorprende in quella
> eternità d'istante —— marmo manna
> e distruzione —— ch'entro te scolpita
> porti per tua condanna e che ti lega
> più che l'amore a me, strana sorella, ——
> e poi lo schianto rude, i sistri, il fremere
> dei tamburelli sulla fossa fuia,
> lo scalpicciare del fandango, e sopra
> qualche gesto che annaspa....
>
>   Come quando
> ti rivolgesti e con la mano, sgombra
> la fronte dalla nube dei capelli,
>
> mi salutasti —— per entrar nel buio.

In "Lungomare," on the other hand, the poetic symbolism revolves around an intensely personal and sentimental theme treated with an admirable degree of concentration on the essential, as well as a certain sense of detachment from what is felt and suffered:

> The gale gathers force, the dark
> is ripped into gashes, and your shadow
> on the fragile fence curls up.
>
> It's too late to want to be
> yourself! The mouse drops from the palm
> with a thud, and the lightning's on the fuse,
> the fuse of your long lashes.
>
> Il soffio cresce, il buio è rotto a squarci,
> e l'ombra che tu mandi sulla fragile
> palizzata s'arriccia. Troppo tardi
>
> se vuoi esser te stessa! Dalla palma
> tonfa il sorcio, il baleno è sulla miccia,
> sui lunghissimi cigli del tuo sguardo.

The wind and lightning throw into relief the existential pathos and dilemma of the shadow's poignant fragility, not to mention unreality, while at the same time they enforce the poet's yearning to safeguard his and his beloved's identities and to resist the feeling of bewilderment when everything around is dissolving. Thus, the combustion of the elements serves as the objective counterpart or correlative of the poet's emotional drama, and his realization that it is always "too late."

All this is clinched by the way in which personal experience is presented in its immediate as well as distancing character through the suggestive banality of the detail—the mouse dropping from a palm-tree, which brings to an abrupt end the poet's colloquy with the imagined woman. Then both counterbalancing and offsetting the prosaic nature of this image is the superb detail of the lightning on the fuse—the fuse of the woman's lashes.

Separation from the woman loved as well as the impossibility of communicating with her is also the theme of "Su una lettera non scritta." The poet's desire to flee from the splendor of her lashes is not only a poetic paradox, but also a lyric and dramatic form of asserting the bond with her. The romantic but poignantly precarious and ineffectual means that he employs for this purpose—an empty bottle thrown into the sea—brings out the emotional and metaphysical possibilities of the theme. And the interplay between the symbolic and the pictorial details and imagery is most suggestive and convincing:

> Is it for a cluster of dawns,
> or a few wires on which the flakes
> of life are entangled, weaving
> themselves into hours and years,
> that the dolphins sport with their young
> today? Oh that I might
> hear nothing of you, might flee
> from the splendor of your lashes.
> It's all so different on earth.
>
> I can neither vanish nor reappear.
> The night's crimson furnace delays
> and the evening is prolonged.
> Prayer is a torment, and the bottle
> hasn't yet reached you from the sea
> among the protruding rocks.
> And the empty waves break against
> the cape at Finisterre.

> Per un formicolìo d'albe, per pochi
> fili su cui s'impigli
> il fiocco della vita e s'incollani
> in ore e in anni, oggi i delfini a coppie
> capriolano coi figli? Oh ch'io non oda
> nulla di te, ch'io fugga dal bagliore
> dei tuoi cigli. Ben altro è sulla terra.
>
> Sparir non so nè riaffacciarmi; tarda
> la fucina vermiglia
> della notte, la sera si fa lunga,
> la preghiera è supplizio e non ancora
> tra le rocce che sorgono t'è giunta
> la bottiglia dal mare. L'onda, vuota,
> si rompe sulla punta, a Finisterre.

The poem represents a closely interwoven pattern of descriptive and symbolical imagery as well as of such simple and direct but pregnant statements as "Oh that I might / hear nothing of you, might flee," "It's all so different on earth," "I can neither vanish nor reappear," and "Prayer is a torment."

They are so integrated within the context of poetic symbols and imagery as to
have both a certain autonomy of their own and an intensely realized relevance to the whole structure of the poem. Thus, in Montale's poetry whatever is stated is almost always justified and illustrated in symbolic and metaphorical terms; so that, for instance, when he states his predicament—"I can
neither vanish nor reappear"—it immediately finds its metaphorical counterpart in such images as "the night's crimson furnace delays," "the evening is
prolonged," and "the bottle hasn't reached you." But some images, besides
supporting straightforward statements, also support other images. For instance, the image of the bottle not reaching the beloved is reinforced by the
empty wave breaking against the cape at Finisterre. The word *empty*, coming
as it does at the end of the line, clinches the pathos and the ineffectuality of
the effort to send the woman loved a message—a message that is all but
poetically nonexistent.

In the poem "Nel sonno," with its apparently disconnected and almost incongruous images, memories, and dreams presented with sharp precision and
concreteness of detail, the poet succeeds in realizing, at least partly, what
he could not realize with the help of the bottle thrown into the sea. For these
dreams and images not only remind him of the woman loved, but also make
him "awake to your voice [desto / alla tua voce]," so that what he sees in
sleep—her image pulsating with "blood beyond death [sangue oltre la
morte]"—acquires an even greater substance and reality than her living form
and personality could have done.

In "Serenata indiana" the theme of romantic attachment to the woman
merges with that of discovering and analyzing her individuality by means
of concrete yet subtle and intricate aspects of analogy, symbolism, and imagery.
For instance, the sentimental link between the poet and the woman comes
out through such reminiscences as "the dissolving of the evenings [il disfarsi
delle sere]" or "the streak that rises from the sea / to the parks and wounds
the aloes [la stria che dal mare / sale al parco e ferisce gli aloè]." However,
neither the link nor the feeling behind it is enough for the poet to be able
to give her a face and a form, although he yields to her witchery:

> You can lead me my the hand,
> if you pretend you are with me, if I am
> so fond as to follow you far
> away . . .

> Puoi condurmi per mano, se tu fingi
> di crederti con me, se ho la follia
> di seguirti lontano . . .

But the illusion that she is with him is itself short-lived and his wish is soon frustrated:

> I wish your life were that
> which holds me on the threshold and I
> could lend you a face, fashion you
> a figure. But it's not so,
> not so.

> Fosse tua vita quella che mi tiene
> sulle soglie —— e potrei prestarti un volto,
> vaneggiarti figura. Ma non è,
> non è così. . . .

And yet such is the intensity of his yearning that despite the fact that he cannot give her a face and a form, he still somehow manages to possess her completely, and what yearning and desire could not achieve, is achieved with the help of the tentacles of his imagination. They enmesh her like the polyp emmeshing the rock with its inky tentacles:

> . . . The polyp that insinuates inky
> tentacles among the rocks
> can make use of you.
> You belong to it, yet don't know,
> you are it, but think
> you are you.

> . . . Il polipo che insinua
> tentacoli d'inchiostro tra gli scogli
> può servirsi di te. Tu gli appartieni
> e non lo sai. Sei lui, ti credi te.

The same theme of the belovèd's haunting presence and its moral and poetic impact is dealt with in "Gli orecchini," which displays an even greater stylistic and metaphorical ingeniousness than "Serenata indiana." However, the element of ingeniousness tends to preponderate over the creative and moral impulse, and lyric intensity seems to be somewhat sacrificed in the interest of a brilliantly manipulated pattern of symbolic and realistic imagery for its own sake. Nor is the logical or intuitional link between one object or image and another always clear. The implied aim of this pattern is to capture and define the elusive and intangible essence of the woman loved:

The lamp-black of the mirror doesn't retain
the shadow of the flights. (And there's
no trace of yours.)

Non serba ombra di voli il nerofumo
della spera. (E del tuo non è più traccia.)

And yet in a way the poet seems to run away in despair from the very thing he seeks: "I flee from the goddess / that doesn't become incarnate, cherish / desires until they are consumed / by your flash [fuggo / l'iddia che non s'incarna, i desideri / porto fin che al tuo lampo non si struggono]." But this note of despair is counterbalanced by the hope that "your image will come down [la tua impronta / verrà di giù]" with its "strong reign [il forte imperio]" and claim the poet again.

In spite of the elaborate stylistic and structural comment and analysis to which this poem has been subjected by D'Arco Silvio Avalle,[4] its obscurity remains. And the obscurity can be traced to a certain tendency in Montale's images (as manifest in some of the poems in *Le occasioni* and also in this volume)—a tendency which F. R. Leavis, for instance, was to criticize in Shelley, namely, that of forgetting "the status of the metaphor or simile that introduced them" and of assuming "an autonomy and a right to propagate, so that we lose in confused generations and perspectives the perception or thought that was the ostensible *raison d'être* of imagery." [5]

"La frangia dei capelli . . ." too, in a way, deals with the same theme as "Gli orecchini." For all her pervasiveness, the haunting presence of the "transmigratory Artemis" (a Montalian variant of Dante's Beatrice) remains perpetually elusive, although she is presented with a sharper individuality in this poem than in "Serenata indiana" or "Gli orecchini":

The fringe of hair that covers
your childlike forehead you shouldn't
put back with your hand. This too
reveals to me something of you,
is the only sky on my path,
the only light together
with the jade you wear on your wrist,
the curtain that your pardons spread
in the tumult of my sleep; the only

4. See " 'Gli orecchini di Montale,' " in *Tre saggi su Montale* (Turin: Einaudi, 1970), where Avalle analyzes exhaustively "l'unità del componimento e di riflesso il sistema di interazioni su cui essa si regge."
5. "Shelley," in *Revaluation* (London, 1936), p. 206.

wing on which you fly,
transmigratory Artemis, safe
amidst the wars of the stillborn, and
if now that depth is adorned
with airy down, it's you
who suddenly descend to marble it,
and your restless forehead becomes
one with the dawn and hides it.

La frangia dei capelli che ti vela
la fronte puerile, tu distrarla
con la mano non devi. Anch'essa parla
di te, sulla mia strada è tutto il cielo,
la sola luce con le giade ch'ài
accerchiate sul polso, nel tumulto
del sonno la cortina che gl'indulti
tuoi distendono, l'ala onde tu vai,
trasmigratrice Artemide ed illesa,
tra le guerre dei nati-morti; e s'ora
d'aeree lanugini s'infiora
quel fondo, a marezzarlo sei tu, scesa
d'un balzo, e irrequieta la tua fronte
si confonde con l'alba, la nasconde.

In "Finestra fiesolana," on the other hand, there is no explicit reference to
the theme of love. But the conceptually pregnant images of "another light
[altra luce]" and "other flames [altre vampe]," as well as the emotional
warmth of the apostrophe to "my scarlet ivies [mie edere scarlatte]," contrast
with the details of the cricket making holes in the clothes, the smell of camphor, the moths pulverizing the books, and the dark sun becoming entangled among painted foliage. And the contrast somehow suggests the
hidden or underlying impulse of love:

Here where the insidious cricket
makes holes in the clothes of vegetable
silk and the smell of camphor
doesn't put to flight the moths
that pulverize the books,
the little bird climbs the elm tree
by spirals and the dark sun becomes
entangled among the painted foliage.

Another light that doesn't teem,
other flames, oh my scarlet ivies.

Qui dove il grillo insidioso buca
i vestiti di seta vegetale
e l'odor della canfora non fuga
le tarme che sfarinano nei libri,
l'uccellino s'arrampica a spirale
su per l'olmo ed il sole tra le frappe
cupo invischia. Altra luce che non colma,
altre vampe, o mie edere scarlatte.

In "Il giglio rosso" it is the red lily that symbolizes love and youth as well
as the hereafter. The idea of its putting down roots in the heart of the woman
is conveyed through a vivid and concrete impressionism of detail and imagery
graphically capturing a specific aspect of Florence (of which the red lily is
the emblem) during World War II:

(the weir shone among the sieves
of the sand-diggers, bright moles plunged
making holes among the reeds,
towers and banners routed the rain,
and in the new sun the grafting was happily
accomplished and you did not know it);

(brillava la pescaia tra gli stacci
dei renaioli, a tuffo s'inforravano
lucide talpe nelle canne, torri,
gonfaloni vincevano la pioggia,
e il trapianto felice al nuovo sole,
te inconscia si compì);

This much in the past. But the red lily also symbolizes salvation in the hereafter, being

the flower of the ditch which will open
on the solemn banks where the hum
of time no longer wearies . . . :
in order to touch the celestial
harp and make death friendly.

fiore di fosso che ti s'aprirà
sugli argini solenni ove il brusìo

del tempo più non affatica...: a scuotere
l'arpa celeste, a far la morte amica.

In "Il ventaglio" the past is symbolically projected on to a fan, as the poet
pictures to himself

. . . the lips that confound, the looks,
the gestures and the days gone by—
I try to fix them there,
as in the lens of a telescope turned
upside down, mute and immobile,
but more living.

. . . Le labbra che confondono,
gli sguardi, i segni, i giorni ormai caduti
provo a figgerli là come in un tondo
di cannocchiale arrovesciato, muti
e immoti, ma più vivi.

On such a picture the reality of the war—"jousting of men and arms / flying
about in that smoke / blown by the sirocco [una giostra / d'uomini e ordegni
in fuga tra quel fumo / ch'Euro batteva]"—casts a sombre and poignant
light. But then "already the dawn empurples / with a start and breaks
through that mist [già l'alba l'inostra / con un sussulto e rompe quelle
brume]," which is the angel-woman's symbolic way of intimating the defeat
of the enemy and the salvation of humanity:

The mother-of-pearl shines,
the deep and precipitate gully
still swallows the victims, but the plumes
become white on your cheeks and perhaps
the day is saved.

Luce la madreperla, la calanca
vertiginosa inghiotte ancora vittime,
ma le tue piume sulle guance sbiancano
e il giorno è forse salvo. . . .

The day is saved because being the kind of amulet that it is, the fan, with the
angel-woman depicted on it, becomes a weapon which brings about the defeat of the enemy:

. . . Oh heavy blows, the moment
you reveal yourself, the cruel

bolts, the lashing showers on the hordes!
(Does he die who recognizes you?)

. . . O colpi fitti,
quando ti schiudi, o crudi lampi, o scrosci
sull'orde! (Muore chi ti riconosce?)

In "Personae separatae" it is not so much the woman's role as an angel
and a savior as her real character and personality that are brought into relief
by the war which has turned the world into a "tormented human forest." In
the context of war the pangs of separation from her are felt all the more
keenly and memories of her treasured all the more, as it comes out through
the intensely vivid evocation of geographical and topographical detail.

Like a disc of gold
spinning out of a dark background,
then melting into an avenue
of locust-trees reduced to skeletons,
do we also—*personae separatae*—
look like that to others?
Words count little and so
does space in these raw and foggy
new moons: but what's missing,
what wrings the heart and makes
me linger among the trees, while waiting
for you, is a lost sense or
a fire, if you like, which might
print parallel figures on the earth,
—like-minded shades, the hands
of a sundial, new trunks of
a clearing—and which might even
suffuse the hollow stumps, ants' nests.

Come la scaglia d'oro che si spicca
dal fondo oscuro e liquefatta cola
nel corridoio dei carrubi ormai
ischeletriti, così pure noi
persone separate per lo sguardo
d'un altro? È poca cosa la parola,
poca cosa lo spazio in questi crudi
noviluni annebbiati: ciò che manca,
e che ci torce il cuore e qui m'attarda

> tra gli alberi, ad attenderti, è un perduto
> senso, o il fuoco, se vuoi, che a terra stampi,
> figure parallele, ombre concordi,
> aste di un sol quadrante i nuovi tronchi
> delle radure e colmi anche le cave
> ceppaie, nido alle formiche.

Thus, the present has meaning for the poet only insofar as it is illuminated by gleams of a past life or by the vision of the woman loved, without which he is lost in the "dark forest." Even the "perennial voice"—the voice embodying the message of hope—seems "too hollow," and the places and objects associated with her have an anxious and desolate look:

> . . . The human forest
> is too tormented, the perennial
> voice too hollow, and the gash
> that looms across the snowy
> peaks of Lunigiana
> has an anxious look.
> Your form passed here, and paused
> for a while by the stream, among
> the lobster-pots sitting on the bank,
> then dissolved like a sigh in the air.
> There was no gurgling horror—in you
> the light still found light,
> but today even in the early morning
> it has already become dark.

> . . . Troppo
> straziato è il bosco umano, troppo sorda
> quella voce perenne, troppo ansioso
> lo squarcio che si sbiocca sui nevati
> gioghi di Lunigiana. La tua forma
> passò di qui, si riposò sul riano
> tra le nasse atterrate, poi si sciolse
> come un sospiro, intorno —— e ivi non era
> l'orror che fiotta, in te la luce ancora
> trovava luce, oggi non più che al giorno
> primo già annotta.

"L'Arca" takes us back to the poet's childhood, evoked through such characteristic ties as a willow, a steaming ladle in the kitchen, dogs, and old servants. It is they, more than the poet's kith and kin, that represent the poet's sense of loyalty to the past as well as to the world of his childhood. The violence of the spring storm convulsing "the willow's umbrella" and disturbing "the garden's / golden fleece that hides / my dead" both rocks that world of old ties and sentiments, and at the same time renews and revitalizes it to such an extent that the poet is led to hope that one day all those who are gone will be reunited "under the same roof as of old, / but somewhere far-off, much farther / than in this parched land where / each human footprint seethes / with blood and lime." That there is something poignantly ineffectual about such a hope is conveyed through the wishful thinking intimated by the words *no doubt,* which has only a poetic value. It is this illusory hope as well as his contrasting sense of loss and despair which gives a peculiar intensity of pathos to such phrases as "fallen alive into the pit" or "the bark of loyalty." The word *alive* conveys the idea of something disappearing suddenly or being wrenched away by some rude force. Added to this feeling is the fear of the second death—the death of oblivion against which the poet struggles in order to save his "faithful dogs / and old servants":

> The spring storm has convulsed
> the willow's umbrella and the garden's
> golden fleece that hides
> my dead, my faithful dogs
> and old servants—how many since
> have fallen alive into the pit,
> when the willow was pale and I
> would slash off its curls with a sling!
> No doubt the storm will unite
> them again
> under the same roof as of old
> but somewhere far off, much farther
> than in this parched land where each human
> footprint seethes with blood
> and lime.
> The ladle steams in the kitchen,
> and its bowl reflects sharp snouts
> and bony faces, which the magnolia
> protects under its shadow, if a gust
> of wind bends it that way.
> The spring storm rocks my boat
> with a bark of loyalty, oh lost souls!

La tempesta di primavera ha sconvolto
l'ombrello del salice,
al turbine d'aprile
s'è impigliato nell'orto il vello d'oro
che nasconde i miei morti,
i miei cani fidati, le mie vecchie
serve —— quanti da allora
(quando il salce era biondo e io ne stroncavo
le anella con la fionda) son calati,
vivi, nel trabocchetto. La tempesta
certo li riunirà sotto quel tetto
di prima, ma lontano, più lontano
di questa terra folgorata dove
bollono calce e sangue nell'impronta
del piede umano. Fuma il ramaiolo
in cucina, un suo tondo di riflessi
accentra i volti ossuti, i musi aguzzi
e li protegge in fondo la magnolia
se un soffio ve la getta. La tempesta
primaverile scuote d'un latrato
di fedeltà la mia arca, o perduti.

In "Giorno e notte" the poet's interest shifts to the present, which the haunting presence of Clizia renders both rich and meaningful:

Even a flying feather can outline
your figure, or the ray that plays
hide and seek among the furniture,
the reflection of the child's mirror
from the roofs. Around the walls
trails of smoke elongate the spires
of the poplars and down below
on a trestle the knife-grinder's parrot
preens itself.
Then the sultry night on the square
and the steps and this perpetual toil
of sinking only to reemerge
the same, from centuries or seconds
of nightmares that cannot find
again the light of your eyes
in the incandescent cave —
and still the same cries

and long laments on the veranda
if the shot suddenly echoes out
that reddens your throat and breaks
your wing, o dangerous harbinger
of the dawn,
and the cloisters and hospitals awake
to a blaring of trumpets —

Anche una piuma che vola può disegnare
la tua figura, o il raggio che gioca a rimpiattino
tra i mobili, il rimando dello specchio
di un bambino, dai tetti. Sul giro delle mura
strascichi di vapore prolungano le guglie
dei pioppi e giù sul trespolo s'arruffa il pappagallo
dell'arrotino. Poi la notte afosa
sulla piazzola, e i passi, e sempre questa dura
fatica di affondare per risorgere eguali
da secoli, o da istanti, d'incubi che non possono
ritrovare la luce dei tuoi occhi nell'antro
incandescente —— e ancora le stesse grida e i lunghi
pianti sulla veranda
se rimbomba improvviso il colpo che t'arrossa
la gola e schianta l'ali, o perigliosa
annunziatrice dell'alba,
e si destano i chiostri e gli ospedali
a un lacerìo di trombe....

The varied interplay of perception and intuition on the one hand, and of inventive realism and symbolic evocativeness on the other, that characterizes
"Giorno e notte," characterizes "Il tuo volo" to an even greater extent, and
the chance apparitions and fugitive glimpses of the woman are conveyed
through an elaborate framework of imagery which is at once realistic and
metaphysical:

If you appear in the fire
(amulets hang from your forelock
and stud it) two lights contend
for you in the gully that makes
its way through the vault of the thorns.

The clothes are in tatters, the trampled
frutices spark up again

and the inflated fishpond of human
tadpoles opens to the furrows
of the night.

Oh don't disturb the filthy
selvage, leave around
the burning stacks, the heavy
smoke on the survivors!

If you break the fire (the ash-blond
hair on the tender wrinkle
that has left the sky)
how will the hand with its silk
and gems be able to find
again its faithful among the dead?

Se appari al fuoco (pendono
sul tuo ciuffo e ti stellano
gli amuleti)
due luci ti contendono
al borro ch'entra sotto
la volta degli spini.

La veste è in brani, i frùtici
calpesti rifavillano
e la gonfia peschiera dei girini
umani s'apre ai solchi della notte.

Oh non turbar l'immondo
vivagno, lascia intorno
le cataste brucianti, il fumo forte
sui superstiti!

Se rompi il fuoco (biondo
cinerei i capelli
sulla ruga che tenera
ha abbandonato il cielo)
come potrà la mano delle sete
e delle gemme ritrovar tra i morti
il suo fedele?

The last poem in *Finisterre* is "A mia madre." The transcendental nature
of the hereafter and the image of death as eternal sleep are not only concretely
particularized, but also rendered familiar by the topographical details of "the

chorus of the quails" and "the harvested slopes of the Mesco." Thus, the familiar and the transcendental, the personal and the symbolic blend together against the background of a world where "the strife of the living / is raging ever more fiercely." Such a world offers a suggestive contrast with the image of the "Elysium crowded with souls and voices," where the poet's mother has taken refuge:

> Now that the chorus of the quails,
> in their gay disbanded flight
> over the harvested slopes of the Mesco,
> lulls you in eternal sleep;
> now that the strife of the living
> is raging ever more fiercely,
> who will protect you if
> you surrender your remains like a shade
> (but it's not a shade, o tenderhearted,
> it's not what you believe).
> The empty road is not
> a path, but two hands, a face,
> —*those* hands, *that* face, the gestures
> of a life that is true to itself.
> Only this puts you in the Elysium,
> crowded with souls and voices,
> and the question that you leave unanswered—
> even that is a gesture of yours
> in the shadow of the crosses.

> Ora che il coro delle coturnici
> ti blandisce nel sonno eterno, rotta
> felice schiera in fuga verso i clivi
> vendemmiati del Mesco, or che la lotta
> dei viventi più infuria, se tu cedi
> come un'ombra la spoglia
>   (e non è un'ombra,
> o gentile, non è ciò che tu credi)
> chi ti proteggerà? La strada sgombra
> non è una via, solo due mani, un volto,
> *quelle* mani, *quel* volto, il gesto d'una
> vita che non è un'altra ma se stessa,
> solo questo ti pone nell'eliso
> folto d'anime e voci in cui tu vivi;

> e la domanda che tu lasci è anch'essa
> un gesto tuo, all'ombra delle croci.

The poet's concern for his mother's personal identity in an "Elysium crowded with souls and voices" humanizes the extrahuman and confers a lyric warmth on what is impersonal about the hereafter. This, however, doesn't make the question of identity any less uncertain, and the poem ends by hinting at this metaphysical uncertainty, which remains unresolved and which clinches the pathos and poignancy of the poem as a whole.

Finisterre is followed by another section called *Dopo,* consisting of three poems—"Madrigali fiorentini" (parts 1 and 2), "Da una torre," and "Ballata scritta in una clinica." The first of "Madrigali fiorentini" (dated 11 September 1943) refers to the hope and enthusiasm aroused by the signing of the Armistice, as a result of which someone had made so bold as to write an anti-Hitler slogan on a wall in Florence. However, it was rubbed out when the Germans reoccupied the city. The detail of the airplane distributing propaganda pamphlets refers to the activity of the reinstated Fascist regime. The poet asks the woman-angel—she is called Herma in this poem—to seal "with ribbons and sealing-wax / the hope that was vainly revealed, / hardly budding forth in your mornings [con nastri e ceralacca / la speranza che vana / si svela, appena schiusa ai tuoi mattini]." The second madrigal (dated 11 August 1944) was occasioned by the blowing up of Trinity Bridge at Florence. The poet turns again to this woman, hoping that she may come down to earth from the "corridor of paradise [corsia del paradiso]" and bring an end to the catastrophe of war. In "Da una torre," too, the havoc wrought by the war is implicit in the indifference that the birds and animals show to what is happening all around them, which, together with the image of the dead dog coming back to life, metaphorically enacts the poet's own feelings both as victim and as witness of the war. These feelings assert themselves even more strongly through the powerfully evocative image of "a lip of blood becoming more mute [un labbro / di sangue farsi più muto]."

In "Ballata scritta in una clinica" the poet's awareness of the war finds a new dimension, namely, that of personal sorrow and anguish surrounding the serious illness of his wife. The year is 1944 and she is recovering in a clinic in Florence. The war is coming to an end, but before it does, it passes through one of its cruelest phases. Thus both the contingency of the war and that of his wife's illness [6] were to reflect and complement each other through the apocalyptic symbolism of such images as "the mad August comet [la

6. Montale's wife died in 1963. Apart from *Xenia,* this poem is the only one that can be identified with absolute certainty as being inspired by her.

folle cometa agostana]" melting beyond the mountains, the roof-terraces and
bridges collapsing, and the flag of the Red Cross flying over the hospital:

> I turned to look in the mirror
> and found that I wasn't the same
> anymore, since your throat and chest
> had suddenly disappeared behind a plaster cast.
>
> In the depths of your eyes shone lenses
> of tears that were thicker than your
> heavy tortoise-shell glasses which I
> remove each night and place
> beside the phial of morphine.

> ed io mi volsi e lo specchio
> di me più non era lo stesso
> perchè la gola ed il petto
> t'avevano chiuso di colpo
> in un manichino di gesso.
>
> Nel cavo delle tue orbite
> brillavano lenti di lacrime
> più spesse di questi tuoi grossi
> occhiali di tartaruga
> che a notte ti tolgo e avvicino
> alle fiale della morfina.

Through a semi-ironical and semipoetic blend of astronomical, religious, and
realistic details and allusions, the poet seeks a way out from this state of
double emergency—the emergency of the war and of his wife's illness:

> It wasn't ours—the god in the form
> of a bull, but the God who soaks
> the lilies of the ditch in fiery
> colors; I invoked the Ram
> and the horned monster's flight swept away
> the last vestige of pride and crushed
> the heart broken by your coughing.
>
> I am waiting for a sign to tell me
> that the hour of the final abduction
> has come. I am ready and the penitence
> starts even now in the hollow
> sobs of the vales and precipices
> of the *other* Emergency.

L'iddio taurino non era
il nostro, ma il Dio che colora
di fuoco i gigli del fosso:
Ariete invocai e la fuga
del mostro cornuto travolse
con l'ultimo orgoglio anche il cuore
schiantato dalla tua tosse.

Attendo un cenno, se è prossima
l'ora del ratto finale:
son pronto e la penitenza
s'inizia fin d'ora nel cupo
singulto di valli e dirupi
dell'*altra* Emergenza.

In the end the personal and historical, the moral and realistic details and elements merge together and find a common voice—the mute howl of the wooden bulldog standing on the bedside table of his wife's hospital room.

The third section of *La bufera e altro* is called *Intermezzo*. It consists of one poem, "Due nel crepuscolo," and two prose pieces, "Dov'era il tennis . . ." and "Visita a Fadin." The poem was published in 1943 although, as Montale points out in his note, "a rough draft already existed as early as September 1926. I recopied it, giving it a title somewhat reminiscent of Browning's 'Two in the Campagna' and inserting a few words where there were blank spaces or erasures. I also removed two superfluous verses. Thus I did what I should have done long ago, had I known that the draft could one day interest me." Apart from the title, this poem, like many others by Montale, has another link with Browning in that its form is rather like that of a dramatic monologue. Moreover, while depicting the person he is talking to in all her elusive form and personality and unraveling the threads of what their relationship signified in the past and what it means now, he probes into the dilemmas and complexities of his own nature and experience by bringing out the metaphysical symbolism of ordinary acts and gestures through such conceptually pregnant images as "the torpor of the rocks."

I surrender myself to the power
weighing all around, yield
to the sorcery of recognizing nothing
of me except myself.
No sooner do I raise my arm,
than the act turns out to be
quite different, breaks itself
asunder against a crystal,

its memory gone or estranged
and the gesture no longer belongs to me.
If I talk, I'm astonished to hear
my own voice descend to the lowest
pitch, or fade away
in air that cannot support it.

. . . Ed io riverso
nel potere che grava attorno, cedo
al sortilegio di non riconoscere
di me più nulla fuor di me; s'io levo
appena il braccio, mi si fa diverso
l'atto, si spezza su un cristallo, ignota
e impallidita sua memoria, e il gesto
già più non m'appartiene;
se parlo, ascolto quella voce attonito,
scendere alla sua gamma più remota
o spenta all'aria che non la sostiene.

What saves the poet from being completely lost in this metaphysical reverie is his strong hold on the physical world—a world represented by the wind, the valleys, the leafy branches, the smoky rapids, and the port:

Such is the bewilderment that lasts
up to the point where it resists
the final dissolution of the day;
then a gust of wind lifts up the valleys
to the crest of a frenzy and brings out
from the leafy branches a tinkling
sound that is lost amidst
the smoky rapids, and
the first lights outline the port.

Tale nel punto che resiste all'ultima
consunzione del giorno
dura lo smarrimento; poi un soffio
risolleva le valli in un frenetico
moto e deriva dalle fronde un tinnulo
suono che si disperde
tra rapide fumate e i primi lumi
disegnano gli scali.

The end of the reverie, however, does not mean any reconciliation between the two "in this late return." On the contrary, it merely serves to emphasize the deep division between them:

> Words fall lightly between us.
> I see you through a soft mist,
> but don't know if I recognize you.
> All I know is that
> I was never so divided from you
> as now in this late return.
> Just a few seconds have sufficed
> to burn everything of us
> except our two faces—two masks
> upon which a forced smile is carved.

>   ....le parole
> tra noi leggere cadono. Ti guardo
> in un molle riverbero. Non so
> se ti conosco; so che mai diviso
> fui da te come accade in questo tardo
> ritorno. Pochi istanti hanno bruciato
> tutto di noi: fuorchè due volti, due
> maschere che s'incidono, sforzate,
> di un sorriso.

The artistic and technical raison d'être for the two prose pieces in this section is perhaps the poet's desire to stretch to the utmost limit the respective characteristics of prose and verse and blend the two with a view to achieving something like a prose poem. Thus the graphic matter-of-factness of prose realism is wedded to a lyric intensity that is more implicit than explicit. There is also a subtle but pervasive suggestion of ethical or philosophical irony which gives these pieces an edge of pondered seriousness and emotional integrity. Take, for instance, this passage from "Dov'era il tennis . . .":

It is curious to think that each of us has a country like this or perhaps a country quite different from this, that must remain one's unchanging landscape; it is curious that the physical order should be so slow in filtering through to us and then so difficult to cancel. But what about the rest? All things considered, to ask oneself the why and the wherefore of the interrupted game is like asking the cloud of vapor that issues from the wornout cargo down there on the lines of the Palmaria. Soon the first night-fishing boats will be lighting up in the bay.

The artistic ease and unpretentiousness with which Montale deals with what might have led another writer to indulge in an elaborate philosophical moralizing is at once characteristic and remarkable. In the last passage an autobiographical element is introduced without its interfering with the generally impersonal tone and ethos of the piece:

> These objects and houses still formed part of the circle of life as long as it lasted. At first only a few felt that the cold was coming; among them perhaps was my father who, even in the hottest day in August, would finish his dinner in the open, surrounded by mayflies and other insects, throw a woollen shawl around his shoulders, and repeat invariably in French, goodness knows why, *il fait bien froid, bien froid;* and then he would retire to his room in order to finish smoking his Cavour in bed.

In "Visita a Fadin" Montale describes his visit to a poet friend, Sergio Fadin, who is lying seriously ill in a hospital. Ths tragic circumstance coupled with the oppressive atmosphere of the hospital inspires in him philosophical reflections, which he expresses in a language that has about it both a lyric pathos and a prosaic lucidity:

> I found him on the balcony for the incurable, taking the sun. He saw me at once and didn't seem surprised. His hair was short as usual, and seemed to have been recently cut, but his face was thinner and flushed at the cheekbones. His eyes, though just as beautiful as before, had deeper sockets around them. I arrived without notice and on an awkward day. Even Carlina, "his musical angel," couldn't be there.
>
> The sea below was deserted and along the coast were scattered the marzipan edifices of the nouveaux riches.
>
> . . . .
>
> I don't remember what we talked about. Certainly he had no need to apply his mind to the supreme universal questions—he who had always lived in a humane way, that is to say, both simply and silently. Exit Fadin. And now to say that you are no more simply means that you have entered a different order of being, however much the one in which we move should, for all its madness, seem to us, the latecomers, the only order in which the Divine can realize its attributes, recognize itself, and test itself within the limits of an assumption whose significance we do not know. (Should the divine power, too, need us then? If it is blasphemy to say so, alas, it is not even our worst.)
>
> To be always among the first and to *know* it, this is what counts, even if the why and the wherefore of the phenomena escapes us. Whoever has learned from you this lofty lesson of everyday decency (the most difficult

of virtues) can wait without impatience for the book of your memoirs.
But perhaps your word was not among those that are written.

The fourth section of *La bufera e altro* is entitled *Lampi e dediche*. It consists of fifteen poems written between 1948 and 1952. Like the *Mottetti* in *Le occasioni,* they are based on a richly interwoven pattern of insights and intuitions as well as of moments of vision or recollection that both relate to and delineate the form and presence of the woman loved. Underlying practically all of these poems is the vividly realized Montalian "occasion" treated in its particularity of temporal and topographical detail. Like a flash of lightning, memory evokes a particular episode or situation from the past, which illumines the various facets of the poet's moral and imaginative life.

In "Verso Siena," for instance, spurred on by memory—"Alas that no one can / hold back memory at its peak [Ohimè che la memoria sulla vetta / non ha chi la trattenga!]"—the poet reconstructs a scene from the past that pinpoints certain characteristically peculiar circumstances, such as "The flight of the pigs on the Ambretta / by night [la fuga dei porcelli sull'Ambretta notturna]," or "the carillon of San Gusmè / and a May moon, all stains [il carillon di San Gusmè / e una luna maggenga, tutta macchie]." These images in turn evoke the image of the woman in the form of the enigmatic god who "threw down his mask and struck / the rebel with his lightning [gittò la maschera / e fulminò il ribelle]." In "Sulla Greve," on the other hand—the Greve is a tributary of the Arno—the various forms and modes in which the woman loved used to reveal herself in the past, present themselves again in a more pervasively symbolic way, so that the poet can say:

> Now I do not feed
> only on your looks, as when
> you used to appear at my whistle
> and I would hardly see you.
> A rock, a furrow with a funnel,
> the black flight of a swallow, a cover
> for the world . . .
>
> That velvet bud unfolding
> at the glissade of a mandolin
> is bread for me, the flowing
> rustle, water, and your
> deep breathing, wine.
>
> Ora non ceno solo con lo sguardo
> come quando al mio fischio ti sporgevi
> e ti vedevo appena. Un masso, un solco

> a imbuto, il volo nero d'una rondine,
> un coperchio sul mondo....
>
> E m'è pane quel boccio di velluto
> che s'apre su un glissato di mandolino,
> acqua il frùscio scorrente, il tuo profondo
> respiro vino.

The next five poems were all inspired by the poet's visit to England and Scotland. In "La trota nera" he is in the vicinity of the University of Reading, where the graduates in economics and doctors of divinity are fishing of an evening. Even this scene is enough to set his mind thinking of the woman loved:

> Graduates in economics,
> doctors of divinity, intent
> on the evening water—the trout
> sniffs them and goes by,
> its ruby flash is your curl
> dissolving in the water,
> a sigh rising from the vaults
> of your office.

> Curvi sull'acqua serale
> graduati in Economia,
> Dottori in Divinità,
> la trota annusa e va via,
> il suo balenio di carbonchio
> è un ricciolo tuo che si sfa
> nel bagno, un sospiro che sale
> dagli ipogei del tuo ufficio.

In "Di un Natale metropolitano" the scene shifts to London during Christmas. The poet is visiting a friend. Describing her room with graphic vividness, he imbues each object in it with a wistful evocativeness:

> Mistletoe, a bunch of faith
> and hoarfrost hanging from childhood
> over your washstand and the oval mirror,
> shaded by your shepherdess-style curls
> among holy pictures and snaps
> of boys slipped rather hurriedly
> into the frame, an empty decanter,

little glasses of ash and rind,
the lights of Mayfair and then,
at a crossing, souls, bottles that couldn't
be opened, no longer war or peace,
the slow whirring of a pigeon that couldn't
follow you on the escalator
which carries you down . . .

Un vischio, fin dall'infanzia sospeso grappolo
di fede e di pruina sul tuo lavandino
e sullo specchio ovale ch'ora adombrano
i tuoi ricci bergère fra santini e ritratti
di ragazzi infilati un po' alla svelta
nella cornice, una caraffa vuota,
bicchierini di cenere e di bucce,
le luci di Mayfair, poi a un crocicchio
le anime, le bottiglie che non seppero aprirsi,
non più guerra nè pace, il tardo frullo
di un piccione incapace di seguirti
sui gradini automatici che ti slittano in giù....

Similarly, while visiting Ely Cathedral ("Lasciando un 'Dove'") or Glasgow
("Argyll Tour"), he is pursued by the vision of the woman, which transforms everything he sees into something rich and strange: "Dawns and
lights suspended [Albe e luci, sospese]," "this tomb that does not fly [questa
tomba / che non vola]," "clouds of naphtha hanging / over the walled canals
[nafta a nubi, sospese / sui canali murati]." In "Vento sulla mezzaluna" he
is at Edinburgh, where the sense of physical distance from the woman adds to
the intensity of his craving to rejoin her:

The great bridge didn't lead to you.
Yet at your command I would have
reached you even by navigating
the drains. But my strength
was ebbing away as fast as the sun
dyed crimson the panes of the verandas.

Il grande ponte non portava a te.
T'avrei raggiunta anche navigando
nelle chiaviche, a un tuo comando. Ma
già le forze, col sole sui cristalli
delle verande, andavano stremandosi.

The second stanza is a poetic résumé of the experience on which the story "Sosta a Edimburgo" in *Farfalla di Dinard* is based. A man preaching on the crescent asks the poet if he knows where God is,—a question that is more explicitly answered in "Verso Finistère," but which here affords him the opportunity of linking the concept of God with that of the woman loved. The preacher, however, is not convinced by the poet's answer, shakes his head, and disappears

> in the storm
> which tossed both men and houses
> and lifted them to the pitch-dark height.

> nel turbine che prese uomini e case
> e li sollevò in alto, sulla pece.

In "Sulla colonnna più alta" the scene shifts from Edinburgh to Damascus. (Montale visited the Middle East as a foreign correspondent for *Corriere della sera,* in the company of his wife). Here again the theme is the transformation, or rather assimilation, of the woman loved into something angelic or divine. And such a process is all the more favored by the foreign place and setting, which are quintessentially rendered in the first stanza:

> Christ the judge will have
> to alight up there to preach
> his word. And amidst the rubble
> of the seven riverbeds, crows,
> blackcaps, nettles, and sunflowers
> will all bow humbly.

> Dovrà posarsi lassù
> il Cristo giustiziere
> per dire la sua parola.
> Tra il pietrisco dei sette greti, insieme
> s'umilieranno corvi e capinere,
> ortiche e girasoli.

The second stanza brings about a subtle transition from the image of Christ to that of the woman loved:

> But in the twilight on that peak
> it was you, dark, wings encrusted
> and maimed by the frost of the Antelebanon;
> and your flash still transformed the black diadems
> of the tree stumps into mistletoe,

and the column spelt out the Law
for you alone.

Ma in quel crepuscolo eri tu sul vertice:
scura, l'ali ingrommate, stronche dai
geli dell'Antilibano; e ancora
il tuo lampo mutava in vischio i neri
diademi degli sterpi, la Colonna
sillabava la Legge per te sola.

In "Verso Finistère" the intuition of God is achieved through an even more intimately realized sense of identity between God and the woman loved. The quintessential brevity and concreteness of style and imagery connects this poem with some of the *Mottetti:*

> With the belling of the deer in the rain
> at Armor, the arc of your lashes
> is blotted out by the dusk,
> and filters through to the dawn's plaster
> where cycle wheels, spindles, rockets
> and fronds of swinging trees
> whirl. Perhaps I have
> no other proof that God
> sees me through your bluish-green eyes.

> Col bramire dei cervi nella piova
> d'Armor l'arco del tuo ciglio s'è spento
> al primo buio per filtrare poi
> sull'intonaco albale dove prillano
> ruote di cicli, fusi, razzi, frange
> d'alberi scossi. Forse non ho altra prova
> che Dio mi vede e che le tue pupille
> d'acquamarina guardano per lui.

The touch of intimacy about such details as "the arc of your lashes" and "your bluish-green eyes" serves to emphasize the transition from the personal to the impersonal and from the human to the divine, not so much in spite of as because of the matter-of-fact concreteness of such objects as "cycle wheels, spindles, rockets," etc.

"Siria" and "Luce d'inverno" offer variations on the same theme. In the former, while traveling through Syria, the poet is reminded of the old saying that poetry is a ladder to God. He is not sure, however, if his own poetry can

be regarded as such. But, inspired by the thought of the woman loved, he discovers a new voice that enables him to add what was missing in his poetry—
a new dimension, as it were:

> In ancient times they thought
> that poetry is a ladder to God.
> Perhaps it's not so if you read mine.
> But the day I knew it, I found
> a voice for you, lost in a flock
> of clouds and goats emerging
> from a ditch to browse, slaver on thorn
> and bog-grass, and the wasted faces
> of the sun and moon melted into each other,
> the car had broken down, and
> on a stone an arrow of blood
> pointed the way to Aleppo.

> Dicevano gli antichi che la poesia
> è scala a Dio. Forse non è così
> se mi leggi. Ma il giorno io lo seppi
> che ritrovai per te la voce, sciolto
> in un gregge di nuvoli e di capre
> dirompenti da un greppo a brucar bave
> di pruno e di falasco, e i volti scarni
> della luna e del sole si fondevano,
> il motore era guasto ed una freccia
> di sangue su un macigno segnalava
> la via di Aleppo.

In "Luce d'inverno" it is the novel setting and landscape—the sky of Palmira
or of the acropolis, together with "the pygmy palms / and candied gateways"
or "miles and miles of baskets / full of octopuses and eels," that serve as a
foil to the ecstasy of love, which acquires an almost physical intensity: "you
scratched my throat with your nails / to warn me that you were going to
ravish me." And when the poet juxtaposes this life-giving passion of love with
"the inhuman auroras" or "the icy museums / of mummies and scarabs," it
is like juxtaposing pumice and jasper, sand and sun, mud and divine clay.
What emerges from the juxtaposition is a spark that at once consumes and
renews the poet:

> When I stepped down from Palmira's
> sky to the pygmy palms

and candied gateways and you scratched
my throat with your nails to warn me
that you were going to ravish me;
when I came down from the acropolis's sky
and saw miles and miles of baskets
full of octopuses and eels
(oh the sawing of those teeth on the benumbed
heart!); when I took leave of the peaks
of the inhuman auroras to enter
the icy museums of mummies
and scarabs (oh how you suffered,
my only life!) and compared
pumice with jasper, sand
with the sun, and mud with divine clay —
it was then that the spark went off
and I was burnt to ashes, renewed.

Quando scesi dal cielo di Palmira
su palme nane e propilei canditi
e un'unghiata alla gola m'avvertì
che mi avresti rapito,
quando scesi dal cielo dell'Acropoli
e incontrai, a chilometri, cavagni
di polpi e di murene
(la sega di quei denti
sul cuore rattrappito!),
quando lasciai le cime delle aurore
disumane pel gelido museo
di mummie e scarabei (tu stavi male,
unica vita) e confrontai la pomice
e il diaspro, la sabbia e il sole, il fango
e l'argilla divina ——
                              alla scintilla
che si levò fui nuovo e incenerito.

In "Per un 'Omaggio a Rimbaud' " Montale outlines the course he feels his
own muse, symbolized by the butterfly, should take as distinct from the path
Rimbaud's muse followed. The poem is a tribute to Rimbaud's poetry insofar
as it sums up what he achieved and what his poetry stood for. However,
Montale's own muse is to avoid the course followed by Rimbaud's "in its
violent partridges' / flight [nel suo rapinoso / volo di starna]" and to avoid

"letting fall mauled wings, leaves of gardenia / on the black ice of the asphalt [lasciar cadere / piume stroncate, foglie di gardenia / sul nero ghiaccio dell'asfalto]." Its flight will be more terrible because of the more arduous task it has to perform, namely, that of creating a living link between the human and the extrahuman universe. In other words, Montale wants his muse to be more or less like Wordsworth's lark, a "Type of the wise who soar, but never roam; / True to the kindred points of Heaven and Home!" [7]

The poem "Incantesimo," with which *Lampi e dediche* closes, sums up with lyric simplicity the theme of love based on the identification or interplay of the real and the ideal, the human and the divine:

> O stay safe and free in the isle
> of your thoughts and mine,
> in the light flame which encircles you
> and which I didn't know until
> I met Diotima who so resembles you!
>
> Oh resta chiusa e libera nell'isole
> del tuo pensiero e del mio,
> nella fiamma leggera che t'avvolge
> e che non seppi prima
> d'incontrare Diotima,
> colei che tanto ti rassomigliava!

Lampi e dediche is followed by another group called *Silvae*. Written between 1948 and 1950, it includes some of the better known and more complex poems in *La bufera e altro,* such as "Proda di Versilia," "La primavera hitleriana," and "Voce giunta con le folaghe." In "Iride" and some other poems in this group the concept of the woman loved and her identification with God or an angelic messenger is expressed through more elaborate and more sustained religious symbolism. The woman, Montale tells us in his note, is the one who appeared in "Il giglio rosso" and the *Finisterre* series. "She returns in 'La primavera hitleriana,' in other *Silvae* (under the name of Clizia), and in 'Piccolo testamento,' and she was present in some of the poems in *Le occasioni* such as *Mottetti* and "Nuove stanze". 'Iride' is a poem that I dreamt and then translated into a nonexistent language. I am perhaps more a medium than an author." The poem deals with the figure of Iris, the messenger of the gods, who is supposed to have come from the East in order to illuminate the ice and fog of the North, and who now embodies the concept of the Christian sacrifice:

7. "To a Skylark."

When Saint Martin suddenly scatters
its embers and pokes them deep
into the gloomy furnace of Ontario,
the crackling of green pinecones
among the ashes or the smoke of an infusion
of poppies and the bloodstained Face
on the shroud that divides me from you;
this and little else (for there's
no other sign of yours
than a wink, in the struggle which drives me
into the charnel-house, shoulder to the wall,
where bright blue sapphires, palms,
and storks on one leg don't shut out
the horrible sight from the poor lost Nestorian);

is what reaches me of you
from the shipwreck of my people and yours,
now that a fire of ice brings to my mind
the soil that is yours and that
you didn't see; and I have
no other rosary in my hand,
nor has another flame assailed you
than this of resin and berries.

Quando di colpo San Martino smotta
le sue braci e le attizza in fondo al cupo
fornello dell'Ontario,
schiocchi di pigne verdi fra la cenere
o il fumo d'un infuso di papaveri
e il Volto insanguinato sul sudario
che mi divide da te;

   questo e poco altro (se poco
è un tuo segno, un ammicco, nella lotta
che me sospinge in un ossario, spalle
al muro, dove zàffiri celesti
e palmizi e cicogne su una zampa non chiudono
l'atroce vista al povero
Nestoriano smarrito);

   è quanto di te giunge dal naufragio
delle mie genti, delle tue, or che un fuoco

di gelo porta alla memoria il suolo
ch'è tuo e che non vedesti; e altro rosario
fra le dita non ho, non altra vampa
se non questa, di resina e di bacche,
t'ha investito.

The symbolic forms through which the woman loved reveals herself are also
to some extent indicative of the recent tragedy of the war. Moreover, the
objects and the landscape in their grim desolation form a screen on which
the poet projects his thoughts and feelings, the stresses and dilemmas of his
times, and the message of hope embodied by Iris. However, in spite of its
dream origin, there is something too conscious and too elaborate about the
symbolic and imagistic pattern on which the poem is based for it to achieve
the compelling intensity of conviction. It offers something more in the nature
of a technical and artistic tour de force depending on set concepts and beliefs
of a religious and spiritual nature, than something impelled by a creative urge
and rooted in a fully realized personal experience.

The poem "Nella serra," on the other hand, brings out the sudden and
transient visions through which the woman manifests herself—sometimes as a
messenger of God, sometimes as a symbol of hope and salvation. And both
what she stands for and what her multiple modes and forms of manifestation
amount to are more poetically and more convincingly fused than was the
case with "Iride." "Ravished and gay," the poet tells her,

> I was intoxicated by you, your form
> was my hidden breathing, your face
> melted into mine,
>
> and the obscure thought of God
> descended on the few who were alive,
> amidst celestial sounds, childish drum-beats
> and the spheres of lightning hanging
>
> over me, over you, over the lemons . . .

> Rapito e leggero ero intriso
> di te, la tua forma era il mio
> respiro nascosto, il tuo viso
> nel mio si fondeva, e l'oscuro
>
> pensiero di Dio discendeva
> sui pochi viventi, tra suoni
> celesti e infantili tamburi

> e globi sospesi di fulmini
> su me, su te, sui limoni....

In "Nel parco" the perceptive minuteness of detail with which the poet observes the natural phenomena and transforms them into so many modes of
externalizing his feelings, serves to consolidate the link between him and the
woman loved:

> Laughter that isn't mine
> pierces through hoary branches
> into my breast and shakes it,
> thrills my veins,
>
> I laugh with you on the distorted
> shadow of the wheel, and freed
> from myself I stretch on the bone-like
> roots that protrude, and prick
>
> your face with wisps of straw.

> Un riso che non m'appartiene
> trapassa da fronde canute
> fino al mio petto, lo scuote
> un trillo che punge le vene,
>
> e rido con te sulla ruota
> deforme dell'ombra, mi allungo
> disfatto di me sulle ossute
> radici che sporgono e pungo
>
> con fili di paglia il tuo viso....

In "L'orto" we have more or less the same theme brought out through a
subtle blending of naturalism and symbolism. The various objects in the
orchard seem to be suffused by the woman's presence, which they help to
define in terms of the minute particularity of moral and psychological characteristics:

> Where the acorns rain
> and where beyond the wall
> the airy garlands of hornbeams
> are unraveled,
> revealing the waves' frothy rim.

> dove le ghiande piovano e oltre il muro
> si sfioccano, aerine, le ghirlande

> dei carpini che accennano
> lo spumoso confine dei marosi . . .

The woman's muffled footstep becomes one with "the blind incubus with which / I've grown toward my death / ever since I saw you [il cieco incubo onde cresco / alla morte dal giorno che ti vidi]." One association or memory is enough to evoke other memories and associations, so that

> I don't know if your footstep,
> which makes my veins throb as it approaches
> this tangle, is the one that had
> overtaken me some other summer,
> before a gust of wind
> grazing the rugged peak
> of the Mesco shattered my mirror.

> io non so se il tuo passo che fa pulsare le vene
> se s'avvicina in questo intrico,
> è quello che mi colse un'altra estate
> prima che una folata
> radente contro il picco irto del Mesco
> infrangesse il mio specchio——

Nor does the poet know if

> . . . the hand that lightly touches
> my shoulder is the same as that
> which once responded on the celesta
> to the cries of other nests,
> from a thicket now burnt.

> . . . la mano che mi sfiora la spalla
> è la stessa che un tempo
> sulla celesta rispondeva a gemiti
> d'altri nidi, da un fòlto ormai bruciato.

However, for all its abstract and intangible character, the presence of the woman is not unaffected by the tragedy and dilemmas of suffering humanity; on the contrary, it fully participates in "the hour of torture and lament / that struck down on the world [L'ora della tortura e dei lamenti / che s'abbattè sul mondo]." In the last stanza the poet's feeling of identification with the woman—an identification both physical and moral—finds a lyric culmination:

> O mute lips
> parched by the long journey through

the airy path which bore you,
O limbs that I can hardly tell
from mine, O fingers that quench
the thirst of the dying and
inflame the living, O will
that has led you to create, beyond
your limit, the hands of the dial,
by which you expand yourself
into human time and human
space, into the furies of demons
incarnate and the foreheads of angels
swooping down in their flight——
If the force that moves the record
already cut were another,
your fate would surely be joined
to mine to form a single groove.[8]

O labbri muti, aridi dal lungo
viaggio per il sentiero fatto d'aria
che vi sostenne, o membra che distinguo
a stento dalle mie, o diti che smorzano
la sete dei morenti e i vivi infocano,
o intento che hai creato fuor della tua misura
le sfere del quadrante e che ti espandi
in tempo d'uomo, in spazio d'uomo, in furie
di démoni incarnati, in fronti d'angiole
precipitate a volo....Se la forza
che guida il disco *di già inciso* fosse
un'altra, certo il tuo destino al mio
congiunto mostrerebbe un solco solo.

"Proda di Versilia" is one of the major lyrics in *La bufera*. It has the organic compactness as well as the complexity of a characteristically Montalian theme, realized through an impressive variety of verbal and imagistic modes. It invokes the dead, and prays that they might pray for him and for his people

8. The last four lines in this quotation convey the same degree of wistful intensity, both of a personal and metaphysical nature (although expressed in characteristic Montalian diction and imagery), as that which lies behind the words Dante addresses to Brunetto Latini:

> "Se fosse tutto pieno il mio dimando,"
> rispuosi lui, "voi non sareste ancora
> de l'umana natura posto in bando."
>
> *Inferno,* canto 15, lines 79–81

who are still alive, just as he prays for them, "not resurrection / but the fulfillment of that life which they had, / unexplained and inexplicable." However, with the passage of time the visitations of the dead become increasingly
infrequent, and the only way the poet can communicate with them is by
deliberately recalling the past of which they were once an integral part. Thus
Montale relives, and makes the dead relive, that past by means of such
associations as have both a realistic familiarity and an evocative uncanniness
about them:

> My dead whom I pray that they
> might pray for me and for my living,
> as I for them, not resurrection,
> but the fulfilment of the life they had,
> unexplained and inexplicable,
> descend more rarely now
> from the open horizons, when a blend
> of water and sky opens windows
> to the evening rays—and still
> more rarely does a white-winged cutter,
> a celestial hawk,
> place them on the sand.

> I miei morti che prego perchè preghino
> per me, per i miei vivi com'io invece
> per essi non resurrezione ma
> il compiersi di quella vita ch'ebbero
> inesplicata e inesplicabile, oggi
> più di rado discendono dagli orizzonti aperti
> quando una mischia d'acque e cielo schiude
> finestre ai raggi della sera,——sempre
> più raro, astore celestiale, un cutter
> bianco-alato li posa sulla rena.

From such a concretely realized evocation the poet turns to fix and define
the past:

> . . . courtyards of hoary brushwood
> where a friar-colored cat enters and is refused
> leftovers by angry voices;
> rubble and flat roof-terraces
> on low houses along an undulating
> descent of dunes and umbrellas

open to a grey sun, sand
that doesn't nourish the trees
sacred to my childhood, fig,
wild pine, and eucalyptus.

. . . cortili di sterpaglie
incanutite dove se entra un gatto
color frate gli vietano i rifiuti
voci irose; macerie e piatte altane
su case basse lungo un ondulato
declinare di dune e ombrelle aperte
al sole grigio, sabbia che non nutre
gli alberi sacri alla mia infanzia, il pino
selvatico, il fico e l'eucalipto.

The close union between recollection and realization, between the paradoxical
reality of the past with its "reefs and narrow horizons / guarding lives still
human / and recognizable gestures," and the equally paradoxical unreality
of the present as symbolized by "this infinite sea of clay / and refuse," is force-
fully evident in the last paragraph:

Years of reefs and narrow
horizons, guarding lives
still human and recognizable gestures,
breathing or final panting
of submarine creatures, similar
to man and like him even
in name: the priest-fish, the swallow-fish,
the lobster—wolf of the creels—
which forgets its pincers when Alice
approaches—and the trapeze flight
of the familiar mice from palm
to palm; time that was measurable
until this infinite sea of clay
and refuse opened up.

Anni di scogli e di orizzonti stretti
a custodire vite ancora umane
e gesti conoscibili, respiro
o anelito finale di sommersi
simili all'uomo o a lui vicini pure
nel nome: il pesce prete, il pesce rondine,

l'àstice——il lupo della nassa——che
dimentica le pinze quando Alice
gli si avvicina.... e il volo da trapezio
dei topi familiari da una palma
all'altra; tempo che fu misurabile
fino a che non s'aperse questo mare
infinito, di creta e di mondiglia.

In "Ezekiel saw the wheel" the poet again takes up the theme he had dealt
with in "L'orto" and "Nella serra": namely, the separation of the poet and
the woman loved. In trying to put the thought of unattainable love out of
his mind, he actually buries it "under a cumulus, a mountain of sand." But
then comes the rain, breeding in him memory, desire and love. I had tried,
the poet tells the woman loved,

to suffocate your voice, thrust it down
within the brief circle that
transforms everything . . .

a soffocar la tua voce,
a spingerla in giù, dentro il breve
cerchio che tutto trasforma, . . .

But the rain

scraped, brought to the open,
with the print of slippers on the hardened
mud, the splinter, the fiber
of your cross in the rotten pulp
of old broken iron beams,
the smile of the skull interposing
itself between us when
the threatening Wheel appeared
among the reflexes of the dawn
and the petals of the peach were turned
into blood and descended on me,
and, with them, your claws, as now.

raspava, portava all'aperto
con l'orma delle pianelle
sul fango indurito, la scheggia,
la fibra della tua croce
in polpa marcita di vecchie

> putrelle schiantate, il sorriso
> di teschio che a noi si frappose
> quando la Ruota minacciosa apparve
> tra riflessi d'aurora, e fatti sangue
> i petali del pesco su me scesero
> e con essi
> il tuo artiglio, come ora.

This poem is followed by "La primavera hitleriana." Montale's succinct note on it runs as follows: "Hitler and Mussolini at Florence. A gala evening at the municipal theatre. On the Arno a cloud of white moths falling like snow." For all its quintessential brevity, the note sums up the sinister atmosphere and significance of the historic meeting between the two dictators. And the first seven lines of the poem are a poetic elaboration of the note:

> A thick white cloud of moths whirls madly
> round the pale street-lamps and embankments,
> spreading a blanket on the ground
> on which the foot crunches as though walking on sugar.
> The summer's prospect releases
> the night's cold, hitherto imprisoned
> in the dead season's innermost caves,
> or in the orchards extending
> from Maiano down to these sandbanks.

> Folta la nuvola bianca delle falene impazzite
> turbina intorno agli scialbi fanali e sulle spallette,
> stende a terra una coltre su cui scriccia
> come su zucchero il piede; l'estate imminente sprigiona
> ora il gelo notturno che capiva
> nelle cave segrete della stagione morta,
> negli orti che da Maiano scavalcano a questi renai.

The image of the moths whirling round the pale street-lamps and forming a white blanket on the ground strikes an ominous note, suggesting the grip of a cold and ruthless determinism over men and objects. Against such a portentous background Hitler, the "infernal messenger," makes his appearance. Thus both the imagery and the ethos behind it bring out the poet's moral involvement in the situation as well as his sense of outraged humanity. But however indignant he might be, he does not indulge in any sentimental effusions. Instead, he expresses his feeling of the tragic futility and inhumanity of the war through such casual yet ominously eloquent details as

the butcher decking the slaughtered goats' heads with berries or "the poor
harmless shops / armed with cannons and war toys":

> An infernal messenger has
> just shot through the street amid
> the cheering of cut-throats; a mystical
> gulf laced with swastikas opens
> to devour him. Even the poor harmless shops,
> armed with cannons and war toys, are shut.
> And the butcher who was decking
> the slaughtered goats' heads with berries
> has bolted the door.
> The ritual of the mild hangmen
> who do not yet know blood,
> has turned into a filthy reel
> of meshed wings and wraiths on the river edge,
> while the water corrodes the banks
> and no one is free from blame
> anymore.

> Da poco sul corso è passato a volo un messo infernale
> tra un alalà di scherani, un golfo mistico acceso
> e pavesato di croci a uncino l'ha preso e inghiottito,
> si sono chiuse le vetrine, povere
> e inoffensive benchè armate anch'esse
> di cannoni e giocattoli di guerra,
> ha sprangato il beccaio che infiorava
> di bacche il muso dei capretti uccisi,
> la sagra dei miti carnefici che ancora ignorano il sangue
> s'è tramutata in un sozzo trescone d'ali schiantate,
> di larve sulle golene, e l'acqua sèguita a rodere
> le sponde e più nessuno è incolpevole.

The last phrase, "and no one is free from blame anymore," overtly states the
ethical concern implicitly present throughout the poem, and illustrates the
efficacy of the transition from the imagistic to the conceptual and from the
pictorial to the moral plane. If the inexorability of the war is conveyed by
the evocatively simple image of the water corroding the banks of the Arno,
it is no less implicit in the way the lyric tone and emphasis shifts from the
ethical to the personal and from the personal to the symbolic:

Was it then all in vain?
And what about the Roman candles
at San Giovanni, slowly illumining
the horizon, and what about the pledges
and the long farewells
strong as a baptism in
the dismal waiting of the hordes,
(but a gem's glitter cut across the air,
oozing upon the ice and your native
shores, the angels of Tobias,
the seven, the seed of the future),
and what about the heliotropes
growing from your hands?
Everything's burnt, sucked dry
by a pollen that shrieks like fire,
and is armed like a blizzard—

Tutto per nulla, dunque?——e le candele
romane, a San Giovanni, che sbiancavano lente
l'orizzonte, ed i pegni e i lunghi addii
forti come un battesimo nella lugubre attesa
dell'orda (ma una gemma rigò l'aria stillando
sui ghiacci e le riviere dei tuoi lidi
gli angeli di Tobia, i sette, la semina
dell'avvenire) e gli eliotropi nati
dalle tue mani——tutto arso e succhiato
da un polline che stride come il fuoco
e ha punte di sinibbio....

The note of personal symbolism itself develops into something vaster and impersonal, and the topographical particularity of the detail "the Roman candles / at San Giovanni, slowly illumining / the horizon" leads to the morally as well as sentimentally pregnant line, "the pledges / and the long farewells / strong as a baptism."

In the last stanza the note of hope for deliverance from the tragedy of the war culminates in the lyric apostrophe to Clizia, who has kept her love unchanged "even though you yourself are changed." Her love for the poet symbolizes her as well as the poet's love for humanity in its dire plight, which makes even the "cankerous spring" welcome insofar as "it freezes to death this death":

Oh even this cankerous spring is something
to rejoice at, if it freezes to death
this death. Look up again Clizia,
it's your destiny, you who keep your love
unchanged, even though you yourself
are changed, until the blind sun you carry
in you is dazzled by the Other,
perishes in Him and not
for you alone. Perhaps the bells
and the sirens that salute the monsters
tonight in their witches' sabbath
are already mingling with the sound
that, released from the sky, conquers,
becomes one with the breath of the dawn—
white dawn, without wings of terror—
which may show up again tomorrow for everyone
smiling on the dry river-beds of the south.

Oh la piagata
primavera è pur festa se raggela
in morte questa morte! Guarda ancora
in alto, Clizia, è la tua sorte, tu
che il non mutato amor mutata serbi,
fino a che il cieco sole che in te porti
si abbàcini nell'Altro e si distrugga
in Lui, per tutti. Forse le sirene, i rintocchi
che salutano i mostri nella sera
della loro tregenda, si confondono già
col suono che slegato dal cielo, scende, vince——
col respiro di un'alba che domani per tutti
si riaffacci, bianca ma senz'ali
di raccapriccio, ai greti arsi del sud....

The sound that comes from above and mingles with the bells and sirens does
not so much symbolize a religious or mystical concept as such, as the essence
of moral ardor, love, and hope embodied by Clizia in her role as a modern
Beatrice. In fact, in few other poems does Clizia's composite role receive such
an intensely lyrical and symbolical treatment as in "La primavera hitleriana."

"Voce giunta con le folaghe," one of the best and most accomplished poems
in *La bufera,* takes us back to the poet's past. The theme is what Montale
calls "the sudden jerk of memory [lo scatto del ricordo]." Guided by the

shade of the woman loved, he visits his father's tomb and listens to the
dialogue between the two spirits without saying anything himself, rather like
Paolo listening to the conversation between Dante and Francesca in *The
Inferno*. But when the poet tries to embrace his father's spirit, his hands are
repulsed by "the uninhabited void which we / occupied once and which
awaits us [il vuoto inabitato / che occupammo e che attende fin ch'è tempo /
di colmarsi di noi, di ritrovarci]." Thus some of the major themes of Montale's poetry—recollection of the past, communion with the dead, the presence
of the woman loved as a guiding spirit, and the Ligurian landscape—are
superbly orchestrated in this poem. In the first paragraph, as indeed throughout the whole poem, prosaic images mingle with metaphysical concepts with
an unobstrusive ease and convincingness; for instance, "the road I have
traversed [la via percorsa]," "the goat path [sentiero da capre]," and the
place "where we shall melt like wax [dove ci scioglieremo come cera]." The
shade of the dead father turns up in a characteristically familiar garb:

> . . . upright in the glare,
> without shawl or beret,
> in the deafening roar that announced
> the miners' barges in the dawn,
> half submerged under their great load,
> and looming black on the high waves.

> . . . erto ai barbagli,
> senza scialle e berretto, al sordo fremito
> che annunciava nell'alba
> chiatte di minatori dal gran carico
> semisommerse, nere sull'onde alte.

The description of the female shade, too, is both vivid and evocatively delicate:

> The shade that accompanies me,
> vigilant, to your tomb,
> leans on a bust of Hermes
> and with a proud toss of the head,
> removes a childish curl
> from her burning eyes and strong
> eyebrows; it weighs no more
> than you, buried long ago,
> the first rays of the sun
> pierce it, lively butterflies

cross it and the sensitive plant
grazes it without shrinking.

L'ombra che mi accompagna
alla tua tomba, vigile,
e posa sopra un'erma ed ha uno scarto
altero della fronte che le schiara
gli occhi ardenti ed i duri sopraccigli
da un suo biocco infantile,
l'ombra non ha più peso della tua
da tanto seppellita, i primi raggi
del giorno la trafiggono, farfalle
vivaci l'attraversano, la sfiora
la sensitiva e non si rattrappisce.

In the penultimate paragraph the female shade converses with the poet's
father and tries to persuade him to return whence he came. The poignancy
of the encounter between the poet and his father's shade is summed up by
the latter's reluctance to return to "the uninhabited void," whereas the precariousness of the survival of the dead, or of what Montale in one of his prose
pieces [9] calls their limited immortality in the minds and memories of those
who survive them, is expressed by means of words that have both the warmth
of familiarity and the somberness of a moral admonition:

—I have thought for you, remembered
for everyone. Now go back
to the free heaven that transmutes you.
Does this cliff tempt you still?
Yes, the shoreline is the same
as ever, the sea that united you
to my shore, before I had wings,
doesn't dissolve. I remember
these shores of mine, and yet
I have arrived with the coot
to take you away from yours.
Memory isn't a sin
so long as it serves.
Then it's the lethargy of the mole,
abjection that feeds on itself—

9. In "Il regista" (*Farfalla di Dinard*).

——Ho pensato per te, ho ricordato
per tutti. Ora ritorni al cielo libero
che ti tramuta. Ancora questa rupe
ti tenta? Sì, la bàttima è la stessa
di sempre, il mare che ti univa ai miei
lidi da prima che io avessi l'ali,
non si dissolve. Io le rammento quelle
mie prode e pur son giunta con le folaghe
a distaccarti dalle tue. Memoria
non è peccato fin che giova. Dopo
è letargo di talpe, abiezione
che funghisce su sé... ——

In "L'Ombra della magnolia" Clizia again reasserts her hold on the poet
and aids him in his quest for self-realization in a world torn by the war and
its aftermath, which brings challenges that are no less arduous than those of
the war itself. While recalling the period of war, the poet remembers how
at that time

It was easier to use up oneself
and to die at the first
flutter of wings, or at
the first encounter with the enemy,
a game. But now
a harder life begins . . .

Spendersi era più facile, morire
al primo batter d'ale, al primo incontro
col nemico, un trastullo. Comincia ora
la via più dura . . .

The harder life calls for courage and maturity in dealing with the new trials
and tribulations of peacetime; but these cannot affect Clizia who has taken
up abode in the beyond. Hence the gulf between her and the poet, brought
out by the imagery with its religious undertones. You are one, the poet tells
her,

. . . for whom zenith, nadir, Cancer
and Capricorn were all one,
for the war was in you, and in him
who adores through you
the stigmata of your Spouse . . .

> . . . cui zenit nadir cancro
> capricorno rimasero indistinti
> perchè la guerra fosse in te e in chi adora
> su te le stimme del tuo Sposo . . .

The poet's awareness of Clizia's uniqueness and his desire to distinguish himself from the people around him prompt him to undertake the task of self-exploration and self-realization:

> Others fall back, give in.
> The blade that cuts sharply will be
> silenced, the empty rind
> of him who sang will soon
> be glass dust under foot.
> The shadow is livid—it's autumn,
> it's winter, it's the beyond which draws you
> and into which I throw myself,
> a mullet leaping clear of the water
> in the new moon. Goodbye.

> . . . Gli altri arretrano
> e piegano. La lima che sottile
> incide tacerà, la vuota scorza
> di chi cantava sarà presto polvere
> di vetro sotto i piedi, l'ombra è livida,——
> è l'autunno, è l'inverno, è l'oltrecielo
> che ti conduce e in cui mi getto, cèfalo
> saltato in secco al novilunio.
>
>   Addio.

"Il gallo cedrone" offers another variation on the same theme. The poet is disillusioned about what he had hoped would happen after the war had ended, but didn't. The disillusionment makes him realize that "it was better to live / than to be drowned in this magma, / easier to dissolve in the wind / than in this slime, encrusted on the flame [Era più dolce / vivere che affondare in questo magma, / più facile disfarsi al vento che / qui nel limo, incrostati sulla fiamma]." In other words, the moral and political regeneration he had hoped would follow the end of the war hasn't occurred. While contemplating the tragedy of the war, he identifies himself with the wounded blackcock that puts up a final heroic struggle before meeting its violent end:

> I feel in my breast your wound,
> under a clot of wing;

my heavy flight attempts a wall
and all that remains of us
are a few feathers on a frosted ilex.

Tussle of nests, loves,
nests of eggs, marbled, divine!
Now the gem of the perennial plants
sparkles in the dark like a glow-worm.
Jove is buried.

Sento nel petto la tua piaga, sotto
un grumo d'ala; il mio pesante volo
tenta un muro e di noi solo rimane
qualche piuma sull'ilice brinata.

Zuffe di nidi, amori, nidi d'uova
marmorate, divine! Ora la gemma
delle piante perenni, come il bruco,
luccica al buio, Giove è sotterrato.

It is curious that "L'anguilla," a poem concerned neither with war nor the reevocation of the past, should conclude *Silvae,* which is largely dominated by such themes. Like the second stanza in Leopardi's "Canto notturno," with which it has rhythmic and prosodic affinities as well as affinities of verse movement, it consists of one long sentence with its energetic progression of lyric intensity on the one hand and its descriptive perspicuity and concreteness of detail on the other, as the poet traces the eel's journey from the Baltic to "our seas [nostri mari]," "our estuaries [nostri estuari]." And just as the Leopardian stanza allegorizes the journey of man's life, so this poem may be regarded as allegorizing the development and the achievement of a poet's art:

. . . swimming deep down under the crosscurrent,
from ever-thinning branch to branch,
hairline to hairline, plunging
deeper and deeper into the heart
of the rock and filtering through
ruts of slime until
one day a light explodes
from the chestnuts, illumines its wriggle
in ponds of stagnant water,
in ditches that slope from the cliffs
of the Apennines down to the Romagna;

the eel, torch, whip,
arrow of Love on earth,
that only our gullies or dried up
Pyrenean streams lead back
to the paradise of fecundation;
the green soul looking for life
where only burning heat
and desolation bite, the spark
that says that all begins
when everything seems to be carbonized,
a buried stump; . . .

. . . risale in profondo, sotto la piena avversa,
di ramo in ramo e poi
di capello in capello, assottigliati,
sempre più addentro, sempre più nel cuore
del macigno, filtrando
tra gorielli di melma finchè un giorno
una luce scoccata dai castagni
ne accende il guizzo in pozze d'acquamorta,
nei fossi che declinano
dai balzi d'Appennino alla Romagna;
l'anguilla, torcia, frusta,
freccia d'Amore in terra
che solo i nostri botri o i disseccati
ruscelli pirenaici riconducono
a paradisi di fecondazione;
l'anima verde che cerca
vita là dove solo
morde l'arsura e la desolazione,
la scintilla che dice
tutto comincia quando tutto pare
incarbonirsi, bronco seppellito; . . .

The vivid multiplicity and concreteness of detail are proof not only of the poet's creative strength and vitality but also of his ability to mold them into a technically ingenious pattern and rhythm.

Madrigali privati forms the penultimate section of *La bufera e altro*. It originally contained five poems, but to subsequent editions was added the poem "Se t'hanno assomigliato." In this poem Montale finds that there is something about the woman loved which others cannot see and which he himself continues to discover every day. If she has been compared to a fox, it is, he tells her, because of her marvelous stride, her "flying footstep that unites and divides," or perhaps because of "that wave of light / which your soft almond eyes diffuse" or "the tangle of your torn feathers / which you hold in your infant hands." And if she was compared to "a blond carnivorous animal," it is because others could not see her angelic characteristics— "the wings on your delicate shoulders, / the omen on your burning forehead." The fact that the poet can see what others cannot adds to his sense of desolation because of the loss of the woman, which he cannot share with anyone else. Thus the poem moves under the pressure of characteristically Montalian themes and sentiments—admiration for the woman loved, the sudden jerk of memory,[10] and the sense of pride due to the full and intimate awareness of what the woman means and represents. On account of these as well as certain features of style and imagery, the poem anticipates *Xenia:*

> If they compared you to a fox,
> it is because of your marvelous stride,
> your flying footstep that unites
> and divides, upsets and reanimates
> the pavement (your terrace, the streets
> near the Cottolengo, the lawn,
> the tree that bears my name—
> all vibrated with it, happy, moist,
> subdued)—or perhaps
> because of the wave of light
> that your soft almond eyes diffuse,
> the astuteness of your quick surprise,
> the tangle of your torn feathers
> which you hold in your infant hand;
> if they compared you to a blond carnivorous
> animal, to the perfidious genius
> of the thicket (and why not to the torpedo,
> the ugly fish that gives a shock?),
> it is because the blind did not see
> the wings on your delicate shoulders,
> the omen on your burning forehead,
> the furrow I scratched in blood,
> cross confirmation enchantment
> calamity vow farewell

10. "Lo scatto del ricordo" ("Voce giunta con le folaghe").

perdition and salvation;
if they couldn't believe you were something
more than a weasel or a woman,
with whom shall I share my discovery,
where shall I bury my gold
and the embers which grate in me
if turning from the stair you leave me.

Se t'hanno assomigliato
alla volpe sarà per la falcata
prodigiosa, pel volo del tuo passo
che unisce e che divide, che sconvolge
e rinfranca il selciato (il tuo terrazzo,
le strade presso il Cottolengo, il prato,
l'albero che ha il mio nome ne vibravano
felici, umidi e vinti)—o forse solo
per l'onda luminosa che diffondi
dalle mandorle tenere degli occhi,
per l'astuzia dei tuoi pronti stupori,
per lo strazio
di piume lacerate che può dare
la tua mano d'infante in una stretta;
se t'hanno assomigliato
a un carnivoro biondo, al genio perfido
delle fratte (e perchè non all'immondo
pesce che dà la scossa, alla torpedine?)
è forse perchè i ciechi non ti videro
sulle scapole gracili le ali,
perchè i ciechi non videro il presagio
della tua fronte incandescente, il solco
che vi ho graffiato a sangue, croce cresima
incantesimo jattura voto vale
perdizione e salvezza; se non seppero
crederti più che donnola o che donna,
con chi dividerò la mia scoperta,
dove seppellirò l'oro che porto,
dove la brace che in me stride se,
lasciandomi, ti volgi dalle scale?

In "Le processioni del 1949," too, the loved woman's "furiously angelic virtue [virtù furiosamente angelica]" flashes through the pomp, clamor, and

stuffiness of a religious procession, embodying what is truly meaningful—at
any rate for the poet—as distinguished from what the procession represents
for others:

> Flashes of sultriness
> on the point of separating, livid,
> misty hour, then an even
> worse halo, a rumbling of wheels
> and laments from the first ramps of
> the hill, a regurgitation, a bitter
> stench polluting the clods
> consecrated to us. . . .

> Lampi d'afa sul punto del distacco,
> livida ora annebbiata,
> poi un alone anche peggiore, un bombito
> di ruote e di querele dalle prime
> rampe della collina,
> un rigurgito, un tanfo acre che infetta
> le zolle a noi devote . . .

In a more explicitly romantic vein and by means of a pervasive lyricism, the
poet celebrates three episodic moments from the past in "Nubi color magenta . . .". The tone of personal warmth and the delicacy of feeling blend
in a characteristic specificness of detail, as he imagines himself being borne
on the wings of his beloved, who moves or stops at his command. However,
he realizes that it is really she who commands him and that his happiness
consists in his surrendering himself to her charm. Montale's own comment on
the woman who inspired this poem is as follows: "She was a young woman,
and she comes out in this poem as someone who is very earthy—quite different from Clizia. Compared with her, I felt like an abstract man beside
a concrete woman: she lived with all the pores of her skin, and inspired in
me a sense of freshness, above all a sense of being alive." The poet translates
this feeling in terms of rhythmic nimbleness and vivid and vital concreteness
of imagery:

> Magenta-colored clouds gathered beyond
> the coast over Fingal's cave
> when I said "Pedal my angel!" and at once
> the tandem freed itself from the mud,
> and flew among the berries on the mound.

Bronze-colored clouds formed a bridge
across the spirals of the Agliena
on the rusty heath, when I said:
"Stop!" and your ebony wing
convulsed the horizon with its long
unbearable shudder.

Like Paphnutius in the desert,
I wanted to win you too much, though vanquished.
Now I fly or stay with you; living
and dying are the same, a knot
tinged with your color and warm
with the breath of the cavern, deep
and hardly audible.

Nubi color magenta s'addensavano
nella grotta di Fingal d'oltrecosta
quando dissi "pedala,
angelo mio!" e con un salto
il tandem si staccò dal fango, sciolse
il volo tra le bacche del rialto.

Nubi color di rame si piegavano
a ponte sulle spire dell'Agliena,
sulle biancane rugginose quando
ti dissi "resta!", e la tua ala d'ebano
occupò l'orizzonte
col suo fremito lungo, insostenibile.

Come Pafnuzio nel deserto, troppo
volli vincerti, io vinto.
Volo con te, resto con te; morire,
vivere è un punto solo, un groppo tinto
del tuo colore, caldo del respiro
della caverna, fondo, appena udibile.

In "Per album" the poet's memory seems to be intoxicated by what it re-members, the image of the woman loved when she was alive and the fact that he saw the light which, once seen, can never be forgotten. He now tries to recapture her—or her image—with a fishhook:

But I noticed no wriggling tail
in the muddy wells, no wind
brought your sign from the hills
of Monferrato.

I spent my day spying upon you
—larva, tadpole, gazelle,
zebra, okapi, black cloud,
hail before the vintage—
and gleaning through the drenched rows of vine,
without finding you.
I continued late without knowing
that the three boxes—Sand Soda Soap,
the dovecote whence you took
your flight: from a kitchen—would have opened
for me only. Thus you vanished
on the uncertain horizon.

Ma nessun guizzo di coda
scorgevo nei pozzi limosi,
nessun vento veniva col tuo indizio
dai colli monferrini.
Ho continuato il mio giorno
sempre spiando te, larva girino
frangia di rampicante francolino
gazzella zebù ocàpi
nuvola nera grandine
prima della vendemmia, ho spigolato
tra i filari inzuppati senza trovarti.
Ho proseguito fino a tardi
senza sapere che tre cassettine
—— SABBIA SODA SAPONE, la piccionaia
da cui partì il tuo volo: da una cucina, ——
si sarebbero aperte per me solo.
Così sparisti nell'orizzonte incerto.

In "Da un lago svizzero" the evocation of the past brings in its train the sharply outlined features and qualities of the woman loved: "your open life, bitter, and atrociously / fragile, yet strong [tua vita aperta, amara, / atrocemente fragile e pur forte]." And yet the poet is not clear as to whether what shines in the dark is she herself or merely a reflex of his own imagination. This perplexity contributes to the lyric depth of the poem, which culminates in the second stanza:

Is it you who are gleaming in the dark?
Within that pulsating furrow,
in a red-hot track, brisk on the trail

of your light predatory paw
(a mark invisible as a star)
I, a foreigner, plunge still;
and a black duck flying from the depth
of a lake shows me the path
to the new fire, and burns itself.

Sei tu che brilli al buio? Entro quel solco
pulsante, in una pista arrevontata,
àlacre sulla traccia del tuo lieve
zampetto di predace (un'orma quasi
invisibile, a stella) io, straniero,
ancora piombo; e a volo alzata un'anitra
nera, dal fondolago, fino al nuovo
incendio mi fa strada, per bruciarsi.

"Anniversario" closes *Madrigali privati*. The tragedy of the war that engulfed the poet and the woman loved has acted upon him as a chastening influence, enabling him to realize the ethical and spiritual dimension of love:

A flame burned long; on your roof,
on mine, I saw horror overflow.
A young stem, you grew, and in the truce's
light breeze I watched your plumage.

I'm on my knees: the gift
I dreamed not for me but
for everyone belongs to me only,
God divided from men, from the clotted
blood on the high branches, on the fruit.

Arse a lungo una vampa; sul tuo tetto,
sul mio, vidi l'orrore traboccare.
Giovane stelo tu crescevi; e io al rezzo
delle tregue spiavo il tuo piumare.

Resto in ginocchio: il dono che sognavo
non per me ma per tutti
appartiene a me solo, Dio diviso
dagli uomini, dal sangue raggrumato
sui rami alti, sui frutti.

The seventh and last section of *La bufera* is called *Conclusioni provvisorie*, and it consists of the two well-known poems "Piccolo testamento" and "Il sogno del prigioniero." They sum up Montale's quest for spiritual identity and for stoic independence in the face of such a catastrophic challenge as that of World War II. However, whatever hope the poet might cherish, or whatever faith he might profess, it is, he tells us in "Piccolo testamento," certainly not that of "the light of the church or the workshop / that may nourish a black or red cleric"—a typically Montalian way of referring to the two reigning creeds of Catholicism and communism in Italy. For his is "a faith that was hard fought for [una fede che fu combattuta]," and a hope "that burnt more slowly / than a hard log in the fireplace [che bruciò più lenta / di un duro ceppo nel focolare]." Thus while attempting, as it were, a moral and philosophical stock-taking of what his own life has meant to him ond how, through all the vicissitudes of the war, he has been able to maintain his belief in himself and his sense of pride, he sums up the only kind of testament he can possibly leave behind him—a testament based on the philosophical realization that "a story lasts only in ashes / and persistence is merely extinction [una storia non dura che nelle cenere / e persistenza è solo l'estinzione]." And it is this faith which the poet wants to leave as an inheritance for the woman loved—an inheritance which may stand her in good stead when with

> . . . every lamp extinguished,
> the sardana will become infernal
> and a shadowy Lucifer will descend
> on a prow on the Thames or Hudson
> or the Seine,
> fluttering his bituminous wings
> half-shorn through fatigue,
> to tell you: the hour has come.

> . . . spenta ogni lampada
> la sardana si farà infernale
> e un ombroso Lucifero scenderà su una prora
> del Tamigi, del Hudson, della Senna
> scuotendo l'ali di bitume semi-
> mozze dalla fatica, a dirti: è l'ora.

The poet's concern for the fate of the woman angel—a recurrent theme in Montale—and his conviction that the course he followed in his life, as well as the causes he espoused, were the only way he could have realized his humanity comes out with moving dignity in the last four lines:

> and pride was not an escape,
> nor was humility mean,
> and the tenuous ray that glimmered
> down there was not a spark from a match.

. . . l'orgoglio
non era fuga, l'umiltà non era
vile, il tenue bagliore strofinato
laggiù non era quello di un fiammifero.

"Il sogno del prigioniero," the last poem in *La bufera*, was written in 1954.
Stylistically and also to some extent thematically, it is linked with "Piccolo
testamento." The poet imagines himself to be a prisoner in the real as well as
in the moral and metaphysical sense of the term, a prisoner, that is, of the
historical and political contingencies of his age and country. To this theme
is added the theme of love and his dream of the woman loved is inseparably
bound up with his hope for liberation. Thus he keeps dreaming of both,
and it is these dreams which console him in his plight. The prison conditions
are described with such a wealth of concrete detail that one can interpret
the whole poem purely in terms of a real prison. But the symbolical and
allegorical significance becomes manifest in the way the prisoner transforms
the grim features of the prison into something ineffably sweet the moment he
imagines himself to be lying at the feet of the woman loved.

Few signs distinguish the dawn
from the night over here. In the days
of the battle my only wings
the zigzag flight of starlings
around watchtowers, a current of arctic
air, the head-guard's eye
peeping through the spy-hole,
the cracking sound of nuts,
an oily sizzling from the pits,
and real or imagined roasting-jacks—
but the straw is gold,
the wine-red lantern a hearth,
the moment I fall asleep
and imagine myself at your feet.

Albe e notti qui variano per pochi segni.

Lo zigzag delgi storni sui battifredi
nei giorni di battaglia, mie sole ali,
un filo d'aria polare,
l'occhio del capoguardia dallo spioncino,
crac di noci schiacciate, un oleoso
sfrigolìo dalle cave, girarrosti

> veri o supposti——ma la paglia è oro,
> la lanterna vinosa é focolare
> se dormendo mi credo ai tuoi piedi.

It is not only the straw and the prison lamp that undergo this romantic transformation, but also the morally oppressive atmosphere of the prison:

> The purge goes on for ever,
> and there's no reason why.
> They say that by retracting
> and signing one can save oneself
> from the slaughter of the geese, that he
> who accuses himself, but betrays
> and sells the others, rules the roost,
> instead of ending up in the pâté
> destined for the pestilential gods.

> La purga dura da sempre, senza un perchè.
> Dicono che chi abiura e sottoscrive
> può salvarsi da questo sterminio d'oche;
> che chi obiurga se stesso, ma tradisce
> e vende carne d'altri, afferra il mestolo
> anzi che terminare nel *pâté*
> destinato agl'Iddii pestilenziali.

Under such conditions not only does living lose its significance, but even dying is reduced to "the slaughter of the geese." The only way the prisoner can escape both moral and physical oppression is by letting his imagination gild the bleak walls of the prison and evoke rainbows on the horizon of cobwebs and petals stuck to the bars of the grating:

> Dull-witted, and sore from the prickly
> mattress I've become one
> with the moth that pulverizes
> my sole on the pavement,
> and with the changing kimonos of the light
> displayed to the dawn from the towers,
> I've smelt in the wind the burnt
> odor of bread from the ovens,
> and have looked around and evoked
> rainbows on the horizon of cobwebs
> and petals on the bars of the grating.

I got up, then fell again
at the point where a minute is a century—

and the blows and the footsteps continue,
and I still don't know whether
I shall be stuffer or stuffed at the banquet.
The waiting is long and my dream
of you is not yet finished.

Tardo di mente, piagato
dal pungente giaciglio mi sono fuso
col volo della tarma che la mia suola
sfarina sull'impiantito,
coi kimoni cangianti delle luci
sciorinate all'aurora dai torrioni,
ho annusato nel vento il bruciaticcio
dei buccellati dai forni,
mi son guardato attorno, ho suscitato
iridi su orizzonti di ragnateli
e petali sui tralicci delle inferriate,
mi sono alzato, sono ricaduto
nel fondo dove il secolo è il minuto—

e i colpi si ripetono ed i passi,
e ancora ignoro se sarò al festino
farcitore o farcito. L'attesa è lunga,
il mio sogno di te non è finito.

In conclusion, one can see why Montale, in a remark quoted at the beginning of this chapter, should have considered *La bufera e altro* his best book, insofar as "it vividly reflects my historical as well as my human condition." The years of World War II were also the years of Montale's maturity—he was in his late forties—and his emotional life, while at its most intense, was subjected to such pressures and dilemmas as those of the Fascist regime and the war. These necessarily must have had such a profound effect on him, as well as on his moral and poetic sensibility, as to charge whatever he wrote at that time with a special emotive significance. And this in turn must have colored, not only his creative reaction to his own experiences and impressions, but also his evaluation of them in moral and artistic terms. But whether because of all these things one can, in an objective and dispassionate appraisal, concur with Montale's own predilection for this book as his best, especially compared to *Ossi di seppia,* is another matter.

5: *Satura*

Broadly speaking, *Satura*,[1] Montale's latest volume consists of two distinct books: the poems collectively called *Xenia,* which Montale wrote on the death of his wife and which were published for the first time in book form, together with my verse translation by the Black Sparrow Press, (Los Angeles) and New Directions, (New York) in 1970; and the poems that fall outside this category and have not, for the most part, been published before. *Xenia* and related poems are love poems; the others are satirical or semiphilosophical verse. In the former a lyrical and autobiographical element prevails; in the latter a critical intelligence, in the widest and most flexible sense of the term, operates within the framework of a commentary on the *Zeitgeist.*

"Love," Robert Graves has said, "is the main theme and origin of true poems. . . . For me poetry implies a courtship of the Muse prolonged into a magical principle of living. . . . Rare and hidden correspondences between the soul of a poet and the Muse woman are what matter in poetry; they give him courage not to die while still alive." [2] As a love poet, Montale would surely agree with this. For whatever else he might be, he is essentially a love poet. His method of treating the theme of love, however, is more subtle and complex than one normally finds in the genre. In our own century, the best love poems in English have been written by Hardy, Yeats, Pound, and Graves. But none of these poets, with the possible exception of Graves, is regarded as primarily a love poet, as Montale is.

1. The fourth book of Montale's poems, *Satura* (1971) bears the same title as the group of five poems privately published in 150 copies at Verona in 1962. Of the five poems, only one, "Botta e risposta I," is included in the present book. For Montale, the title *Satura* represents "una mescolanza di generi diversi o vari tipi di poesia; una miscellanea." The satirical character of a great many poems in the volume is also suggested by this title. Regarding the title *Xenia,* Montale uses it in the sense of "offerta, dono." Cf. also Goethe's satirical epigrams entitled *Xenien,* written in collaboration with Schiller. More recently, Pound also used the title *Xenia* for a group of seven poems ("The Street in Soho," "The Cool Fingers of Science Delight Me," "A Song of Degrees," I-III, "Ité," and "Dum Capilolium Scandet") published in *Poetry* 3, no. 2 (November 1913).
2. Robert Graves, *Poetic Craft and Principle* (London: Cassells, 1967), pp. 116, 118, 134.

Although love existed as a theme or a source of inspiration in most of Montale's earlier poetry, in *Xenia* it is expressed with a degree of frankness and familiarity that has its own peculiarly personal tone and accent. The death in 1963 of Montale's wife Drusilla Tanzi—who was generally known as Mosca—transformed her into a "presence that is not to be put by," [3] into someone who has come to mean "perhaps more than before [Forse più di prima]." [4] While evoking the circumstances and episodes of their past life together, Montale relives them with an added intensity and crystallizes them in art. The dual realization that what he is evoking belongs irretrievably to the past and at the same time has come to acquire a new freshness and creative potency in memory, confers a hallucinatory and poignant significance even upon the most banal and prosaic details and incidents.

In terms of technique, style, and diction the result is a strikingly unique achievement for which there is no parallel in Italian poetry. Even in English poetry the only parallel that comes to mind are the poems Hardy wrote on the death of his first wife in 1912—poems that Montale himself has described as "one of the peaks of modern poetry." [5] However, the simplicity of tone in *Xenia* seldom borders on sentimentality, as it sometimes does in Hardy; there is little or no romantic aura about what is evoked; and instead of letting loose a flood of emotions and passions, Montale keeps them down to a remarkably low ebb.

Hardy's sense of bereavement and his recollection of the past were always weighed down by the feeling of what might have been; Montale's are enriched by the awareness of what was actually realized. Faced with the same challenge as Hardy and at about the same point in his life and career, Montale acquits himself with superb poise, dignity, and strength, both moral and artistic. The past and the present assume a new purpose and dimension, and a renewed hold on the poet.

Although these poems stand apart not only in the context of Italian poetry as a whole but also in relation to Montale's previous verse, they are in fact as essentially typical of him, both as a man and as an artist, as his previous verse. Using the word in the Goethian sense, Montale called the second volume of his verse *Le occasioni* (1939). *Xenia,* too, is written under the stress

---

3. The phrase is Wordsworth's. See "Ode on Intimations of Immortality."

4. *Xenia* II, "Riemersa da un'infinità di tempo."

5. In his preface to my Italian translation of Thomas Hardy's poems, entitled *Poesie di Thomas Hardy* (Parma: Guanda, 1968). "Le liriche che egli scrisse," says Montale of Hardy, "negli anni 1912–1913 in memoria della sua prima moglie, sono una delle vette della poesia moderna, e non di quella poesia vittoriana alla quale si sarebbe tentati di ascrivere un poeta già operante nel 1870." See F. R. Leavis's acute critique on *Xenia* and his comments on Hardy and Montale, in *The Listener,* 16 December 1971, London.

and inspiration of an occasion—an occasion that, in the singular intensity of
its tragic impact, is not to be compared with any other in the past. The
uniqueness of the occasion—and of the experience underlying it—engenders a
strikingly different tone, inflection, and pathos which have about them
something at once personal and impersonal. To have written on such a theme
and at the same time to have achieved the impersonality of art was a challenge
that only a mature artist like Montale could have met.

The poems offer a verse portrait of Mosca, who is seen as both dead and
alive, a portrait drawn not face to face but from various side angles. On the
poetic and psychological plane there is a vivid interfusion of what his wife
was when alive and what she has come to mean after her death. Although it
is the poet who is always talking, we feel that the presence of his dead wife
amounts to something more than a merely passive listener.

It is for the most part the apparently prosaic details and events of everyday life when Mosca was alive that come back to the poet's mind, throbbing
with a new life and intensity. The theme of love, however, is neither directly
nor indirectly stated. In this, too, the poems differ from Hardy's. There the
theme of love—whether realized or not—and the sense of regret concerning
what might have been are always to the fore. In Montale, on the other hand,
the feeling of deep emotional involvement rarely comes to the surface. Rather,
the apparently trivial details and associations that are evoked convey a sense
of something deeper which the poet has deliberately left unsaid. For instance,
it may be a visit to Paris, "At the Saint James's in Paris / I shall have to ask
for a single room / and they don't like single customers [Al Saint James
di Parigi dovrò chiedere / una camera 'singola'. Non amano / i clienti
spaiati]"; or "the fake Byzantium of your hotel in Venice [nella falsa bisanzio
del tuo albergo / veneziano]"; [6] "the logistic problems of Summer [i problemi
logistici d'Estate]"; [7] the oval portrait of his wife as a child, with disheveled
hair; [8] or the surgical details—"the poisonous antibiotics, / the rivet in your
thigh-bone [antibiotici / velenosi . . . chiodo del tuo femore]," [9] and Mosca's

6. *Xenia* I, "Al Saint James di Parigi dovrò chiedere."
7. In the original series of *Xenia* I, as it appeared in my translation in *London Magazine,*
June 1967. Later included in the book *Xenia* (New York: New Directions; and Los Angeles: Black Sparrow Press), poem number 12 was the one entitled "La primavera sbuca
col suo passo di talpa," and the present line, "the logistic problems of summer," comes
from there. In *Satura,* for personal reasons, this poem was omitted and replaced by the
poem "Il grillo di Strasburgo notturno col suo trapano"—a pity since "La primavera" is a
more beautiful lyric and in fact one of the most intense in either *Xenia* I or II. Similarly,
in this book Montale effected certain changes in the texts of the *Xenia* poems that, in my
opinion, are not always changes for the better. I therefore quote from the original text.
8. *Xenia* I, "Tuo fratello morì giovane."
9. Ibid., "La primavera sbuca col suo passo di talpa."

being "imprisoned among bandages and plasters [imprigionata tra le bende e i gessi]." [10]

Some of the images or situations recur in their symbolic as well as realistic significance in the poet's inner world: the "stuccos and pinchbecks [i similori e gli stucchi]" at the Hotel Danieli in Venice; [11] for instance, journeys with the "connections, bookings, traps [le coincidenze, le prenota-zioni, / le trappole]"; [12] the image of Mosca's brother Silvio's music being submerged by the flood at Florence; [13] or Mosca's father watching the poet "From morning till evening / from the miniature effigy on the wall [da una minieffigie / (mi sorveglia) dal muro sera e mattina]." [14]

The psychological and poetic significance of these glimpses from the past lies in their bringing out, not so much the nature of the relationship between the poet and Mosca, as the individual traits of Mosca's own personality and what they meant and mean to Montale. Such traits are sometimes evoked "through a single gesture or habit [pure in un solo gesto o un'abitudine]," [15] or are summed up through the attitude of friends and acquaintances toward her—friends and acquaintances who thought of her as "only a myopic creature lost / in the babble of high society [un insetto miope / smarrito nel blabla / dell'alta società]." But for Montale

> How ingenuous of those clever people
> not to know it was they
> who were your laughing-stock,
> that you could see them even in the dark,
> and startle them with your infallible flair
> and with your bat's radar.[16]

> . . . Erano ingenui
> quei furbi e non sapevano
> di essere loro il tuo zimbello:
> di esser visti anche al buio e squinternati
> dal tuo fiuto infallibile, dal tuo
> radar di pipistrello.

Thus it is not merely affection and a sense of gratitude, but also mutual understanding and regard that bound the poet and Mosca together. Even

10. Ibid., "Dicono che la mia."
11. *Xenia* II, "L'abbiamo rimpianto a lungo l'infilascarpe."
12. Ibid., "Ho sceso, dandoti il braccio."
13. Ibid., "L'alluvione ha sommerso."
14. Ibid., "La morte non ti riguardava."
15. *Xenia* I, "Al Saint James di Parigi."
16. Ibid., "Non ho mai capito se io fossi."

Mosca's eccentric friends and acquaintances, for instance the lawyer from Klagenfurt "who sends us greetings / and who was supposed to call on us [quello che manda gli auguri. / Doveva venirci a trovare]," [17] who could not understand her and yet who enjoyed her friendship and had a mysterious feeling of attachment to her, indirectly bring out the inexplicable magnetism of her personality. The use of the present tense in "sends us greetings" delicately affirms the continuity between past and present despite Mosca's death. Another strange friend of Mosca's was Celia, the Philippine who, "reemerging from an infinity of time [Riemersa da un'infinità di tempo]," rings "from Manila or some other word / in the atlas [da Manila o da altra / parola dell'atlante]" to ask for news of her. When she asks if Mosca is no more, the poet gives the answer, "Perhaps more than before," [18] which has at once the edge and the delicacy of Montalian irony.

However, the copresence of Mosca before and after her death does not induce any feeling of nostalgic sentimentality, and this partly because there is no feeling of regret or bitterness in Montale, as there is in Hardy. The sense of what was lived and realized in the past gives his lyrics a haunting sense of pathos and tenderness, pride and resignation. All this comes out through a kaleidoscopic pattern of details and incidents which have an air of casualness about them. Take, for instance, the incident of the poet's having left behind a shoehorn in an elegant Venetian hotel:

> For a long time we missed the shoehorn,
> the rusty tin shoehorn that had always
> been with us. It seemed indecent
> to introduce such a hideous object
> among stuccos and pinchbecks.
> It must have been at the Danieli
> that I forgot to put it back in the suitcase
> or the bag. The waitress Hedia surely threw it
> into the Canalazzo. But how could I write
> that they should look for that trifling piece of tin?
> Ours was a prestige to be saved
> and Hedia the faithful had saved it.[19]

> L'abbiamo rimpianto a lungo l'infilascarpe,
> il cornetto di latta arrugginito ch'era
> sempre con noi. Pareva un'indecenza portare

---

17. *Xenia* II, "Spesso ti ricordavi (io poco)."
18. Ibid., "Riemersa da un'infinità di tempo."
19. Ibid., "L'abbiamo rimpianto a lungo l'infilascarpe."

tra i similori e gli stucchi un tale orrore.
Dev'essere al Danieli che ho scordato
di riporlo in valigia o nel sacchetto.
Hedia la cameriera lo buttò certo
nel Canalazzo. E come avrei potuto
scrivere che cercassero quel pezzaccio di latta?
C'era un prestigio (il nostro) da salvare
e Hedia, la fedele, l'aveva fatto.

Instead of giving vent to the feeling of love and loyalty between him and
Mosca, the poet lets the apparently banal incident of the shoehorn, which
has a symbolic significance like "the white ivory mouse" or "the ever-green
laurel in the kitchen" (in "Dora Markus), reenact the human and emotional
aspects of that bond in terms of concretely realized details of time, place, and
circumstance. The degree of prosaicness is thus a measure of the unexpressed
symbolism underlying what is recollected, as well as the mode of recollecting
it.

In another poem the scene is set in Portugal, which the poet visited along
with his wife. [20]

After a long search
I found you in a bar in Avenida
da Libertade; you didn't know
a word of Portuguese, or rather
just one word: Madeira.
And a glass of wine arrived with shrimps.

In the evening I was compared to the greatest
Lusitanians with unpronounceable names
and to Carducci in addition.
Not in the least impressed,
I saw you crying for laughter, hidden in a crowd
perhaps bored but reverent.[21]

Dopo lunghe ricerche
ti trovai in un bar dell'Avenida
da Libertade; non sapevi un'acca
di portoghese o meglio una parola
sola: Madeira. E venne il bicchierino
con un contorno di aragostine.

20. See Montale's article "Portogallo" in *Fuori di casa*.
21. *Xenia* II, "Dopo lunghe ricerche."

La sera fui paragonato ai massimi
lusitani dai nomi impronunciabili
e al Carducci in aggiunta.
Per nulla impressionata io ti vedevo piangere
dal ridere nascosta in una folla
forse annoiata ma compunta.

The deeper the affinity and understanding between the poet and Mosca, the more he distances and depersonalizes them by using details and circumstances that have an autonomy and relevance of their own, and that at the same time form a weft, as it were, through which personal emotions and sentiments seldom break out:

The hawks
were always too far from your sight,
and you seldom saw them at close range.
One at Étretat watching
its young ones' clumsy flights.
Two others in Greece on the road to Delphi,
a mere scuffle of soft plumes and two
young, bold, harmless beaks.

You liked life torn to shreds,
life breaking out from
its unbearable weft.[22]

I falchi
sempre troppo lontani dal tuo sguardo
raramente li hai visti davvicino.
Uno a Étretat che sorvegliava i goffi
voli dei suoi bambini.
Due altri in Grecia, sulla via di Delfi,
una zuffa di piume soffici, due becchi giovani
arditi e inoffensivi.

Ti piaceva la vita fatta a pezzi,
quella che rompe dal suo insopportabile
ordito.

Rarely do the emotional tone and coloring come to the fore and contrast with the prosaicness and impersonality of the general tenor and substance of the

22. Ibid., "I falchi sempre troppo lontani." The same detail is also mentioned in Montale's article "Sulla via scara" (*Fuori di casa*).

poem, as for instance when, following up the details of Mosca's father's daguerreotype and his pedigree and ancestral data, the poet strikes an emotional chord at the end:

> . . . And so what? Yet the fact
> remains that something happened, perhaps a trifle
> which is everything.[23]

> . . . E allora? Eppure resta
> che qualcosa è accaduto, forse un niente
> che è tutto.

A frank and transparently lyrical tone, however, which all but does away with the objective correlative device is to be found in some of the most touching and beautiful of the *Xenia* poems. For instance, in the following:

> Spring comes out at the pace of a mole.
> I shall hear you talk no more
> of the poisonous antibiotics,
> the rivet in your thigh-bone,
> or the patrimony that shrewd unnamed
> rat nibbled away.

> Spring advances with its thick mists,
> its long light days and unbearable hours.
> No longer shall I hear you struggle
> with the regurgitation of time
> or of phantoms
> or of the logistic problems of summer.[24]

> La primavera sbuca col suo passo di talpa.
> Non ti sentirò più parlare di antibiotici
> velenosi, del chiodo del tuo femore,
> dei beni di fortuna che t'ha un occhiuto omissis
> spennacchiati.

> La primavera avanza con le sue nebbie grasse,
> con le sue luci lunghe, le sue ore insopportabili.
> Non ti sentirò più lottare col rigurgito
> del tempo, dei fantasmi, dei problemi logistici
> dell'Estate.

---

23. Ibid., "Ho appeso nella mia stanza il dagherròtipo."
24. "La primavera sbuca col suo passo di talpa."

In such lyrics autobiographical realism and psychological intimacy of detail
serve to heighten the intensity of bereavement and at the same time to focus
the immediacy of the impact it makes on him. It revives in him the old
existential problems and preoccupations, in describing which he displays a
firm and subtle grasp of the concrete and the abstract blending into each
other—"the poisonous antibiotics, / the rivet in your thigh-bone," "the regurgi-
tation of time / and of phantoms," and "the logistic problems of summer."
Another such poem is the following:

> With my arm in yours I've descended at least a million stairs,
> and now that you are no more, a void opens at each step.
>
> Even so our long journey has been brief.
> Mine continues still, though I've no more use
> for connections, bookings, traps,
> and the disenchantment of him who believes
> that the real is what one sees.
>
> I have descended millions of stairs with my arm in yours,
> not, of course, that perhaps with four eyes one might see better,
> but because I knew
> that even though so bedimmed
> yours were the only true eyes.[25]

> Ho sceso, dandoti il braccio, almeno un milione di scale
> e ora che non ci sei è il vuoto ad ogni gradino.
> Anche così è stato breve il nostro lungo viaggio.
> Il mio dura tuttora, nè più mi occorrono
> le coincidenze, le prenotazioni,
> le trappole, gli scorni di chi crede
> che la realtà sia quella che si vede.
>
> Ho sceso milioni di scale dandoti il braccio
> non già perchè con quattr'occhi forse si vede di più.
> Con te le ho scese perchè sapevo che di noi due
> le sole vere pupille, sebbene tanto offuscate,
> erano le tue.

The subtle and almost imperceptible interpenetration of the literal and the
metaphorical elements in the concept of the journey with its "connections,"
"bookings," and "traps" leads the poet to claim an immunity from the "dis-
enchantment of him who believes / that the real is what one sees." Thus,

25. *Xenia* II, "Ho sceso, dandoti il braccio."

while indicating that his poetry is not a poetry of religious or philosophical commitment, he strikes a note of philosophical maturity which is fully vindicated in terms of lyric art, with Mosca's image serving as a focal point of reference and realization:

> They say that mine
> is poetry of nonbelonging.
> But if it was yours, it was someone's:
> not your form any more but your essence.
> They say that poetry at its highest
> glorifies the Whole in its flight
> and deny
> that the tortoise is swifter than lightning.
> You alone knew
> that motion is not different from stillness,
> that the void is the same as fullness,
> that the clearest sky is but
> the most diffused of clouds.
> Thus I understand better your long journey
> imprisoned among bandages and plasters.
> Yet it gives me no rest to know
> that alone or together
> we are one.[26]

> Dicono che la mia
> sia una poesia d'inappartenenza.
> Ma s'era tua era di qualcuno:
> era di te non più forma ma essenza.
> Dicono che la poesia al suo culmine
> magnifica il Tutto in fuga,
> negano che la testuggine
> sia più veloce del fulmine.
> Tu sola sapevi che il moto
> non è diverso dalla stasi,
> che il vuoto è il pieno e il sereno
> è la più diffusa delle nubi.
> Così meglio intendo il tuo lungo viaggio
> imprigionata tra le bende e i gessi.
> Eppure non mi dà riposo
> sapere che in uno o in due noi siamo una sola cosa.

26. *Xenia* I, "Dicono che la mia."

The sense of oneness, while being inseparable from the sense of what he owed
to her ("my courage was the first / of your gifts and perhaps you didn't
know it [il mio coraggio fu il primo / dei tuoi prestiti e forse non l'hai
saputo]," he says in "L'alluvione ha sommerso"), was something more than
that. It sprang from a peculiar kind of affinity with Mosca which even he
could not always grasp or analyze:

Death didn't concern you.
Your dogs had also died, and the doctor
for the insane, known as crazy uncle,
your mother with her "speciality"
of rice and frogs—a Milanese triumph—
and your father who now watches me from morning till evening,
from a miniature effigy on the wall.
Yet death didn't concern you.

It was I who would go to the funerals,
hidden in a taxi and staying aloof
to avoid tears and bother.
Even life mattered little to you,
with its fairs of vanity and greed,
and the universal gangrenes that turn
men into wolves, still less.

A *tabula rasa*—except
that a point there was, though beyond my grasp,
and this point *did* concern you.[27]

La morte non ti riguardava.
Anche i tuoi cani erano morti, anche
il medico dei pazzi detto lo zio demente,
anche tua madre e la sua "specialità"
di riso e rane, trionfo meneghino;
e anche tuo padre che da una minieffigie
mi sorveglia dal muro sera e mattina.
Malgrado ciò la morte non ti riguardava.

Ai funerali dovevo andare io,
nascosto in un tassì, restandone lontano
per evitare lacrime e fastidi. E neppure
t'importava la vita e le sue fiere
di vanità e ingordige e tanto meno le

27. *Xenia* II, "La morte non ti riguardava."

cancrene universali che trasformano
gli uomini in lupi.

Una tabula rasa; se non fosse
che un punto c'era, per me incomprensibile,
e questo punto *ti riguardava.*

The point may have been beyond the poet's grasp, but it somehow served to forge a lifelong bond between them, giving a pattern and a meaning to what they shared in suffering and enjoyment.

Another poem rich in evocativeness as well as in autobiographical details is the one inspired by the disastrous 1966 flood in Florence. Montale lived in Florence for about twenty years before he came to settle in Milan, and it was there that he met Mosca. When they both moved to Milan in 1948, he had to leave part of his belongings (including books and furniture) with his Florentine friends. This is how he refers to the damage done to his belongings by the flood, thereby making what is personal impersonal, and vice versa:

> The flood has submerged
> the muddle of furniture, papers, paintings,
> crammed in a double-locked cellar.
> Perhaps the red morocco volumes
> fought blindly and Du Bos's
> interminable dedications,
> the wax seal with Ezra's beard,
> Alain's *Valéry,* the original
> of the *Canti Orfici,* some shaving brushes,
> and a thousand trifles and all
> your brother Silvio's music.
> Ten or twelve days under the atrocious
> bite of oil-dregs and naphtha. I am sure
> they strove hard before losing their identity.
> I too am encrusted up to the neck,
> since my personal status has been doubtful from the outset.
> It isn't mud has besieged me, but the events
> of an incredible reality which was never believed.
> In the face of these my courage was the first
> of your gifts and perhaps you didn't know it.[28]

> L'alluvione ha sommerso il pack dei mobili,
> delle carte, dei quadri che stipavano

28. Ibid., "L'alluvione ha sommerso."

un sotterraneo chiuso a doppio lucchetto.
Forse hanno ciecamente lottato i marocchini
rossi, le sterminate dediche di Du Bos,
il timbro a ceralacca con la barba di Ezra,
il Valéry di Alain, l'originale
dei Canti Orfici — e poi qualche pennello
da barba, mille cianfrusaglie e tutte
le musiche di tuo fratello Silvio.
Dieci, dodici giorni sotto un'atroce morsura
di morchia e nafta. Certo hanno lottato
tanto prima di perdere la loro identità.
Anch'io sono incrostato fino al collo se il mio
stato civile fu dubbio fin dall'inizio.
Non torba m'ha assediato, ma gli eventi
di una realtà incredibile e mai creduta.
Di fronte ad essi il mio coraggio fu il primo
dei tuoi prestiti e forse non l'hai saputo.

Thus while each detail, concept, or object represents a link with the past, it also stands out as a poetically and pictorially realized autonomous entity.

Xenia marks a special phase in Montale's career. When he wrote it the poet was seventy; the most fertile period of his creative life (though in Montale's case fertility did not really mean prolificity) and of his technical and linguistic innovations lay in the past. His status as a major twentieth-century Italian poet —in the opinion of some the greatest since Leopardi—had been amply vindicated by the first three volumes of his verse and by the impact they made on contemporary Italian poetry. And now with Mosca's death he was faced with the greatest challenge in his creative as well as personal life. The floods of memory and recollection were unloosed. The past acquired a new dimension and a new vitality and almost completely overshadowed the present. He found himself, both poetically and existentially speaking, in a situation where he could say with Hardy that "the past is all to him." [29] No wonder, then, that the language of recollection in these poems is strictly and artlessly *that* and nothing more or less. What he recollects and what it means to him undergoes as little transformation—emotional, artistic or moral—as possible. And since Mosca's posthumous presence is always there in the form of a mute visitor or interlocutor, the nature of the communion between them takes the form of a monologue—a monologue with a poetically convincing intimacy of tone.

There are also some other poems in *Satura* which belong to the *Xenia*

29. Thomas Hardy, "The Haunter" (*Satires of Circumstance*).

group in terms of style, technique, and ethos. The more important among
them are "Il tu," "Lettera," "Gli ultimi spari," "Le revenant,' "La belle dame
sans merci," "A tarda notte," "L'Arno a Rovezzano," "Gli uomini che si
voltano," "Ex voto," the series of eight lyrics grouped under the title *Dopo
una fuga,* "Il primo gennaio," and "L'Altro." In the first, the poet answers
those critics who wonder what particular person the use of "tu" refers to and
what bearing the question of identity may have on the interpretation of his
poetry. He compares the person referred to as "tu" with a bird which

> caught in the net doesn't know
> if it's he or if it's one
> of his many duplicates.

> . . . preso nel paretaio
> non sa se lui sia lui o uno dei troppi
> suoi duplicati.

In "Lettera," through a rich medley of personal names and references and a
subtle blend of lyricism and irony—

> Respighi's widow
> the heirs of Toscanini,
> Tetrazzini's pall-bearer, a namesake
> of Malpighi's, Ramerrez-Martinelli
> with his nimbus of silver hair,
> and Tullio Carminati,
> a glory for some surviving initiate—

> la vedova di Respighi, le eredi di Toscanini,
> un necroforo della Tetrazzini, un omonimo
> di Malpighi, Ramerrez-Martinelli,
> nube d'argento, e Tullio Carminati,
> una gloria per qualche superstite iniziato—

he resuscitates the past and relives it with a nostalgic pathos and intensity,
as he recalls a particular trait or aspect of Mosca's personality. In "Gli ultimi
spari," while recalling his Florentine years, he exploits the literary and autobiographical circumstance of his wife's taking English lessons from James
Joyce's brother Stanislaus, who helped them settle on "hellish fly" as a more
appropriate nickname for her than either "midge" or "fly," which were
nicknames "not always consonant / with your sweetly tenacious nature [non
sempre pertinenti al tuo carattere / dolcemente tenace]."

In "Le revenant," while going through an old clandestine periodical "with faces and pictures of artists / 'nipped in the bud' at the outset / of the century [volti / e pitture di artisi 'stroncati in boccio' / ai primi del 900]," the poet recognizes a painter who had paid court to his wife, and he wonders

> why the threads of the two
> spools became so entangled;
> and if that phantasm's not
> the lost original and I
> its facsimile.

> . . . perchè i fili di due rocchetti
> si sono tanto imbrogliati; e se non sia quel fantasma
> l'autentico smarrito e il suo facsimile io.

One of the most intense moments of recollection in the Montalian *Canzoniere,* as one might call *Xenia* and related poems, is to be found in "La belle dame sans merci," which by virtue of its evocative realism of detail, may be compared with some of the best *Mottetti:*

> To be sure the cantonal seagulls
> must have waited in vain
> for the crumbs I used to throw
> on your balcony, that you might
> hear their cries even in sleep.

> Today no one turns up at the appointment,
> our breakfast is frozen among piles
> of my useless books and your knick-knacks:
> calendars, cases, phials,
> and creams.

> Your amazing face lingers still,
> carved against the morning's chalky
> background; but a life without wings
> can't reach it and its suffocated fire
> is nothing but the flash of a lighter.

> Certo i gabbiani cantonali hanno atteso invano
> le briciole di pane che io gettavo
> sul tuo balcone perchè tu sentissi
> anche chiusa nel sonno le loro strida.

> Oggi manchiamo all'appuntamento tutti e due
> e il nostro breakfast gela tra cataste

per me di libri inutili e per te di reliquie
che non so: calendari, astucci, fiale e creme.

Stupefacente il tuo volto s'ostina ancora, stagliato
sui fondali di calce del mattino;
ma una vita senz'ali non lo raggiunge e il suo fuoco
soffocato è il bagliore dell'accendìno.

In "A tarda notte" a wrong telephone call serves as an incentive for poetic ingeniousness. The poet finds himself in Venice, conversing with an unknown woman in Vancouver, while he was expecting a call from Milan. At first he is taken aback by the incident, but he is soon intrigued and wants the misunderstanding to continue. The underlying lyricism comes out through the semifacetious and semi-ironical concern about who is going to pay the bill for this long-distance call:

> Nor did we ever know
> who would foot the bill.
> . . . .
> Now after all these years
> the other voice has forgotten
> and perhaps thinks I'm dead. I think
> it's she who is dead, but she was
> alive for a second at least,
> and did not know it.
>
> . . . Nè sapemmo mai
> su quali spalle poi gravasse il prezzo
> di quel miracolo.
> . . . .
> Ormai dopo tanti anni l'altra voce
> non lo rammenta e forse mi crede morto.
> Io credo che lo sia lei. Fu viva almeno un attimo
> e non se n'è mai accorta.

In "L'Arno a Rovezzano" the particularized familiarity of geographical and topographical detail subtly enriches the underlying pathos of what is recalled years after the woman loved has ceased to be:

> . . . when I'd sing to you on the phone:
> "toi qui fais l'endormie"
> amidst immoderate peals of laughter.
> Your house was a lamp seen from

the train, leaning on the Arno
like the Judas tree that wanted to protect it.
Perhaps it's still there, or there
only in ruins. Full of insects,
you would tell me, and quite uninhabitable.
Other comforts are our lot now, other
discomforts.

da quando ti cantavo al telefono "tu
che fai l'addormentata" col triplice cachinno.
La tua casa era un lampo visto dal treno. Curva
sull'Arno come l'albero di Giuda
che voleva proteggerla. Forse c'è ancora o
non è che una rovina. Tutta piena,
mi dicevi, di insetti, inabitabile.
Altro comfort fa per noi ora, altro
sconforto.

Thus the delicate balance between the poignant evocation of the past and the
realization of the blankness of the present is achieved through the symbolically
suggestive contrast between the house in ruins and the perpetual continuity
of the Arno.

"Gli uomini che si voltano" is linked with "Forse un mattino andando"
(*Ossi di seppia*) insofar as it deals with men who do turn around, whereas the
poem in *Ossi di seppia* finds Montale going quietly among men who do not.[30]
This poem also links itself with some of the *Mottetti*—especially "Non
recidere forbice"—by virtue of its dealing with the corrosion of the memory
of the dead person compared, with an almost dramatic efficacy, to the
scraping of glass-paper:

Maybe
you no longer are what you have been
and rightly so. The glass-paper
has scraped us too, and the line that was left
gets thinner.
Yet something was written on the pages of our life.
To hold them up against the light is to magnify that sign,
form a hieroglyph bigger than the diadem
that used to dazzle me.

---

30. "Ma sarà troppo tardi; ed io me n'andrò zitto / tra gli uomini che non si voltano, col
mio segreto" ("Forse un mattino andando").

No more shall I see you emerge
from the hovercraft or from the seaweed's depth
—skindiver amidst muddy rapids—
to give meaning to the living. You would walk
down Woolworth's escalator,
the only living person among
masked corpses, and wouldn't even ask
if it was an encounter, choice, or message,
and which of us two was the bull's-eye
they shoot at in the fairground booths.
Nor would I ask, since
I have seen for an instant,
and that's enough for those walking in a crowd.
as it happens with us, if we are still alive,
or thought we were. All's uncertain.[31]

Probabilmente
non sei più chi sei stata
ed è giusto che così sia.
Anche noi ha raschiato la carta a vetro
e assottiglia la linea che v'era rimasta.
Pure qualcosa fu scritto
sui fogli della nostra vita.
Metterli controluce è ingigantire quel segno,
formare un geroglifico più grande del diadema
che mi accecava.
Non apparirai più dal portello
dell'aliscafo o da fondali d'alghe,
sommozzatrice di fangose rapide
per dare un senso ai vivi. Scenderai
sui gradini automatici dei templi di Mercurio,
tra cadaveri in maschera,
tu, la sola vivente,

31. Before it was included in *Satura,* or indeed was published anywhere, this poem appeared in my English translation in the *Times Literary Supplement* (January 23, 1969), with the title "In Retrospect." Montale has revised the text of this poem here and there. My translation is of the original version given here, which is, in my opinion, better than the revised version. There are other similar variants in *Satura* in respect of the Italian text that had either been published in periodicals such as *Strumenti critici* or had never been published before my translation and text appeared in the New Directions and Black Sparrow volume of 1970.

> e non ti chiederai
> se fu incontro, fu scelta, fu comunicazione
> e chi di noi fosse il centro
> a cui si tira con l'arco nel baraccone.
> Non me lo chiedo neanch'io. Sono colui
> che ha veduto un istante e tanto basta
> a chi cammina incolonnato come ora
> accade a noi se siamo ancora vivi
> o se credemmo di esserlo. Tutto rimane incerto.

But what they had both actually lived through and experienced was so rich that even today, when recalled, it forms "a hieroglyph bigger than the diadem / that used to dazzle me," and makes the poet look upon her as "the only living person among / masked corpses" and capable of "giving meaning to the living" even after death.

In "Ex voto" the woman loved is dead, the very fact of her physical absence acts, as it were, as a leaven for the spirit's affinities, which may "fall short of words and gestures, / but diffuse like magnetism." Through a technical and prosodic *tour de force* and a series of creatively pregnant antitheses and paradoxes, the poet succeeds in capturing what is at once elusive and unanalyzable, namely, the magic and essence of the woman loved:

> It happens
> that the spirit's affinity may
> fall short of words and gestures,
> but diffuse like magnetism—something
> rare, but it happens.
>
> It may well be
> that only distance and oblivion
> are real, that the dry leaf is
> more real than a green shoot. This
> and much more may well be.
>
> I quite understand
> your obstinate wish to be always
> absent, for only thus
> can your magic be revealed. Your innumerable tricks
> I quite understand.
>
> I will
> insist on looking for you in the twig, never

in the full-grown tree; in the void
but not in fullness; in that
which would even resist the drill.

It was, or it wasn't
the will of the gods who preside
on your far-off hearth—strange, multiform,
multispirited pets;
perhaps it was as it seemed to me,
or it wasn't.

I do not know
if my nonexistence soothes
your destiny, or if yours
overflows mine, if innocence is a fault,
or if one perceives on the threshold of your home.
All this about you, about me,
I know, and I do not know.

Accade
che le affinità d'anima non giungano
ai gesti e alle parole ma rimangano
effuse come un magnetismo. È raro
ma accade.

Può darsi
che sia vera soltanto la lontananza,
vero l'oblio, vera la foglia secca
più del fresco germoglio. Tanto e altro
può darsi o dirsi.

Comprendo
la tua caparbia volontà di essere sempre assente
perchè solo così si manifesta
la tua magia. Innumeri le astuzie
che intendo.

Insisto
nel ricercarti nel fuscello e mai
nell'albero spiegato, mai nel pieno, sempre
nel vuoto: in quello che anche al trapano
resiste.

Era o non era
la volontà dei numi che presidiano

il tuo lontano focolare, strani
multiformi multanimi animali domestici;
fors'era così come mi pareva
o non era.

Ignoro
se la mia inesistenza appaga il tuo destino,
se la tua colma il mio che ne trabocca,
se l'innocenza è una colpa oppure
si coglie sulla soglia dei tuoi lari. Di me,
di te tutto conosco, tutto
ignoro.

Dopo una fuga, a series of eight poems, revolves around the same theme as *Xenia,* namely the death of the woman loved, who continues to have a second life in the poet's recollection and imagination. In *Xenia,* however, the woman in question was Montale's wife, whereas in *Dopo una fuga* she doesn't have any specific identity. And although the ethos and emotional grip of the situation on the poet are more or less the same in these two series, they are rendered by means of a more subtle and complex symbolism. Moreover, there is something too consciously contrived about the way in which the various details, circumstances, and episodes are brought together in an interplay of response, recollection, and recognition. Thus while this series gains in terms of conceptual, intellectual, and even verbal subtlety and ingenuity, it loses that quality of spontaneous yet delicately controlled evocativeness of moral and emotional pathos which characterizes *Xenia.* In other words, it is lacking in that effortless ease and naturalness which *Xenia* has and which was, to a large extent, the result of the immediacy of the impact that his wife's death made on Montale. Actually, in this case, as in the case of some motets and other poems in *Le occasioni* and *La bufera,* one might even quote Montale's own dictum at his own expense—namely, that a poet "needn't write a series of poems when a single poem can exhaust a particular psychological situation." For *Dopo una fuga* does deal with "a particular psychological situation" which *Xenia* had already exhausted.

To affirm this, however, is not to detract from the artistic and technical merit of *Dopo una fuga,* but merely to emphasize that, so far as the psychological or emotional aspect is concerned, it doesn't register any signficant moral or technical development; nor does it cover any new ground. Nevertheless, to maintain that some of the lyrics—for instance "C'erano le betulle," "Mentre ti penso si staccano," "Quando si giunse al borgo," "Non posso respirare se sei lontana"—compare favorably with the most intense and accomplished lyrics in *Xenia,* is not to overestimate their worth. In "C'erano le betulle," the poet recalls a situation similar to the one he had already dealt with in some of the *Mottetti,* the woman loved recovering in a Swiss sanatorium, and recalls the essence of the circumstance by means of details that are dexterously presented: "a cricket / housed in an annex of the clinic" or "an album of exotic birds" lying on the table along with the telephone and some chocolates:

> Thick birches sheltered the sanatorium
> where someone suffering from too much
> love of life, and hovering
> between all and nothing
> was feeling bored. A cricket
> housed in an annex of the clinic
> chirped along with the cuckoo
> that you had heard in Indonesia
> at lesser expense.
> There were these birches, a Swiss nurse,
> three or four madmen in the courtyard,
> an album of exotic birds,
> the telephone, and some chocolates on the table.
> And of course I too was there
> with other bores to give you
> the solace which you could have given us
> in abundance, if we had had eyes.
> I had.

> C'erano le betulle, folte, per nascondere
> il sanatorio dove una malata
> per troppo amore della vita, in bilico
> tra il tutto e il nulla si annoiava.
> Cantava un grillo perfettamente incluso
> nella progettazione clinica
> insieme col cucù da te già udito
> in Indonesia a minore prezzo.
> C'erano le betulle, un'infermiera svizzera,
> tre o quattro mentecatti nel cortile,
> sul tavolino un album di uccelli esotici,
> il telefono e qualche cioccolatino.
> E c'ero anch'io, naturalmente, e altri
> seccatori per darti quel conforto

che tu potevi distribuirci a josa
solo che avessimo gli occhi. Io li avevo.

In "Mentre ti penso" the urgency of time that is wasted in the absence of the
woman loved makes its impact through a characteristically bizarre juxtaposition of such objects and details as "lentisks, blackberries, streams / the croak-
ing of frogs," etc., and "the desire to retrace the years / and beat fleet-footed
Time":

> While I think of you
> the leaves of the calendar rapidly
> fall off. The weather this morning
> is bad and Time is even worse.
> The best of you exploded
> among lentisks, blackberries, streams,
> the croaking of frogs and the short
> flights of stilt-birds unknown to me
> (the Cavaliers of Italy, as they call them!),
> and I lay sleepless amidst
> the moldy smell of books and ledgers.
> The worst of me also exploded:
> the desire to retrace the years
> and beat fleet-footed Time
> with a thousand clever tricks.
> They say that I believe in nothing
> if not in miracles.
> I don't know what you believe
> and whether you believe in yourself
> or let others see and create you.
> But this is something more than human,
> it's the privilege of him who sustains
> the world and doesn't know it.

> Mentre ti penso si staccano
> veloci i fogli del calendario. Brutto
> stamani il tempo e anche più pestifero
> il Tempo. Di te il meglio
> esplose tra lentischi rovi rivi
> gracidìo di ranocchi voli brevi
> di trampolieri a me ignoti (i Cavalieri
> d'Italia, figuriamoci!) e io dormivo

insonne tra le muffe dei libri e dei brogliacci.
Di me esplose anche il pessimo: la voglia
di risalire gli anni, di sconfiggere
il pièveloce Crono con mille astuzie.
Si dice ch'io non creda a nulla, se non ai miracoli.
Ignoro che cosa credi tu, se in te stessa oppure
lasci che altri ti vedano e ti creino.
Ma questo è più che umano, è il privilegio
di chi sostiene il mondo senza conoscerlo.

"Quando si giunse al borgo" achieves a remarkably smooth and convincing synthesis of historical, political, and literary elements and allusions that form a lyrically effective pattern, with a touch of irony:

On reaching Sant'Anna, the village
of the Nazi massacre, on which
a peak suddenly gravitates, I saw you
climb to the top like a roebuck
in the company of a slender Polish woman,
and a water-rat, your guide, more like
an ibex than either of you.
I waited five hours in the square,
counting the dead on the stele,
and including myself among them
ad honorem for a joke.
In the evening the outboard motor
jolted us to Burlamacca,
a dam of excrement on which
a pseudo oil-mill pours out
boiling water. Perhaps
a preview of hell. The Burlamacchi,
and the Caponsacchi . . . spectres
of heresy and of unreadable poems.
Poetry and the sewer,
two problems that can never be separated
(but I didn't tell you about this).

Quando si giunse al borgo del massacro nazista,
Sant'Anna, su cui gravita un picco abrupto
ti vidi arrampicarti come un capriolo
fino alla cima accanto a un'esile polacca
e al ratto d'acqua, tua guida, il più stambecco di tutti.
Io fermo per cinque ore sulla piazza

enumerando i morti sulla stele, mettendomici
dentro ad honorem ridicolmente. A sera
ci trasportò a sobbalzi il fuoribordo
dentro la Burlamacca,
una chiusa di sterco su cui scarica
acqua bollente un pseudo oleificio.
Forse è l'avanspettacolo dell'inferno.
I Burlamacchi, i Caponsacchi.... spettri
di eresie, di illeggibili poemi.
La poesia e la fogna, due problemi
mai disgiunti (ma non te ne parlai).

Another poem where literary allusions and echoes are interwoven against a
lyrical background is "Non posso respirare":

I cannot breathe if you are far away.
Thus Keats to Fanny Brawne whom
he rescued from oblivion.
It's strange—*si parva licet*—
that I cannot say the same.
I can breathe much better
if you are away. Nearness only
brings back memories of events:
but not as they happened, foreseen
by us as future smelling-salts,
if needed, or aromatic vinegar
—(now nobody faints for trifles,
like a broken heart). It's the mass
of facts on which the impact falls,
and the present being a corpse,
the planking doesn't hold.
I don't want to discuss it with you,
for I am sure that if you read me
you'd know that you have given me
the necessary propellant, and the rest
(so long as it *isn't* silence)
doesn't count.

Non posso respirare se sei lontana.
Così scriveva Keats a Fanny Brawne
da lui tolta dall'ombra. È strano che il mio caso
si parva licet sia diverso. Posso

respirare assai meglio se ti allontani.
La vicinanza ci riporta eventi
da ricordare: ma non quali accaddero,
preveduti da noi come futuri
sali da fiuto, ove occorresse, o aceto
dei sette ladri (ora nessuno sviene
per quisquilie del genere, il cuore a pezzi o simili).
È l'ammasso dei fatti su cui avviene l'impatto
e, presente cadavere, l'impalcatura non regge.
Non tento di parlartene. So che se mi leggi
pensi che mi hai fornito il propellente
necessario e che il resto (purchè *non sia* silenzio)
poco importa.

Dopo una fuga is followed by two other significant lyrics in *Satura, Due prose veneziane.* Together with Genoa, Florence, and Milan, Venice has held an important place in Montale's life and creative work. It figures in "Sera difficile" (*Farfalla di Dinard*), in some motets, and in some lyrics both in and outside *Xenia.* In the first of the *Due prose veneziane,* memories of Venice are evoked in such a way as to achieve a poetic synthesis between the personal and autobiographical allusions and incidents on the one hand, and the characteristic features of the life and atmosphere of the city, on the other: for instance, the typists seen from the window of a hotel in Venice and the nauseating smell from the canal; the poet and the woman loved walking along amidst the pigeons and carrying "the heavy catalogue of / the Biennial Exhibition, which was / never consulted and which / wasn't easy to get rid of [col peso del catalogo della biennale / mai consultato e non facile da sbarazzarsene]"; and such personal details as her loving only Gesualdo Bach and Mozart, while the poet loved "a horrible operatic repertoire / with a preference for the worst [l'orrido repertorio operistico con qualche preferenza / per il peggiore]"; the clock showing five o'clock, when it was only four; or the fact that the two rooms in the hotel they occupied did not even connect with each other. And the feeling of pathos and nostalgia underlying what is recollected is clinched in a typically Montalian way; that is to say, through the detail of the particular year, which helps the poet to fix his experience at a specific point in time as well as in place, and to stress its essentially dual character—realistic as well as symbolical, personal as well as impersonal:

We come back by the boat
stepping over birdseed, buying

souvenirs, picture cards, and
sunglasses at the stalls.
I think it was in '34 and
we were too young or too strange
in a city that wants tourists and old lovers.

Torniamo col battello scavalcando becchime,
comprando keepsakes cartoline e occhiali scuri sulle bancarelle.
Era, mi pare, il '34, troppo giovani o troppo strani
per una città che domanda turisti e amanti anziani.

In the second Venetian piece the salient aspects of Hemingway's life and
work are pinpointed, as the poet describes his visit to him in Venice. The
account of the meeting, for all its factual realism, achieves something in the
nature of a poetic and moral summing up of Hemingway's talent and
personality observed by one who is himself a poet, a critic, and a journalist.
The lyric, narrative, and descriptive elements are harmoniously blended so
as to achieve an emotional and psychological unity that is so subtle as to be
hardly noticeable. Every single detail or reference has both a realistic and
an ironic significance, and what emerges is a living portrait of Hemingway
the man and writer as Montale found him just a few years before his death:

Farfarella the garrulous porter,
being observant of his orders,
said that he wasn't allowed
to disturb the man, the lover
of bullfights and hunting expeditions.
I beg him to try and tell him
I'm a friend of Pound's (I exaggerated
a bit) and deserve special treatment.
Who knows . . . He picks up the receiver,
talks, listens, talks again,
and Hemingway the bear takes the bait.
He's still in bed,
from the mass of his beard just his eyes
and the marks of eczema peep out.
Two or three empty bottles
of Merlot, avant-garde of the gallons
that were to come. Down in the restaurant
they are all at table.
We don't discuss him, but

our dear friend Adrienne Monnier,
Rue de l'Odéon. Sylvia Beach, Larbaud,
the roaring thirties and the braying
fifties. Paris, London
a pigsty, New York stinking,
pestiferous. No more hunting
in the marsh, no more wild ducks, no
more girls, not even the idea
of a book along these lines.
We make out a list of mutual friends,
whose names I don't know. All's rotten,
decayed. Almost in tears
he asks me not to send him
people of my sort, still less
if they are intelligent. Then he gets up,
wraps himself in a bathrobe
and shows me the door with an embrace.
He lived a few more years
and, dying twice, had occasion
to read his obituary.

Il Farfarella garrulo portiere ligio agli ordini
disse ch'era vietato disturbare
l'uomo delle corride e dei safari.
Lo supplico di tentare, sono un amico di Pound
(esageravo alquanto) e merito un trattamento
particolare. Chissà che.... L'altro alza la cornetta,
parla ascolta straparla ed ecco che
l'orso Hemingway ha abboccato all'amo.
È ancora a letto, dal pelame bucano
solo gli occhi e gli eczemi.
Due o tre bottiglie vuote di Merlot,
avanguardia del grosso che verrà.
Giù al ristorante tutti sono a tavola.
Parliamo non di lui ma della nostra
Adrienne Monnier carissima, di rue de l'Odéon,
di Sylvia Beach, di Larbaud, dei ruggenti anni trenta
e dei raglianti cinquanta. Parigi Londra un porcaio,
New York stinking, pestifera. Niente cacce in palude,
niente anatre selvatiche, niente ragazze

e nemmeno l'idea di un libro simile.
Compiliamo un elenco di amici comuni dei quali
ignoro il nome. Tutto è rotten, marcio.
Quasi piangendo m'impone di non mandargli gente
della mia risma, peggio se intelligenti.
Poi s'alza, si ravvolge in un accappatoio
e mi mette alla porta con un abbraccio.
Visse ancora qualche anno e morendo due volte
ebbe il tempo di leggere le sue necrologie.

The last two poems in the volume, "Luci e colori" and "L'Altro," share the spirit and ethos as well as the linguistic and stylistic qualities of *Dopo una fuga,* and even more so of *Xenia.* The first is about one of the "mute visitations [visite mute]" of the woman loved who is now no more, in which she shows up "in the red bed-jacket, / with your eyes somewhat swollen like those / of him who has seen [la liseuse rossa, / gli occhi un po' gonfi come di chi ha veduto]," or in the form of

an apricot-colored worm hobbling
uncomfortably on the bedside carpet.
It wasn't easy to make it
glide up a piece of paper
and throw it alive in the courtyard.
You yourself wouldn't weigh much more.

colore di albicocca un vermiciattolo
che arrancava a disagio. Non riuscì facile farlo
slittare su un pezzo di carta e buttarlo giù vivo
nel cortile. Tu stessa non devi pesare di più.

In the second, which is one of the most subtle and delicate as well as artistically and emotionally compact lyrics in *Satura,* the poet tells the woman loved who is now no more how their "dealings with the Other"—a characteristically Montalian way of alluding to God—"were one long subterfuge [furono un lungo inghippo]," which is another way of asserting the indefinable intimacy of the bond, not only between them and God, but also between each other:

I don't know who may have noticed it,
but our dealings with the Other
were one long subterfuge.
To publicize them would be

beseeching clemency, more
than showing obsequiousness.
It isn't our fault that we
weren't him; nor his fault or merit
that we have the form we have.
There isn't even anything to fear.
The shrewd flamingo hides
its head under its tail and imagines
that the hunter cannot see it.

Non so chi se n'accorga
ma i nostri commerci con l'Altro
furono un lungo inghippo. Denunziarli
sarà, più che un atto d'ossequio, un impetrare clemenza.
Non siamo responsabili di non essere lui
nè ha colpa lui, o merito, della nostra parvenza.
Non c'è neppure timore. Astuto il flamengo nasconde
il capo sotto l'ala e crede che il cacciatore
non lo veda.

With the exceptions of *Xenia, Dopo una fuga,* and some related poems—
necessary exceptions when one bears in mind the nature of the occasion
and the inspiration behind them as well as their peculiar quality of tone and
inflection—one is tempted to sum up the rest of *Satura* with the Miltonic
words, "Calm of mind, all passion spent." For in spite of the fact that these
poems make a very effective use of wit, irony, and sarcasm, and represent
the harvest of the "years that bring the philosophic mind," [32] only a few of
them come off. There is something too cerebral about them; the ideas on
which they are based do not organize themselves into a poetically charged
pattern; and in poems like "La storia," "A un gesuita moderno," "Le rime,"
"Fanfara," "Realismo non magico," "Si andava," "La diacronia," and "Rebecca," there is nothing to suggest that the same ideas and concepts could not
have been treated as cogently in the form of prose essays such as those in
Auto da fè, with which they have much in common.

32. Wordsworth, "Ode on Intimations of Immortality."

6: *Farfalla di Dinard*

Farfalla di Dinard is essentially complementary to Montale's poetry and an integral part of his creative work. In this respect it can be compared to Leopardi's *Operette morali,* despite obvious differences in scope and character. Of course, in this work Montale does not have any explicit design—moral, didactic, or philosophical—as Leopardi has in *Operette morali;* but then Montale's poetry itself is not so overtly philosophical as are some of Leopardi's *Canti.* However, by virtue of the similarity of landscape, imagery, and what he calls "mysterious local mythology," [1] *Farfalla di Dinard* is as closely wedded to Montale's poetry as *Operette morali* is to the *Canti.* Moreover, like Leopardi's prose work, it is sui generis, being prose pieces that are also in a way short stories (and among the best of their kind), and at the same time a series of autobiographical vignettes, sketches, and recollections relating to Montale's childhood and to the period between the two world wars. Montale himself calls them something halfway between a short story and a *petit poème en prose,* so that while some of them resemble Baudelaire's prose poems, others remind us of the hallucinatory vividness and perspicuity of Kafka's realism. [2] Regarding the quality of prose in which these pieces are written, it too has an organic link with Montale's poetry insofar as it frequently achieves crystalline neatness and intensity, sophisticated subtlety of

1. See Montale's article "Le Cinque Terre" in *Fuori di casa,* where he talks about the things that constituted the "misteriosa mitologia locale" when he was a child.

2. Montale has suggested that, in some respects, while writing the stories or prose pieces of *Farfalla di Dinard,* he had Logan Pearsall Smith's *Trivia* remotely in mind. Whatever resemblance there may be between the two books—the former could only be the work of a creative artist of Montale's stature while Smith's work can lay no claim to any such title—it is very faint and indirect. *Trivia* must have acted, if at all, as a stimulus to Montale on the purely formal level of trying the idea of writing his own trivia. Montale's pieces are artistically accomplished and both poetically and morally richer than Smith's exercises in witty parlor gossip, which is at bottom what his stories amount to. In such pieces as "Waxworks," "Misapprehension," "Regent's Park," and "St. John's Wood," details may be noted that may have served Montale as suggestions for some of the particulars and circumstances he describes in "Il regista," L'angoscia," and "Honey," respectively.

understatement, unobstrusive delicacy and pathos, and an undercurrent of semiphilosophical irony.

Farfalla di Dinard may therefore be regarded as an original contribution to the development of Italian prose, as *Ossi di seppia* is to that of Italian poetry. Relatively few modern Italian writers have delved into and exploited the hidden resources of the Italian language, both by enriching the vocabulary and loosening the syntax, as successfully as has Montale. Moreover, apart from their creative and linguistic merit these stories tell us practically all we need to know about the poet's early life and background as well as his personality. In the preface to my English translation of *Farfalla di Dinard*,[3] Montale himself describes the nature and genesis of the stories as follows:

> After ten years of unemployment due to political reasons—I didn't belong to the "Party"—I joined in 1948 the editorial staff of an important Milanese daily, which, owing to the shortage of paper as of everything else, used to come out in two or four pages only. The editor's idea was that I should leave literature alone. There was also no question of my being sent out as a foreign correspondent, since others were already doing that job. But still I had to write something. What? I haven't got the imagination of a born novelist; nor can I invent anything. But being a great admirer of the English essayists and being endowed with a sense of humor, which is seldom wanting in the Ligurians—I was born at Genoa where I lived till the age of thirty—I thought that I could perhaps talk about myself and my experiences, without boring the readers with the actual autobiography of an ordinary man—a man who has always tried to move through the history of his times in a clandestine way. This is how these short stories—the *culs de lampe*—of *The Butterfly of Dinard* came to be written. With the exception of a few, placed in Liguria, the stories are placed in Florence where I lived for twenty years in close contact with the English colony, which was quite large in those days. During those years I tried to do something impossible—to live in Florence like an Italian exposed to all sorts of vexations from the political regime; and at the same time to live aloof from the local troubles like a foreigner. After something like twenty years of hard but unsuccessful struggle I gave up. In the meantime I had moved to Milan—the center of business, not art. I had brought along with me a long trail of memories which demanded written expression. If I was not a born storyteller, so much the better; if

3. Both the English edition of my translation of *Farfalla di Dinard* (*The Butterfly of Dinard*), published by Alan Ross in 1970, and the American edition of this translation, published by Kentucky University Press in 1971, carry a preface specifically written for it by Montale.

the space at my disposal was limited, better still. This forced me to write in great haste. To cater to the taste of the general public, which is little accustomed to the allusive and succinct technique of the *petit poème en prose,* created no problem. To write about those silly and trivial things which are at the same time important, to project the image of a prisoner who is at the same time a free man—herein, if I may say so, lies the merit of these instantaneous flashes which are *The Butterfly of Dinard.* These stories *in nuce* were published in book form in 1956; some more stories were added in the subsequent editions of 1961. When they first came out they received the general approval of the public as well as of the critics. But perhaps it is only today that, in their English garb, they can be read and appreciated by a different and a wider public. Some might even think that, thanks to the learned translator, they have at last found a more congenial habitat. Which would no doubt be partly true, although one has to remember that from the age of the Enlightenment onward Italian has enriched itself with such possibilities as would make it second to none. Perhaps it would need other and bigger "Butterflies" (written by others) to confer on our national prose—poetry has already made considerable advances in that direction—that flexibility which too illustrious a literary tradition in the past has prevented it from achieving.

That Montale himself has been able to overcome this obstacle is in large measure due to his possessing in an eminent degree what Pound calls "new subtlety of eyes"[4] (and of ears as well) and that catholicity of interests in the world around him which is the result of a happy combination in him of the poet and the journalist. Another quality to emphasize in Montale as a prose writer is the sureness of instinct with which he has been able to decide what should go into the pages of prose and what should be expressed in verse form. Not that Montale believes in any theoretical or a priori distinction between verse and prose. It is largely a question of the greater or lesser degree of emotional and imaginative involvement on his part in a given theme, situation, or occasion that has made him opt for the one or the other. Thus there is an emotional and psychological as well as creative link between *Farfalla di Dinard* and Montale's poetry. And although it wouldn't make much difference whether one read it before reading the poetry or after, the prose work may be considered an appropriate introduction to Montale's poetical world in general and to the bearing his Ligurian background and his Florentine sojourn have had on his mind and art in particular.

4. See *Pisan Cantos,* no. 81, where Pound says, "there came new subtlety of eyes into my tent."

Each story, while recounting an episode or recollecting a past experience, evokes a particular circumstance, time, and place with a wealth of dramatic or poetic detail. As in some of his poetry, Montale fruitfully exploits the technique of juxtaposing the elements of surprise and recognition, novelty and familiarity, as well as that of introducing frequent shifts of tone in the stories. However, there is nothing abrupt about these shifts of tone, and there is a sureness and inevitability with which the diverse and disparate aspects of a given theme or context blend into one another and form a coherent and accomplished whole.

In the first piece, called "A Stranger's Story," Montale describes some of the scenes and experiences of his childhood in a motherless household at Monterosso on the Ligurian coast. He tells us how "amongst so much discord between my father and myself we had at least one thing in common, a thread which bound us together—namely, that at the end of every week the name of the archpriest Buganza would turn up among the solvers of the logographs, the picture puzzles, and the rebuses of the local periodical called *Amico*." In a characteristic way Montale makes the delicate and difficult relationship between father and son—a son who had "plenty of vague and indefinable ideas about extracommercial vocations," but who had reached "the age of fifteen, then twenty-five, without ever having taken any decision," and who had always been on the lookout for "a job worthy of me and my talent," although "neither I nor my father had ever discovered what that talent was"—depend on an apparently trivial detail, namely, their fondness for Buganza, an unknown solver of the puzzles and rebuses in the periodical. Once, because of the compositor's error, the priest's name did not appear. This resulted in the all too flimsy thread between son and father being broken; so Montale decided to leave home. But in the next issue of the periodical the name reappeared with an apology for the omission from the previous issue, and this changed the whole situation.

> A little later I started unpacking. There was no way out. The thread I had thought broken proved stronger than ever. And now that my father is no more and the *Amico* has disappeared and the archpriest likewise, my house still stands, and only a bomb could . . . but not for the moment I dare say.

Thus in story after story Montale recalls the past by means of what he describes as "this plunge into a life I thought had ended for ever" [5] or "immersion in a time not marked by Signor Frissi's sundial." [6] Scenes, landscapes, images, names of people, local dishes, wines, customs, anecdotes—all are

5. "Le rose gialle."
6. "La casa delle due palme."

recalled with a subtle blend of wistfulness and irony. The atmosphere of a particular occasion or place is depicted in such a way as to bring out both what is dated and what is timeless about it. For instance, Federigo, the protagonist of "The House with the Two Palms," on returning to his native place after "an assiduous and involuntary process of extirpation, a long circumnavigation through modes and ideas of life quite unknown here," finds that there is a family flavor about the food he is going to eat—a flavor that is

> transmitted from generation to generation, which no cook can ever destroy. A continuity this which if destroyed elsewhere endures through the grease of the sauce, the strong garlic smell, the smell of onions and basil, the stuffing pounded in the marble mortar. Attracted by this smell, even the dead, condemned to a much lighter food, return to the earth from time to time.

It is through this nostalgic fidelity to the past, reevoked with a poignant realism of detail, that the poet realizes that "the pleasure of living comes from the repetition of certain acts and habits and from the fact that one can say to oneself: 'I shall repeat everything I've done and it will be more or less the same, but not exactly the same.' The pleasure derives from the element of diversity in what seems identical, and it's the same for an intellectual as for an illiterate person." [7]

In early life it was Montale's ambition to be a singer, but because of the death of his maestro, he gave it up, although his interest in music has lasted all his life, as stories like "In the Key of 'F'," "Success," and "Il lacerato spirito," besides numerous articles and criticisms on various composers and operas, testify.[8] In the first story Montale describes, with characteristic pathos, irony, and realism, the death of the maestro who had tried to bring out the singer in him:

> I saw him lying on a single bed, dressed in a dark suit, his face draped with long silvery hair. He had shrunk into something minute. Diplomas, medals of the tsar, wreaths of artificial flowers, and framed newspaper cuttings were to be seen all round the room. His favorite pupils took it in turn to keep watch by his dead body, uttering small ratlike yelps in "maschera" (*mi mi mi*).

In "Success" the poet appears as an occasional claqueur hired by the local barber Pecchioli, the head claqueur of his town, to whose care, as he tells us, he had entrusted "the future of his music career." He was hired for the

---

7. "La donna barbuta."
8. Montale has, for instance, written something on Purcell, Mozart, Rossini, Donizetti, Bellini, Wagner, Verdi, Strauss, Puccini, and Stravinsky.

particular occasion when a local composer, Rebillo, was giving a performance of his own compositions. Montale's comments on the musical taste of those times in general and on Rebillo's music in particular have a subtle vein of irony:

> In those days modern music was represented almost exclusively by Wagner, whom most people had now come to tolerate. But music like Signor Rebillo's, all dissonance and screeching, had never been heard before. Was Rebillo a genius or a madman? Judging from the titles of his compositions—I remember, for instance, a "ninfea morente" presented like a "musical still-life"—I would have had to conclude that he was at least a precursor. But I would have been even less capable of discerning it then than I am now.

In "Il lacerato spirito" he relates the story of a collector of records cut between 1903 and 1908. The description of his attempts to sing some of the melodies of *Simon Boccanegra,* and especially the invective "il lacerato spirito," brings into play the characteristic qualities of Montale's narrative prose:

> It is not a difficult aria, but it requires an extremely mature voice, and, when he was young, the old man felt that his voice was not mature enough. An inexperienced bass is like a raw, inedible fruit. The years sped by. Innumerable houses, barracks, hotels, boardinghouses, clinics, hospitals, and rented rooms resounded with the thundering invective. The voice, because still loose, kept maturing, until it began to lose first the *funnel* (or *tuba* as it is called), and one fine day, even its tone and resonance. The old man (who was not so old then) realized that the only thing for him to do was to take time by the forelock, grab at the perfection to which he aspired, and impress everybody with the famous aria. He could then sink into dignified silence.

Farfalla di Dinard is divided into four sections, the stories so far referred to belonging to the first. In the second section we have for the most part lively character sketches of certain types of people. And what makes stories like "The Enemies of Mr. Fuchs," "Mr. Stapps," and "Dominico" so memorable is their combination of wit and psychological insight. In the first we are told of one Mr. Fuchs, with his innumerable enemies and his sole occupation as a guest "always in search of rich and possibly aristocratic families who could put at his disposal a room and two daily meals in a castle on the Loire, a tower in the Vosges, a villa in San Sebastian, or at worst an apartment in Florence, Venice, or Milan." A master in the art of making people believe that anyone who invites him does an immense honor to himself, Mr. Fuchs entices Montale into the same trap. But both host and guest end up by quarreling—through no fault of the former—because the spirit heater fails to generate "the ideal atmosphere for conversation." While trying to fix it, Mr. Fuchs breaks it and then accuses his host of blaming him for the accident. They quarrel, or rather Mr. Fuchs quarrels, and then goes away, never to see his host again. "Unwillingly," concludes Montale, "and without my intending to, I too was enrolled in the ever-growing ranks of his enemies. But I consoled myself with the thought that perhaps I was of more use to him that way."

Equally idiosyncratic is the character of Mr. Stapps, "whose origins and way of living were rather obscure; he claimed to be a Bohemian, to have been married three times, to have belonged to the world of Czech diplomacy, and to have quarreled with Masaryk and Benes." "Dominico," on the other hand, is the story of a man half-Sicilian, half-American, who feels the call of the mother country and returns to Florence. Being only half-Italian and carrying an American passport, Dominico finds everything in Italy wonderful. Even the Fascist regime, or "the carnival regime that the Italians in those days had accepted for themselves," was something that Dominico not only did not mind, but which, with "his vaguely democratic principles," heartily approved. He considered it to be "in perfect harmony with the *palio,* with football (which was starting to be popular in those days), and other local manifestations."

In "Clizia at Foggia," one of the more elaborately constructed stories in the book, we find Clizia, the protagonist of the story, waiting for a train at Foggia one hot afternoon:

> The railway lines glittered under the torrid sky of Foggia. Above them the mushed-grape-colored coaches, the dry fountain, the tree trunks tied to each other (an absurd anticipation of winter) seemed on the point of melting like rubber.

She decides to attend a lecture on metempsychosis in the nearby town hall, not because she is interested in the subject, but because she wants to rest in a cool place. She soon falls asleep and has a horrible dream. (In the waiting room she had noticed a spider trapped in "a canopy of yellow fly-catcher" and had wondered how it got there. Her conclusion was that while hanging by its thread it must have dropped down through the gaps in the ceiling and must then have been caught up in the draught which had blown it on to the fly-catcher. Hence the dream.) She imagines she has become, through a dual process of metabolism and metempsychosis, one with the spider, and is about

to meet the same fate. At this point the dream ends, for she is awakened by
one of the lecturers. Taking her for a subject—and an exceptional subject at
that—the two professors want to know what she has dreamt. But they don't
believe what she has to say; for, they maintain, it would be impossible "to
change from a spider to a human being." She is asked to leave with the
admonition that such scientific experiments are too serious for her and that
she should keep away from them. Clizia reaches the station in time to catch
her train.

One of the most humorous stories in this section, however, is "The Stormy
One." The very first two sentences set the tone of the whole story:

> The news that Giampaolo had married Mrs. Dirce F., who had twice
> been a widow and was much older than he, hadn't given rise to any
> unfavorable comments in the town. Giampaolo's had been a trying life,
> and to know that he had now finally settled down (even though at the
> expense of certain inevitable sacrifices) was a source of relief to his many
> friends.

When one of his friends, Federigo, happens to call on them one day, he is
given an extremely cordial welcome by Giampaolo's wife, Signora Dirce. In
describing this welcome, as well as the house, furniture, and habits of the
household, Montale shows himself to be both a painter and—perhaps unin-
tentionally—a caricaturist of upper middle-class Italian society:

> Federigo Bezzica? What an unexpected honor! For years, for two or
> three years in the early stages of her friendship with Giampaolo, when the
> good soul, the second good soul, was still alive (a finger was raised to in-
> dicate a bald man in a large oil portrait) she, Signora Dirce, had learnt
> everything about him, and was full of admiration for his life and char-
> acter. Federigo Bezzica! If only she'd known him before . . . Who
> knows . . . The dearest, the most dignified, the most reserved of Giam-
> paolo's friends. Surely it was he who was to blame for being the last to
> show up. Shyness? Love of a quiet life? She, of course, understood (oh
> how well!) his taste for "blessed solitude," it was on the basis of such an
> affinity that she hoped to establish a solid friendship with him. Giam-
> paolo? Yes, Giampaolo was working, but would come up in a moment.
> In the meanwhile they could talk a little and get to know each other
> better. Can I offer you a port, a dry Martini, a Negroni? Fabrizio,
> where's that lazy Fabrizio got to? Hurry, bring a glass of port for this
> gentleman.

What with one thing and another, Federigo finds that he cannot leave because of the domineering character of his hostess. Before going to bed he
contemplates the various possibilities of escape:

It had stopped raining. Leaning out of the window of his room, Federigo realized that it would be dangerous to jump. Moreover, there was the gate to be negotiated too, the hazard of the fierce dog Tombolo, and other possible obstacles. And what if they took him for a burglar?

Uncertain what to do, he shut the window, taking in as he did so the pyjamas of the second (or perhaps the first) husband laid out on the bed. He picked them up at arm's length, only to drop them hurriedly at the sound of a knock at the door. It was Giampaolo, with a pair of old slippers.

"See you tomorrow then," he said. "On the late side though, as I've work to do. And now, when are you going to get married?"

As in his poetry so in these stories Montale's realism operates not merely by rendering what is trivial interesting but also by deflating what is pompous and pretentious. In "The Women of Karma," for instance, where the vogue of Karma in some circles serves as the leitmotiv, Montale relates the story of a woman called Micky (who is married to an old man) being visited by a former acquaintance Piffi, whom she had once thought of marrying. Introducing the visitor to her friends, Micky offers, as it were, a prose elaboration of what Montale calls the "ambiguities of the possible": [9]

"You don't know that some years ago I would have married this man. Do you remember, Piffi? Then one day he told me: I'm too old for you. He was thirty-three and I was eighteen. What could I say? At the time I couldn't think of what to say, so he left and I married Lucky. How funny! But he is a dangerous witness, you see. When I knew him, I used to believe in psychoanalysis . . . And I thought that earthly love could make me happy."

Of the two stories dealing with widows, "The Limpid Eyes" and "The Widows," the latter comes closer to the Montalian idea of a prose poem. The widows are described as presiding over meetings, cutting the thread at inauguration ceremonies, opening bottles of champagne at launchings, correcting the proofs of their dead husbands' books, distributing scholarships, and thus keeping alive "wicks which for want of oil would rather be extinguished."

"Leave us in peace," the feeble voices of the dead sigh from underground. But the widows insist. And when the first shades of oblivion loom over the tea tables spread out among the pines, in sight of the Apennines, they bend over the canasta and say: "Stand back! *non praevalebunt!*"

9. "Disguidi del possibile" in "Carnevale di Gerti," *Le occasioni.*

Even when they are remarried, they continue the cult of "their *first*."

"Mein mann," says one; "mon mari," says another; "my husband," repeats a third. And a fourth whispers into the ears of a fifth: "even at those particular times . . . you know, he liked me to keep my stockings on . . .

The end of the story strikes a note of lyric pathos and delicacy:

My best friends are all dead. I alone survive and fight against their cult as professed by their widows. I remember them in my own way—getting into a tram or sipping an apéritif, or at the sight of a dog's muzzle, the outline of a palm-tree, the parabola of a firework. Sometimes I come across them in the refuse which the sea carries away towards Calambrone, in the dregs of a glass of old Barolo, in a cat's leap as it chases a butterfly in a square at Massa. There's no voice to say "My husband" and they're quite at home with me.

In the third section, to which "The Widows" belongs, we find another humorous story called "The Bat." It is about an Italian couple staying in an English hotel. At midnight, when the man is about to turn off the light, a bat enters and they both become panicky. The task of driving it out, which turns out to be well-nigh impossible, is described in lively and humorous detail. Between one futile attempt and another, the man sits down exhausted. His wife, lying buried under a heap of blankets for fear of the bat, suggests he should ring the porter for help.

"Hello, hello: *Chauve-souris, pipistrello,* perhaps bat. No, I'm not mad (he says I am), *Chauve-souris,* perhaps bat, in my room. Please come. Help! Help! Help! *Au secours!* Hello, hello!"

(Incomprehensible imprecations and strangled curses issued from the receiver; then there was the sound of someone putting it back).

"What did he say?" inquired the muffled voice.

"He's coming at once, no, not at once, but he's coming . . . perhaps he's coming anyway. I don't know if he understood. But wait, darling, wait a little."

While waiting for the porter they are reminded of the restaurant called The Bat which they used to frequent. The husband on his part suggests, to the horror and mystification of his wife, that the bat might well be the ghost of his dead father.

"I don't know," he said, almost on the verge of tears. "It's the only animal I've ever killed, with the exception, of course, of flies or ants.

The only animal, and my father was very unhappy about it. I think he comes back sometimes to visit me in one form or another.

'We'll meet again somewhere,' he told me the day before he died.

'You're too silly to be able to manage by yourself. Don't worry, I'll take care, I'll find ways and means of doing it.' But I'd almost forgotten it. Only now and then, when I see . . . one of these animals, take aim and *bang!* See it fall like a rag. It's then that the memory of him . . ."

The husband aims an imaginary gun at the bat, which flies out of the window and is swallowed up by the dark. Its departure startles the wife who shrieks and throws herself against the pillow. She then remembers an incident in her own life:

Her eyes wide open, she kept looking where the bat had been, her mind on the restaurant with the black wings. Then, all of a sudden, remembering how years ago her life had been saved by her determination to see Strauss's *Pipistrello*—a bomb had destroyed her house in her absence— she had another wild outburst, before plunging back into the heap of blankets, laughing hysterically.

The same theme of recollection of the past is realized through the delicate blend of the psychological and the sentimental in the story "Relics," which also has husband and wife as protagonists. The wife keeps a box of relics by her bedside, "newspaper cuttings, old letters tied up with a ribbon, and some holy pictures which she dared not destroy (for one never knows . . .)." She is searching anxiously for the photo of Ortello, "a beautiful horse that won the *Grand Prix* at Longchamp." Although the husband seems to be only mildly interested in his wife's relics (which provokes her comment: "You talk of *my* reliquary as if it were only my mania. Naturally, that's just what one would have expected"), he is no less sentimentally attached to his own relics. Thus they rehearse their whole past, recalling, among other things, the apparently casual details and incidents associated with their decision to marry each other. Once, for instance, while visiting a zoo in Zermatt and watching a red fox that had disappeared into its den, the future wife had said to herself: "I'll count twenty; if the fox comes out in the meantime, then what is to happen will happen; but if she doesn't . . . then this man can go to the devil! And so I counted slowly, more and more slowly. At nineteen the fox came out." This becomes the occasion for lively repartee between them:

"And so you decided to marry me," he said, waiting for his tea to cool.

"I see, I see. One never stops learning."

"Don't complain, I deliberately counted slowly. Perhaps after nineteen I would have made an extra long pause. It was I who brought the fox out . . . with my wish. Of course, one had to play a kind of game. I had to slacken the tempo. Like certain musicians."

"Well, since we're in a confessing mood, I'll admit that when Mimì was about to reenter the box, at Vitznau, I told myself: if it enters the box on the right, then what's going to happen will happen; but if it enters the one on the left, then . . . You know what I mean. Mimì, the white and yellow guinea-pig. Don't you remember?"

"Perfectly well. And Mimì, having come out of the conjuror's sleeve, ended up in the righthand box? That means that our union has a very solid basis. Do you want a biscuit?"

No, thanks. Actually it ended up in the lefthand one. But the experiment was repeated three times, and you won two to one; which was enough. There was no trick, you see."

"The fox and the guinea-pig, two interesting godfathers. They must have died long ago without ever having realized what a mess they had been responsible for. Our life is a bestiary, a menagerie in fact. Do you think you've thrown them away? Cats, dogs, birds, blackbirds, turtle-doves, crickets, worms . . .

"Oh worms," he said contemptuously.

". . . even worms and I don't know what else. And the names? Buck Pallino Passepoil Pippo Bubù . . ."

"Lapo Esmeralda Mascotto Pinco Tartufo Margot . . ."

He went on, at times even inventing a name, but then he stopped, noticing that she had closed her eyes, exhausted.

When she falls asleep, he goes out for a stroll.

Behind most of the stories in *The Butterfly of Dinard* a poet's imagination, coupled with a journalist's curiosity and a moralist's instinct to dissect and evaluate is at work. On the autobiographical plane, analysis of things merges almost imperceptibly with self-analysis, and caricature with self-caricature. And the result is that Montale ends up by identifying himself with the character he is talking about or with his interlocutor.

In "The Producer," for instance, the theme of a limited immortality—"for fifty centuries only"—is the basis of a story which despite its uncannily hallucinatory atmosphere, has an unmistakable verisimilitude about it. It recounts a casual meeting between the poet and an old acquaintance of his who had died years before. When on a visit to the earth, he tells Montale that he is going to be here for a few days:

I shouldn't tell you why, because it's confidential, only I haven't forgotten what you did for me that June in Vallarsa, when you sent me off on leave just before the offensive. I know you didn't want to save my skin; in fact you didn't like me; but precisely because of your unreasonable dislike for me you wanted to be a hundred percent fair. So I owe you my life, and my first meeting with Y.—the best bit of luck I've ever had— which took place during that leave. Don't thank me, just listen carefully (and above all keep it to yourself). We're making a film of the next fifty centuries which will be seen, or rather lived by those actually concerned—each in turn and according to the parts they've played. Since you're still alive, you belong to the last film; no, no, not at all a bad film, but rather old-fashioned . . . too many close-ups, too many tracking shots, too many film stars.

Although a poet, Montale cannot, however, expect to be given the role of a Homer. The producer has collected some information about him and it doesn't qualify him for such an honor. As if to counterbalance the uncanniness of this situation, Montale at this point introduces the prosaic and commonplace detail of the poster:

"Of course," I stammered, leaning against a wall covered with posters advertising road safety. "Of course, I understand perfectly well, up there . . . of course, it's natural, a choice, a lot of choice, a very rich choice . . . (The poster against which I was leaning bore the inscription: "Life is short, don't shorten it further").

There is also an element of humor and irony about the way the producer proposes to him the various forms of immortality.

No one would read you in the new film, but you would be remembered as someone who was once alive, as someone who lived in other times. Would you like to become a character in a libretto, only a minor character, naturally, someone like Angelotti in *Tosca?* I think he really existed. Or would you prefer to have your name associated with a beefsteak, like M. Chateaubriant? Or perhaps you'd like your name to be given to a brooch, a tie, a hair-style or a new subspecies of dog. I know you used to have a soft spot for mongrels, we could pick on one and call it after you. But we must decide soon. I'm very busy and if I hadn't met you accidentally I'm not sure I would have been able to fit you into my program at all. Could you give me an idea, a hint?

As he is conversing with the producer, he is approached by a constable who tells him that he has broken a traffic regulation. And as he is in the process of inquiring if the producer has also broken it, the latter disappears in the fog.

Some of the best stories in *Farfalla di Dinard* are to be found in the last section; among them "On the Beach," "The Paintings in the Cellar," "The Snow Statue," and "The Butterfly of Dinard." The first deals with the evocatively vague recollection of a woman whom Montale had met in Florence, and who now, years later, sends him a present from America. The difficulty of identifying her serves as an incentive to unearth some banal but symbolically rich details and circumstances from the past:

> Someone I had completely forgotten had taken me by surprise. It was I who lived on in the mind of Anactoria or Annalena; it was I who survived in her, not she in me. But how on earth can memory fade away so completely? I was always aware of a host of possible spirits living in the casket of my memory—spirits I almost never evoked for fear of reviving shades that were not always pleasant, but that nevertheless did sometimes rise to the surface of my consciousness and enrich it. Reminiscences so formed, castanets snapping unduly late, can be easily accounted for. But what about the creature that springs up like a jack-in-the-box from apparently inert material, a complete oblivion which suddenly reveals itself as a presence? In fact, I've always believed in a relative forgetfulness which is almost voluntary, a sort of Taylorian process by which the mind rejects what is no longer any use, while at the same time retaining the end of the thread. But in this instance there was no doubt at all: Anactoria or Annabella, who had been buried in my mind for four, five, or six years had now come back because she *wanted* to come back. It was she who had chosen to grace me with her presence, not I who had condescended to reawaken her while searching through the past in a desultory way. It was she—the amiable creature, the worthy intruder—who, while digging her past up again, had come across my shade and had tried to reestablish a "correspondence" in the best sense of the term.

Together with the theme of memory, this story also deals with Montale's feeling for the sea, as comes out in the following passage.

> The light blazed on the Apuanians in the interval between one late August storm and the next. There were relatively few people sunbathing on the damp sand. I couldn't manage to get as tanned as I would have liked, but from behind my dark glasses I followed the movement of the last hawkers as they passed by the empty bathing-huts. Their cries reached me, unenthusiastic and monotonous: "Blackberries, raspberries, iced drinks" . . . Then I saw the poodle leading the blind man—a dark

figure *alla Velasquez*—from the folds of whose viscerally groaning har-
monica *Bésame mucho* ground doggedly out. It must have been rather
late.

Here the painter's eye for detail and the poet's intuition are most aptly
interfused and make for the most effective, yet seemingly effortless, prose
lyricism.

In "The Paintings in the Cellar" the scene of the first part of the story is
set in Trieste, and that of the second part in Milan. While taking a stroll in
the company of his friend B.,[10] Montale encounters a tall, slim youth hurrying
by, who makes a sign of greeting. Although there is nothing striking about
him, the poet wants to know who he is. His friend tells him, "Oh nobody in
particular, just a futurist." The boy is the young painter Giorgio Carmelich,
who was to die of consumption in his youth. A couple of years after his death,
Montale went to see an exhibition of his work and bought a couple of paintings, although, he tells us, "his art did not strike me as being particularly
interesting, nor was I particularly keen—at least as regards painting—on discovering new talent." What follows relates to the vicissitudes of the paintings
during and after World War II, and the space problem they created. They
were not precious, he might easily have thrown them away; but the thought
of the unfortunate young artist, whom he had once seen, made it difficult to
do so. Montale took the paintings with him when he moved from Trieste to
Florence, and then, at the end of the war, from Florence to Milan. Things
locked up in chests were brought out. The more important books and paintings found a place in the new apartment, but it was not easy to decide what
to do with the Carmelichs:

> "And now what's to be done with these?" asks the impatient Agatha,
> as she rubs her fingers. What can one do with them, old Agatha? I wish
> I knew. Blessed be the day when I gave away the big painting by Bolaffio
> to a worthy collector of that painter, who offered it a decent and lasting
> shelter; even though because of this gesture of "blind indifference" I
> merited the arrow, a wrathful verse, of an illustrious poet of Trieste, who
> was justly indignant about it. But what can one do with the little
> Carmelichs, Agatha? Can I, perhaps the last custodian of that worthy
> boy's secret and his unhappiness, let them perish like that? I lean against
> the door of the pantry and remain immobile in a draught. The gondola
> and the monument to the great reformer shine at the bottom of the trunk.
> More than twenty years have passed and it seems to be a day. A tall lean

10. Bobi Bazlen. See Montale's article "Ricordo di Roberto Bazlen" in *Montale—Svevo:
Lettere,* Bari, 1966.

youth crosses the square lashed by the wind, the tails of his light over-
coat are flopping around him, he waves with his hand and I ask absent-
mindedly, "Who is he, Bobi?"

"Oh nobody in particular, just a futurist," and we walk off toward
the café.

The last two stories in the book, "The Snow Statue" and "The Butterfly
of Dinard," are set in Saint-Moritz and Brittany, respectively. In the first, the
poet is looking out of the window of the hotel where he comes to stay at the
end of every year, observing a snowman:

> . . . nine feet tall, with a plumed hat, a cigar in his mouth with the ash
> about to fall, two carrots for ears, two onions as eyes, and three turnips
> as the buttons of his jacket. He partly resembles Churchill and partly
> Grock. But what attracts me most are the onion-eyes. From the very first
> day they have called forth in me, by association of ideas, the most lugu-
> brious of sentiments. One thing is certain: the enormous bogey is crying.
> He sheds red, pungent tears—huge drops, like billiard balls. But no one
> sees his tears except me.
>
> .   .   .   .
>
> Standing by the window, tarnished by my breath, I try to speak to this
> wonderful puppet: "May I, Maestro, join in your unrestrainable, total
> and universal weeping? I have come here on purpose to see you; although
> I am not worthy of such an honor, I am perhaps the only person here
> who knows why you cry. I would also dissolve myself into your mud;
> I too have onions in my eye-sockets, a turnip instead of a nose. . . May
> I, Maestro?"

The story has a characteristically deflationary finale:

> A light tap on the door and the maid comes in with the tea. She is a
> Tuscan, matter-of-fact, and not much given to mysticism.
> "Have you seen it?" she asks me, seeing me absorbed by the window.
> "They've made another scarecrow this year."
> "Oh yes," I answer in an indifferent way. "That big puppet. Why on
> earth did they?"

In "The Butterfly of Dinard," with which this book ends, Montale is sitting
in a café in the main square of the town, watching a butterfly. He toys with
the idea that it comes to this café for his sake, bringing him a message from
the woman he loves:

Would the tiny, saffron-colored butterfly, which used to come to see me every day at the café in the square of Dinard, and bring me word about you—or so it seemed—visit the cold, windy little square again after I left? It was incredible that the chilly Breton summer should have brought out so many sparks, all the same color, in those benumbed kitchen gardens. Perhaps what I had seen was not just a butterfly, but *the* butterfly of Dinard. And I was curious to learn if the morning visitor turned up regularly just for my sake, deliberately ignoring other cafés in preference to the one (Les Cornouailles) which I used to frequent, or if this cosy little corner merely happened to be listed in its daily mechanical itinerary. Was it, in short, a morning walk or a secret message? To resolve this doubt I decided to give, before leaving, a handsome tip to the waitress, together with my address in Italy. She was to write to me and tell me if the visitor had come again, or if it had disappeared. I waited for the butterfly to perch on the vase, and then took out a hundred-frank note, a pencil and a piece of paper, and called for the waitress. Stammering in more than usually shaky French, I tried to explain the situation—not, of course, the whole, but only part of it. I gave her to understand that I was an entomologist, and was interested to know if the butterfly would return to the café after I had left, and how long it could survive in this bitter cold. By the time I'd finished explaining, I was exhausted and terrified.

"A butterfly?" asked the charming Filli, her eyes *alla Greuze*. "On that vase? No Monsieur, I don't see anything. Please look again. Merci bien, Monsieur."

She pocketed the note and went away carrying the coffee percolator. I bent my head, and when I raised it again, there was no butterfly on the vase of dahlias.

The prose pieces in *Farfalla di Dinard,* therefore, can be seen as unequivocally representing in a different key and at a different level of creativity, the same control from within, the same sureness and delicacy of perception, and the same grasp of the actual that Montale's poetry displays. The language too is characterized throughout by a mature kind of simplicity and economy which, together with the nuances and subtleties of prose cadences, represent a major and vital link between *Faralla di Dinard* and Montale's poetry.

7: Montale as Critic

Montale is perhaps a unique example of a major poet who has been a professional journalist all his life. Although quite a few poets and critics may start out as journalists, at a certain stage they generally give up journalism in favor of serious literature. Sooner or later they realize that there is a profound variance of aim and scope between the two.

In Italy the situation is very different. Quite a few writers begin as journalists and some remain so until the end of their writing careers. The dividing line between serious literary criticism as such and literary or cultural journalism is more often and more hopelessly blurred than may be the case in England or America. From this one might assume that in Italy the standard of literary journalism is normally higher than in these two countries, without, however, necessarily implying that the standard of literary criticism is lower as a consequence.

What distinguishes Montale's literary journalism are the stimulating and at times original observations interspersed through it—observations that reveal an exceptionally sharp and well-informed mind with a firm analytical grasp as well as subtlety of perception. His literary criticism also differs from much contemporary criticism in Italy, which tends to be either elaborately abstract or pedantically explanatory. That in such a literary and cultural milieu, his criticism should have been, for the most part, direct, constructive, and discriminating is a measure of his independence and acumen. Montale has written on practically all the important twentieth-century Italian writers—with the notable exceptions of Pirandello and Pavese—and on quite a few English, French, and American ones. Even though his criticism does not always achieve a disciplined and coherent rigor of thought, it is invariably informed by maturity of taste and judgment and an unfaltering subtlety and delicacy of response to whatever he is examining. His critical writings neither follow any a priori theory nor become one themselves. The most significant part of Montale's literary criticism deals with modern Italian literature from Pascoli

to contemporary writers. He has, however, also written on Dante and Boccaccio.

In his lecture on Dante, entitled "Dante ieri e oggi," [1] Montale sets out to
demonstrate analytically the continuity of Dante's presence in modern literature, especially Italian literature, and to trace the various phases of his influence through the centuries. However, he does not regard Dante as a
modern poet, and this partly because the tools available to our modern culture
are not adequate to enable us to understand him. In fact, we ourselves no
longer live in a modern era, "but in a new Mediaeval Age whose characteristics it is still very difficult to grasp." Montale then goes on to examine the
various approaches to *The Divine Comedy*—allegorical, philosophical, and
literary—that have been adopted by critics like Foscolo, Parodi, Ferdinando
Neri, T. S. Eliot, Curtius, Auerbach, and C. Singleton. His own comment on
Dante's relevance to and significance for a modern writer is expressed in
semiliterary and semiphilosophical terms. The greatest example, he observes,

of poetic objectivity and rationalism is something extraneous to our times,
because our civilization is subjective and irrational insofar as it puts its
faith in facts and not in ideas. And it is precisely the logic behind these
facts that evades us. Being a concentric poet, Dante cannot furnish models
for a world which is moving progressively away from the center and
which boasts of being in a state of perpetual expansion. Hence the *Divine
Comedy* is and will remain the last miracle of world poetry . . .

That true poetry is always something in the nature of a gift and hence
it presupposes worth and dignity in him who receives it, is the greatest
lesson that Dante has taught us. He is not the only poet to have taught
this lesson, but he is the greatest. And if it is true that he wanted to be
a poet and nothing else, it is we moderns who still can't understand in
our blindness how it is that the further his world recedes from us, the
more we want to understand it and to explain it to those who are blinder
than ourselves.

After Dante, Boccaccio is the only other classical Italian writer on whom
Montale has written. His comments on the "Seventh Day" of *Il Decamerone*
are to be found in the preface he wrote for *Il Decamerone di Giovanni Boccaccio.* [2] Dioneo, the king of the "seventh day," is regarded by Montale as
"perhaps the most living" character in *The Decameron* and the "Seventh

1. In *Atti del Congresso Internazionale di Studi Danteschi*, vol. 2 (Florence: Sansoni,
1966).
2. Preface to the "Settima giornata" of *Il Decamerone* (Milan: Universale Economica,
1952).

Day" itself as offering "that internal harmony of equilibrium and correspondence which animates all great works of art." However, the seventh book is "generally speaking the poorest of the *Decameron.*" Reading it in isolation from the rest of the work would seem to be like "looking at one of Correggio's frescos with only one eye."

> Everything has become flat, has lost that variety of sentiment, those miraculous nuances, that microcosmic richness that turn so many *novelle* and whole books into masterpieces of prose-cum-poetry such as Italian literature has never known since Boccaccio.

As regards the kind of love treated in Boccaccio's work, which together with "the talent, the pure vitality of instincts and power" constitutes one of the four pivots on which "the whole complex and formidable world of characters" rotates, it is something that has "come down to earth again. And just as Parnassus has become secularized in him (if they hadn't resembled women, the Muses would not have had the same worth they have), in the same way the woman has become terrestrial, and she is now very far (even when she is looked upon with chivalrous respect and the utmost human tenderness) from the ideal of the angelic woman, which was still very much alive in the late thirteenth century and which was by no means destined to disappear soon." But apart from the seventh day, which does not have one single figure "so profoundly depicted and inspired as to be able to remain a symbol, and to recall the 'true' (and not the mistaken) tone of *The Decameron,*" Boccaccio's masterpiece as a whole is "so varied, multifaceted, and illuminating, and so rich both morally and imaginatively" that one could say that

> Besides the host of easy adventures, compromises, and amusements, besides the short-lived effect of witticisms, we like to remember the human dimension of his more real characters who live and move in the charmed circle of an ideal, a hope, a love of what is singular and unique that does not content itself with being witty or derivative.

These observations on Boccaccio anticipate the general tone of Montale's criticism of contemporary novels and short stories.

In this article "La fortuna del Pascoli" (*Corriere della sera,* 30 November 1955) written on the occasion of Pascoli's birth centenary, Montale offers a critical revaluation of the poet in the light of what other critics such as Croce, Serra, Cecchi, Borgese, and Debenedetti have written (Montale is, in fact, reviewing the volume *Omaggio a Pascoli* in this article) and what he himself, both as a critic and as a poet, feels about him. He quotes with approval Cecchi's judgment on Pascoli, which he finds "substantially correct" and according to which "Pascoli worked outside any organic idea of style." Montale's own view is that living, as Pascoli did, in an age of Christian positivism and patriotic socialism, he undertook "ventures outside the scope of his inspiration." As to Pascoli's modernity—a point all the more important since Montale has been regarded by some as a continuator of what Pascoli had already done [3]—Montale thinks that Pascoli has already ceased to be modern. In fact, far from being an innovator, he seems to be essentially a nineteenth-century poet, and this largely because of his addiction to strophic patterns. His defects lie not so much in "the frequent drops of tone or the absence of great memorable verse," as in "the constant indecisiveness both on the formal and the psychological plane," which characterizes all his poetry. His lyrics can seldom stand on their own because "only a deep immersion in one's subject will ensure that," whereas Pascoli "leaves too many safety exits open."

It is, however, on Svevo that Montale has written some of his best criticism. Although as many as half a dozen articles appear in the book *Svevo Montale: Lettere* (Bari: De Donato, 1966), the most substantial piece of critical writing is his essay entitled "Italo Svevo nel centenario della nascita," in which he traces the development of Svevo's art and personality. He starts by emphasizing the maturity and originality of Svevo's novels, which have contributed to the development of the modern Italian novel. One proof of Svevo's maturity is that, even though his early work was not recognized—and this because of the D'Annunzian vogue on the one hand and the Pirandellian vogue on the other—he had the patience to wait for the proper climate of critical opinion that could do him justice. A further proof of Svevo's maturity is the balance in him between the man and the writer.

After having analyzed the plot of *Una Vita*—"that singular novel . . . which more than any other bears the traces of the long preparation that went into its making"—Montale discusses its salient qualities: naturalistic detail, the high degree of sobriety and delicacy with which the characters are portrayed, and the role of Trieste as a character in the novel.

Senilità, on the other hand, displays a greater degree of analytical complexity and maturity. If *Una Vita* is a novel which "a reader of today can take to pieces and put together again by rewriting it mentally," *Senilità* impinges upon us as a whole work. In this novel the psychological analysis is not an end in itself, and in any case there is much more to it than "mere psychologism." The analysis merges with the narrative in such a way that the psychological aspect, or what Montale calls "the clinical aspect," is completely transformed

3. For Pascoli's influence on Montale, or for the kind of affinity that can be claimed between the two poets, see Bonfiglioli's articles listed in the Bibliography.

into poetry. And yet Montale would not go so far as to assert, as some critics have done, that this is Svevo's masterpiece. In fact, for him each one of the novels is a masterpiece, and Svevo seems to have written "the same book three times over."

It is, however, in *La coscienza di Zeno* and the subsequent stories that "the quality of the moralist definitely breaks through the crust of the novelist." Zeno Cosini is the protagonist of the novel and an extension of Emilio Brentani. He represents a new way of life—a life which is successful in the practical sense—and also a greater degree of maturity based on his acceptance of the present *and* of the past. According to Montale, such a character could mature only with the years, since he is not a product of fantasy. As to the possible influence of Joyce on Svevo, Montale doubts if it was really profound, and goes on to outline the distinguishing characteristics of the two writers:

> Their roots are very different. Joyce is a Celt, a sophist brought up by Jesuits, a naturalist who put French naturalism on the road to intensely cultural psychology, nourished by psychoanalysis and mythology. He is a rabid philologist, a rebellious romantic, a polemic who looks for the universal through the small lens of a telescope, through the most intricate spirals of his "particular." Joyce represents the nostalgia of the epoch, whereas Svevo remains happily a narrator, of the Goldonian type, let us say, a tragicomic poet who is lucky enough to ignore theoretically what poetry is (literature that expresses itself in verse, in prefabricated poetic forms, was totally extraneous to him). In short, Svevo is a profoundly Italian writer, even though in a very particular sense of the term, and his form (which saves his name from being dragged into any occasional polemics) is that which every great Italian writer could wish for himself.

Although there are traces of the Triestine culture and dialect in Svevo's writings—Montale calls *La coscienza di Zeno* "a city in search of an author" —there is no writer who is more unmistakably Italian than this Triestine "whose cultural formation took place in Germany and who has not read our classics."

Another important critical essay of Montale's is the one on Croce, where he both analyzes the specific impact Croce's thought and philosophy made on him and elucidates its importance to Italian culture in general.[4] Concerning his early contact with Croce's *Estetica,* he tells us that before he read it he had already become in some way "a cautious initiate." What appealed to

---

4. Montale's essay on Croce, entitled "L'estetica e la critica," which originally appeared in *Il Mondo* (Rome, December 11, 1962), is now included in *Benedetto Croce* (Milan: Edizioni di Comunità, 1963).

him most in Croce's aesthetics was the stress he laid on the autonomy of art. According to Montale, his originality lies in his "making art coincide with a primitive auroral intuition." For Croce, literary taste alone cannot be a measuring rod, since "a thought that admits of a material exteriorization, the formation of a work subsequent to the intuition, would lead to an inadmissible dualism in his system." This constitutes the main weakness in his aesthetics. But the main objection against him is that he does not take into account the fact that "the painted picture, the poem written on paper, the music translated into notes are expressions of an ideal work, and as such, they appertain to the realm of the communication of the work, not to its creation." And he does not do so because "to admit that the material of art could in some way act upon an ideal intuition and modify it would have cast doubt on the principle of the fundamental unity of the arts and would have shaken to its foundation the principle of the ideal character of art." In analyzing the consequences of this "absolute formalism," as he calls it, Montale shows himself at his best as a critic who is also a poet. One such consequence, for instance, is that Croce "could not accept any compromise as to the form conceived as material and hence he had to develop his thought in terms of the content, and in terms of its harmony and its congruence with what may be regarded as the central and dominant motif in every poet." Moreover, his own system made Croce diffident of "art that was too lyrical, too passionate, too involved in the impact of rebellious material." Hence his preference for writers like Ariosto and Verga—"completely *unlyrical* artists, adhering absolutely to one fundamental motif, to one single state of mind." It is not, Montale points out, that artists like Ariosto "are without any bone structure, a 'machine' that makes their poetry possible; but in their case fantasy gets the better of abstract imgaination, rendering the content inoffensive, which in itself does not create any problems."

Again because of the rigorously systematic character of his aesthetics, with its emphasis on the ideal nature of form, Croce's criticism is lacking in "formulations of a technical order, in linguistic analysis, and in the contemplation of the particular and the fragmentary that can be isolated and enjoyed for its own sake."

The fact, however, that Croce emphasizes the element of character has something to do with his own temperament rather than with his aesthetics. In this respect Pascoli, for instance, is the very opposite of Croce. For Pascoli's was "an effeminate temperament, unaware of its limits, altogether lacking in that strength of character and inner security that even a poet like Baudelaire (father of so many subsequent decadents) undoubtedly possessed." It is at least partly the tempermental barrier between him and Leopardi that accounts for Croce's lukewarm attitude to the latter. For Croce, Montale observes, "liked those poets whom he would have liked as men, had he known them." As to the relevance of Croce's thought to modern times, it depends, in Montale's view, on the extent to which the Crocean aesthetics is considered valid today, when one no longer sees the world or history in an idealistic light. For his own part, however, Montale finds Croce's thought valid for three reasons: firstly, because it lays emphasis on the autonomy of art; secondly, because of its expounding the theory of the fundamental unity of art; and lastly because it discusses the concept of technique, which is present in every work of art without itself being art. The last, but by no means least, important reason why Montale feels indebted to Croce is that he has been a source of moral guidance and inspiration, with "his defense of human liberty and responsibility" and his conviction "that the forces of right will never be completely overcome."

Even more than what he has said about Croce or Pascoli, it is what Montale says about Gozzano that has a particular bearing on his own poetry, insofar as Gozzano has been considered one of the earliest influences on Montale.[5] Montale himself seems to have been more impressed by Gozzano's art and technique than by Pascoli's. As an innovator, Montale tells us, Gozzano achieved immediate success because "he became popular without arousing suspicion and he could do so because he had effected a reductive operation in respect of the poetry that preceded him. He offered a new kind of poetry, the poetry of grave semitones and harmonies, that was no longer heroic but 'en pantoufles,' which the French, Belgian, and Flemish post-symbolist poets had already been trying for years.[6] Not that Gozzano himself was consistent in practicing his own theories. He had the shrewdness or instinct to be inconsistent when it suited him. For instance, he followed D'Annunzio up to a point, but then ended by reducing him "as Debussy had reduced Wagner, without, however, ever obtaining results that could be called Debussian."[7] Gozzano's strength and originality are best seen when he is compared with Pascoli and D'Annunzio. Montale also compares him with Robert Browning in that he writes verse that is also prose and that is "functional and narrative." While analyzing the inner structure of Gozzano's verse, Montale points out how he "cut entire strophes from some of his poems and successfully transferred them from one poem

---

5. See Sanguineti's article "Da Gozzano a Montale," which originally appeared in *Lettere italiane,* no. 2 (1965) and is now included in his book, *Tra liberty e crepuscolarismo* (Milan: Mursia, 1965).

6. In his preface to Gozzano's *Poesie* (Milan: Garzanti, 1960). The preface had originally appeared in *Il Verri* (Winter 1957), pp. 3–12.

7. Preface to Gozzano's *Poesie,* p. 9.

to another," and how his poetry is based on a "psychologically poor material." [8] It is this insight into the working of Gozzano's art and language that brings out not only Montale's analytical power as a critic but also, in some respects, his instinctive affinity with the poet.

After Pascoli and Gozzano, the other important twentieth-century Italian poets on whom Montale has written are Saba, Campana, Cardarelli, and Sereni. In the course of his critical examination of Saba's poetry, too, Montale makes certain observations that are relevant to his own poetry. The salient quality of Saba's poetry, and especially of *Trieste e una donna,* is "the greater degree of perspective separation about his figurations and the tendency to graphic neatness which confers on our old *canzonetta* a new sense or flavor." At a certain stage in his development as a poet, Saba ceases to be a "poet of occasion" and becomes a "poet of expressive concentration, with a sense of architecture and space." Another prominent characteristic of Saba's poetry is its "impassioned recollection of the vast experience of an artist who no longer needs material for his poetry outside poetry itself." [9]

In 1942, while reviewing the third edition of Dino Campana's *Canti orfici* (originally published in 1928) Montale examined the question raised by Gianfranco Contini as to whether Campana is "a visual or a seeing poet" [10] and found "the horns of this dilemma anything but irreconcilable." In his early cultural formation Campana was open to all the "isms" and influences around him—symbolism, futurism, and D'Annunzianism, for example, or Nietzsche, Whitman, and Rimbaud. However, the obscurity and the fragmentary nature of his poetry is at least partly due to the loss of mental equilibrium that had been threatening him for years and as a consequence of which he was admitted to a mental hospital in 1918 where he remained until his death in 1932.

It is when Montale compares Campana's obscurity and the fragmentary nature of his verse with that of Ungaretti that he makes some highly pertinent comments. In Ungaretti the danger of obscurity is accepted as "the inevitable counterpart of a risky desire for poetic purity," for he regards the fragmentary form of verse as a self-sufficient genre of lyric expression. To a certain extent Campana himself belongs to this school. But the essential characteristics of his poetry at its best, as exemplified in the *Canti orfici,* are "a sense of urgency," "the energetic will and voluptuousness of the nomad," which he shared with Whitman and Rimbaud, and the concept of poetry as "an undifferentiated act of nature that is aesthetic as well as voluntary and

8. Ibid., p. 11.
9. See Montale's article "Ragioni di Umberto Saba," *Solaria,* no. 5 (May 1928), pp. 29–32.
10. See Contini's essay on Campana in *Esercizi di Lettura.*

moral." When he comes to analyze Campana's limitations as a poet, Montale lays his finger on his fundamental weakness—his lack of self-control and the fact that he was distracted by "too many abstract possibilities." Hence one would have to make a rigorous selection from the already small output of his verse in order to save "a few incorruptible pages," [11] where the authentic originality of his inspiration is present in a fully realized and accomplished form.

In 1959 Vincenzo Cardarelli died in Rome and Montale wrote his obituary for the *Corriere della sera* (June 16), an obituary which also happens to be one of his best critical articles. While considering Cardarelli's work, Montale recapitulates the literary and cultural climate in which it developed, as well as the ethos and influence of the famous Italian periodical *La Ronda,* of which Cardarelli was the chief founder and exponent. However, according to Montale, it is for works like *Prologhi* and parts of *Viaggi nel tempo* that Cardarelli will be chiefly remembered. For they illustrate "that low tone, that prosaic form of verse" which was Cardarelli's own invention and which was most congenial to his temperament as a moralist and controversialist. In his later and less successful poems, however, external motifs are introduced which do not organize themselves into a compelling and coherent whole. There are also Leopardian echoes in Cardarelli's poetry, which show "on what a razor's edge [he] had to walk." And then there was his intransigent neoclassicism and his passionate belief that "the spirit of the Risorgimento had adulterated Italian culture, rendering everything unnatural," as a result of which Cardarelli found himself out of place in an age when "a tide of commercial prose beat against an Italy exhausted by its victory in the war."

Of the younger Italian poets about whom Montale has written Vittorio Sereni is the most important. In his review of Sereni's *Strumenti umani* [12] he starts by commenting on the new trends in Italian poetry, and on the growing affinity between the modern techniques and concepts of music and those of poetry. But a poet like Sereni "tends to create complex forms in which the significances are interwoven or superimpose themselves, as happens in that state of drowsiness which represents the life of the man of our times, reduced as he is to the condition of being the object of others and of himself." In Sereni's previous books, *Frontiera* (1941) and *Diario d'Algeria* (1947), the sense of solitude was tempered "by the immersion in his landscape, by his awareness of and perhaps pride in belonging to an ethnic and moral frontier." However, this was poetry "in a minor tone, not rich in color, but rather

11. See Montale's article "Sulla poesia di Dino Campana" in *Italia che scrive* (September-October 1942).
12. In *Corriere della sera,* October 21, 1965.

muted as a painting by the great Ranzoni." As to the metre Sereni used in the first two books, it is for the most part traditional even if "the free alternating of different metres" enabled him to adapt himself "to that concept of poetry that arises out of prose, which is not always the illusory mirage of the poets of today."

In *Strumenti umani,* on the other hand, the traditional verse metre is so molded as to have been brought in line with the prose poem. Hence, while reading this book "the reader must defer bringing the eye in accordance with the ear, and following or inventing the caesuras in the longer lines, after which the polymetre reveals itself as an instrument capable of muffling and interiorizing the sound to the maximum, without descending to the totally horizontal level of prose." Montale then offers a cogent interpretation and evaluation of the nature of the experience this book embodies and the springs of thought and inspiration underlying it. The poems are regarded as so many "pieces, monologues, or snatches of meditation," which express the restlessness and anguish of modern man.

With regard to the novel, apart from what he wrote on Svevo, Montale's views on other novelists such as Palazzeschi, Moravia, Tomasi di Lampedusa, and Calvino are equally penetrating. In an early essay "Palazzeschi ieri e oggi" [13] he deals with the evolution of Palazzeschi's talent as a novelist and poet while taking into account his special relationship with futurism. His shift from poetry to the novel came when he "seemed to have reached the goal of writing poetry as a newspaper item, as poetry in shirt-sleeves." He achieved full maturity as a novelist and prose writer in *Sorelle Materassi* and *Fratelli Cuccoli,* where his qualities both as a poet and as a novelist are best revealed.

Another of Montale's critiques of Palazzeschi appeared in *Corriere della sera* (4 June 1967) in the form of a review of *Il Doge.* The novel is set in, and is Palazzeschi's tribute to, "a completely timeless Venice." The first half of the review is a summary of the plot of the novel. In the second half Montale offers a critical summing up of the novel itself. The only character in the novel, we are told, "is collective language, vociferation." Together with the absence of characters in the accepted sense, there is also the absence of *"Consecutio temporum* and of subordinates and coordinates." This is to be accounted for by what Montale calls "an antigrammatical thought in action, versatile thought which is always in the process of formation." Even the interior dialogue is of a special kind, because "the speaker of the monologue is not a man, nor even the author of the book, but a conglomeration and a

13. In *Immagine* (Rome, March–July 1948), pp. 437–38.

tower of infinite verbiage culled from all sides." However, the high-water mark of Palazzeschi's originality as a writer is reached precisely through the unmistakably personal and authentic quality of his writing, no matter how trivial the argument.

Coming to Tomasi di Lampedusa, Montale recognizes in *Il gattopardo* a book which "the author had carried and developed in himself all his life and which didn't perhaps receive the author's final touches." [14] Although Montale finds this novel "formally almost perfect," he detects a certain lack of harmony and proportion in the grouping or interweaving of individual episodes in it, as well as a certain lack of rapport between the novelist and the moralist in Lampedusa. Montale's own explanation for this unevenness is that *Il gattopardo* is in fact "the reduction of the saga novel that Lampedusa never wrote." But in spite of architectonic looseness and disharmony, the novel has a "surprising degree of spiritual dignity," being, as it is, "the book of a great gentleman, a great snob in the highest sense of the word, a man who had seen all that happened in his life as a poet-narrator with an implacable clarity of vision and a feeling for the vicissitudes of life that is at once stoical and profoundly charitable."

Another writer of fiction from southern Italy on whom Montale has written with sympathy and acumen is Corrado Alvaro. In common with Verga and other writers from the south, Alvaro had, according to Montale, a "secret vein of sadness" which served him as "an inner reserve." The main proof of his individuality lies in the fact that he held himself equally aloof from the two opposing tendencies of his age, "neoclassicism and neorealism." It is not so much in terms of what he actually achieved in the realm of art as in terms of his theoretical and intellectual concern with the nature and meaning of art itself—and narrative art in particular—that Alvaro's historical importance as an innovator lies. Thanks to him and some younger writers, especially Brancati and Pavese, "the problem of the Italian narrative is posed today in altogether new terms."

In discussing Alvaro's best known, though not necessarily best novel, *Gente in Aspromonte,* Montale compares it to Verga's *Cavalleria rusticana,* in that it is a work the public persists in remembering more than any other, even though the author has written better books, including *Vent'anni, L'Età breve,* and a collection of short stories, *Settantacinque racconti.*

In his article "La magia di Bontempelli" (*Corriere della sera,* 23 July 1960), Montale assesses the historical place of Massimo Bontempelli between the two world wars, the secret of his appeal as a writer and his importance as "an innovator of Italian prose," his "magic realism," his "art of watching and of

14. In his review of *Il gattopardo,* in *Corriere della sera,* December 12, 1958.

springing a surprise," and his ability to find amusement in those aspects of the world "which render others miserable and desolate."

On Moravia, too, Montale has written more than once. In his review of *La noia* (*Corriere della sera,* 24 November 1960) Montale refers to Moravia's conviction that "today no one believes anymore in an objective truth and hence the only novel that can interest the reader is the one written in the first person," since there is no way of knowing what another person thinks. Montale's own view is that such observations on the part of the novelist do not help us very much to understand "the character of the protagonist who speaks in the first person." However, the novel has some positive virtues—for instance, the vital presentation of Rome as an archetype of a modern city, or Moravia's ability to turn such characters as Balestrieri, or the feared and victorious rival Luciani into something "living and credible." Thus, in spite of his obsession with the ugly, "which seems today to be the only font of inspiration for those who believe professionally in not believing in anything," Moravia offers in this novel "some of his most successful objective representations."

Italo Calvino is another contemporary writer on whom Montale has written. In commenting on Calvino's *Le cosmocomiche* (*Corriere della sera,* 5 December 1965), a collection of stories dealing with science fiction, or what Montale calls "science fiction turned upside down," Montale singles out for special praise a particular story, and what he says regarding its merit constitutes a valuable insight into the art of story-telling itself. In this story, we are told, "the intellectual game comes closer to poetic illumination." Although one thinks of Borges as a possible author Calvino may have read, there is no comparison between the two, since the former is concerned with "cultural pretexts and paradoxes," whereas Calvino works on "abstract and surrealist hypotheses." Montale also praises Calvino's "stylistic efficacy, his measured use of the spoken language, and his lucid intelligence" no less than his "strong sense of disengagement, of nonbelonging."

Apart from these poets and novelists, the two important critics on whom Montale has written are Emilio Cecchi and Sergio Solmi. Since 1924 he has written as many as eight articles or reviews on the various aspects of Cecchi's work. The first few sentences of the obituary Montale wrote when Cecchi died in 1966 (*Corriere della sera,* September 6) are a testimony to his high esteem for the man:

I have rarely had to face a journey of seven or eight hours (like that from Genoa to Rome) simply for the purpose of visiting a friend. But if

I search my memory, the first, perhaps the only exception that comes to mind, is the occasion of my first meeting with Emilio Cecchi. It must have been in 1924, when I published my first article on the author of *Pesci Rossi*.

In most of these articles Montale rightly emphasizes the creative side of Cecchi's work, as distinguished from the intellectual or critical side, and discusses the process by which Cecchi's prose style on the one hand and his thought and experience on the other become closely integrated so as to offer "authentic life, not literature." In fact, all his writings are characterized by an "extreme spiritual coherence" and a "profound moral seriousness."

In "Due volti di un critico" (*Corriere della sera,* 17 September 1952) Montale draws a distinction between Cecchi as "a critical essayist" and Cecchi as "a lyric essayist." In his early critical essays on Kipling and Pascoli he finds Cecchi's style "involved, difficult, and even obscure"; but later on a new Cecchi emerges, a "clear, perceptive, and exact instructor and a fine judge." Cecchi's talent as a writer of *prosa d'arte* developed side by side with his critical powers, so that he may be described as a major poet in a minor poetic form. What he offers in fact is not a Baudelairian or Mallarmean type of prose poem, but "a sort of colloquial discourse, with a deliberately subdued elegance that is capable of accommodating an almost limitless gamut of themes and contents."

In his obituary on Cecchi (*Corriere della sera,* 6 September 1966) Montale sums up Cecchi's achievement as a critic of art and literature, essayist, and prose stylist. His essential quality as a critic of art lies in "mimesis, the capacity to reproduce stylistically the formal character of the works examined." It is only when this result is not achieved, nor even attempted, that the element of evaluative judgment comes in. But it is a judgment which is "lacking in inner conviction, and is always an act of homage to the good intentions of a writer worthy of respect." What, in fact, Cecchi demanded of a writer or an artist, Montale observes, is "simply this: a style. But a style that was created from within, a style that was the fruit of a vigilant moral conscience and not merely a moralistic conscience."

The first time Montale wrote on Sergio Solmi was when he reviewed his book *Il pensiero di Alain* in *Pegaso* (November, 1930); the second, when he reviewed *La salute di Montaigne* in *Corriere della sera* (18 March 1953). He finds Solmi's critical writings characterized by an "intense inner vibration" and "an ever vigilant attentiveness to the weight and truthfulness of the word," as a result of which his literary criticism "has always a point of arrival, a result: it is not a game that exhausts itself." And in a recent tribute to Solmi on his seventieth birthday, "Sergio Solmi: Man and Poet" (*Corriere della sera,* 14 December 1969), Montale observes: "If clear-sightedness, that is to say, the ability to see before and better than others what is hidden in the many nebulae which have obscured our vision is a gift, then we can say that Solmi has had this gift from the very outset of his career."

When Montale comes to discuss foreign writers his criticism acquires a frankness of tone which is not always evident in his criticism of Italian ones. In the field of English literature, apart from his translations of some of Shakespeare's plays and sonnets and a play by Marlowe, the earliest author he wrote about was Defoe. In his preface to the Italian translation of *Robinson Crusoe,*[15] Montale refers to Defoe's overflowing vitality, his pungent moralistic vein, and his inventive realism, by virtue of which he is "one of the greatest and most typical realist-surrealist writers of all times and of all literatures." The fantastic element in him, however, usually has a substratum of verisimilitude, so that what he offers is "an ingenious narrative stratagem, a happy falsehood." Hence, as regards the plot and story of *Robinson Crusoe,* everything develops "freely and organically, like a trunk round its center. Everything seems natural, irreplaceable." And Robinson Crusoe's common sense never appears to be the result of a "boring foresight" or a "weary resignation," but rather the reflection of "energetic will-power, a joyous natural impulse, a wise, methodical, and characteristically British love of comfort, common sense, and clear-sightedness." Thus the secret of Defoe's popularity lies in "this extreme adherence to the minute gears, the big little miseries of life" coupled with "that continual, inexhaustible heroic resistance to the wear and tear of necessity, adversity, and solitude, which makes us sympathize with Robinson Crusoe as we do with Moll Flanders."

After Defoe, most of Montale's critical comments on English writers are on modern authors from Thomas Hardy onward. In his preface to my translation of a selection of Hardy's poems, Montale considers Hardy as that rare example of "a writer of prosaic prose who has also been a very poetical poet."[16] Another characteristic of Hardy's poetry is "its rigidly closed forms and impeccably traditional stanzas." And as for the poems Hardy wrote after the death of his first wife, Montale considers them "one of the peaks of modern poetry, and not of Victorian poetry, to which one would have thought a poet already writing in 1887 would normally have belonged."

15. In his preface to the Italian translation of *Robinson Crusoe* (Milan: Universale Economica, 1951).
16. See *Poesie di Thomas Hardy,* selected and translated by G. Singh, with a preface by Eugenio Montale (Parma: Guanda, 1968).

Montale's review of the French translation of James Joyce's *Dubliners* goes back to 1926 when it had appeared in *La Fiera Letteraria* (no. 38, 19 September). In it he set out to defend the two stories "A Meeting" and "The Two Gallants" which had scandalized puritanical readers and reviewers of the time. It would be difficult to imagine, he commented, "a more sober and convincing rendering of such delicate themes," which brought out Joyce's superb ability to translate "this concrete provincial Dublin into a rigorously abstract city—a city outside of time."

Many years later Montale reviewed the Italian translation of D. H. Lawrence's poems.[17] As a poet he found Lawrence at his best in those frag ments or lyrics "where the verse is not intrinsically useless, even if it remains always gnomic or descriptive," or where the poet feels himself a child of the sun or identifies himself with a bat or with the growing grass, or when, inspired by the feeling of a deep religious awe for nature, "his old puritanism gives way to a delirious cosmic orgasm."

Another important writer about whom Montale has written more than once is Ezra Pound. Montale's position vis-à-vis Pound is to some extent symptomatic of the general attitudes in Italy toward Pound's work. His earliest article, a review of Alfredo Rizzardi's Italian translation of the *Pisan Cantos,* appeared in November 1953. According to Montale, Pound's interest in Italy was occasioned not so much by the poetic tradition which, so far as Pound was concerned, "had ceased to be fruitful from the Trecento onwards," as by the fact that he regarded Italy as a sort of "archive, not, of course, of erudite information, but of exciting cultures." Italy served him as "a good historical massage" for the preparation of his *Cantos*—"the longest and most comprehensive Dantesque-Joycian poem conceived in our times."

In this interesting but not altogether convincing summing up of Pound's attitude to Italian literature (for instance, Pound did, unlike Landor or Browning, realize the importance of a post-Trecento classic like Leopardi) one can sense a critical rebuke to Pound for ignoring or underestimating everything that had happened "from the Trecento onwards" and for his extremely eclectic, almost gratuitously personal view of Italian history, literature, and criticism.

When he comes to Pound's influence on and attitude toward other poets as well as to his desire to renovate or, as Pound himself put it, to "resuscitate the dead art of poetry,"[18] Montale again makes one or two rather controversial points. For instance, he tells us that "as the leader of imagism and later of vorticism, Pound had exercised an influence even on poets to whom he

17. *Corriere della sera,* 27 May 1961.
18. "E P. Ode Pour L'Election De Son Sepulchre."

himself owed much, namely Yeats and Eliot." Montale doesn't specify exactly what Pound owed or could have owed to Yeats or to Eliot. No doubt Pound read Yeats, who was twenty years older than he, and regarded him as the greatest living poet. He also declared that at that time "one was drunk with 'Celticism,' and with Dowson's 'Cynara.' " [19] But that is as far as one can go by way of mustering any evidence of the influence Yeats may have exercised on Pound or the debt Pound may have owed to Yeats. The influence was, in fact, the other way round insofar as, through advice, admonition, and criticism as well as through his own poetic practice, Pound not only helped Yeats, as Yeats himself admitted, "get back to the definite and the concrete and away from modern abstractions," but also to get away from "the smooth regularity of the Tennysonian tradition . . . this wavering, uncertain langor," etc. And as regards Pound's influence on Eliot, it is enough to think of the major—though not the only—evidence provided by *The Waste Land,* whereas there is not much one can point to in Pound's poetry that may have been the result of Eliot's influence on him.

Again, when Montale observes that Pound and his friends and followers, while importing "modern poetry" to America, remained "extraneous to the Virgilian and Petrarchan traditions of poetry which through Leopardi and Baudelaire have still remained the secret of the European lyric," and that it was perhaps due to "their misunderstanding of these traditions, that they came to detest Swinburne," there are two fallacies involved in this statement. Firstly, in Pound's concept of and attitude toward the form and pattern of the lyric, Leopardi played a role that was no less important than that of Catullus, Villon, Dante, or Cavalcanti. Pound not only translated a poem by Leopardi, but he is also on record as having recommended Leopardi to Miss Iris Barry as "the only author since Dante who need trouble you." And while dismissing Tagore's philosophy, as not having "much in it for a man who has 'felt the pangs' or been pestered by Western civilization," he went on to affirm that Tagore "isn't either Villon or Leopardi" and that "the modern demands just a dash of their insight." As for Baudelaire, there is nothing in Pound's view to suggest that he regarded him as extraneous. What however, he does say is that along with Verlaine, Baudelaire is "the least use, pedagogically, I mean," and this at least partly because, like Petrarch, he and Verlaine "beget imitation and one can learn nothing from them." [20] As to Pound's definition of Virgil as "a Tennysonianized version of Homer," Pound was merely asserting that aspect of the European lyric which traced its

19. See Pound's essay, "Lionel Johnson," in *Literary Essays of Erza Pound* ed. T.S. Eliot (London: Faber & Faber, 1964).
20. Ezra Pound, *Letters,* ed. D. D. Paige (London, 1951), pp. 55, 60.

origin to and derived its sustenance from Dante and Cavalcanti rather than
Petrarch—hardly the same thing as ignoring the secret of the European lyric
in toto. Also, in the case of Swinburne, whatever might have been the attitude
of other American poets, both Pound and Eliot had considerable respect for
him while at the same time being conscious of his defects "by the bushelful,"
as Pound puts it. There are, he observes, "fine passages, like fragments of
fine marble statues" in Swinburne's poetry.[21]

Coming to Montale's views on Pound's own poetry, one finds them no
less interesting or controversial. He regards *Pisan Cantos* as "a symphony, not
of words, but of free phrases . . . tied together by a *montage* which, for all its
apparent incoherence, far exceeds that of some parts of Joyce's *Ulysses* or
Eliot's *Waste Land.*" The whole poem is, for him, no more than "a lightning
recapitulation of the history of the world (or *a* world) without any coherent
link of time and space." In the second article (*Corriere d'informazione,* 18–19
November 1955), Montale deals with Pound's economic theories and his own
personal contact with him between 1925 and 1935. In the third article
(*Corriere d'informazione,* 26 April 1958), written shortly before Pound was
released from St. Elizabeth's Hospital, Montale admits that the treatment
meted out to him is "treatment that does no honor to his country" and that he
is far from believing there was any element of truth in Pound's being mad,
for "as a theorist and critic of poetry, as a translator and recreator of poets,
he argued only too well." In his last article (*Corriere della sera,* 19 December
1965), while reviewing the sixth number of the French periodical *Herme*
which was dedicated to Pound, Montale argues about Pound's attachment to
the past and his evasion of the present. Whatever one might think of Pound's
attitude toward the past—and most poets' attitude toward it would not
stand up to critical scrutiny or analysis any more than does Pound's—it is
hard to see how his poetry, inextricably rooted as it is in the life and ethos of
contemporary civilization, can be regarded—as Montale regards it—as an
evasion of the present.

When dealing with Eliot, on the other hand, Montale shows greater
sympathy and understanding. His earliest essay, entitled "Eliot and Ourselves," came out in 1947.[22] It is partly the feeling of what he calls "immediate intimacy" with Eliot that accounts for his being favorably predisposed
toward a more positive evaluation of Eliot's work and personality. Consequently, Montale's criticism of him is at once more constructive and more
subtle than his criticism of Pound. Eliot, Montale points out, had "that close

21. See "Swinburne Versus His Biographers," in *Literary Essays of Ezra Pound,* p. 294.
22. This article originally appeared in *L'Immagine* (Rome, November–December 1947),
and was later included in English translation in the volume of essays published in honor
of Eliot's sixtieth birthday and edited by Richard Marsh and Tambimuttu (London, 1948).

contact with the lofty European tradition that had been lost for many years," with the result that he made a salutary impact on contemporary Italian culture and readers. Both Eliot and Valéry, Montale adds, "brought Italian readers to a less superficial knowledge of their poetic patrimony, to a more intimate sense of their classicism." Not that this in itself makes them "classical poets," which they are not. But it makes them "strongly vital and significant poets who cannot be reduced to the norms of a school." All this is quite true, but it does not take into account the fact that Eliot's "contact with the lofty European tradition" was itself influenced by Pound's own earlier contact with it, and that it was Pound who did more than Eliot to emphasize the links between past and present and to show their critical and creative relevance, in his seminal essays on Cavalcanti, the Renaissance, the Troubadours, Arnaut Daniel, as well as through his lively translations. Eliot may have owed something to Valéry, but he certainly owed much more to Pound in his realization and interpretation of the crucial role his "contact with the lofty European tradition" played in writing his own poety. Montale's failure to recognize this accounts at least in part for his exclusion of Pound from the group of those he regards as representing the poetic current of the last hundred years, which includes Eliot, Valéry, Yeats, Apollinaire—even Hopkins and Emily Dickinson—but not Pound!

Similarly, in his brief comment on the awarding of the Nobel Prize to Eliot (*Corriere della sera,* November 5, 1948), while singling out precisely those qualities of *The Waste Land* which Eliot achieved thanks to Pound's excisions and modifications, Montale refers to Paul Valéry, Gottfried Benn, and "a few others" who had done the same as Eliot, but not to Pound. In this connection Eliot's own view of Pound's influence on his work may be quoted. In his article "Isolated Superiority" (*Dial,* January 1928) he wrote:

> A man who devises new rhythms is a man who extends and refines our sensibility; and that is not merely a matter of "technique." I have, in recent years, cursed Mr. Pound often enough; for I am never sure that I can call my verse my own; just when I am most pleased with myself, I feel that I have caught up some echo from a verse of Pound's. . . . He enabled a few other persons, including myself, to improve their verse sense; so that he has improved poetry through other men as well as by himself. I cannot think of anyone writing verse, of our generation and the next, whose verse (if any good) has not been improved by the study of Pound's. . . . What is curious is his complete and isolated superiority as a master of verse form. No one living has practised the art of verse with such austerity and devotion; and no one living has practised it with more success.

Montale's last article on Eliot, "Ricordo di T. S. Eliot" (*Corrierre della sera,* 6 January 1965) was written after Eliot's death. No Italian—or for that matter European—poet could find himself in the same cultural situation, Montale points out, in which Pound and Eliot found themselves. While describing the nature of Eliot's poetic objectivity, Montale connects it with his interest in Dante, and goes on to distinguish between Eliot's and Pound's interest in Dante. "A tenacious upholder of objective poetry," Eliot found in *The Divine Comedy* a perfect example of that objectivity "which turns symbols and allegories into something palpable and living." Pound, on the other hand, went further and found in Dante's masterpiece a model for his own "encyclopaedic epic of ancient and above all modern history, a universal bazaar of life presented in the form of poetry."

After Hardy, Lawrence, Pound, and Eliot, W. H. Auden is the only other English poet Montale has discussed. His first and longest article appeared in 1952 (*Corriere della sera,* 12 August). Rather than being the sort of poetry about which Edgar Allan Poe theorized—"poetry which demands strong expressive concentration, a great power of musical transfiguration and a total interfusion of the idea and significance" such as was achieved by Hopkins, Yeats, and Valéry—Auden's poetry is characterized by a "less ascetic nature" and is based on "a wider and more generic concept of poetry," a concept according to which "every composition in verse (or quasi verse) which expressed anything intelligible in conformity with the rules of art" becomes poetry. Montale, however, recognizes Auden as being the most important poet of his generation, representing that sense of anguish which is not "an up-to-date ingredient, but a form of eternal restlessness that is common to all men." In another note (*Corriere della sera,* 17 November 1961), Montale praises Auden for his "indisputable verbal felicity," as a result of which he would be regarded as "an experimentalist" in Italy.

Montale's interest in American literature is not merely an offshoot of his interest in English; it is also symptomatic of the general vogue that American literature has increasingly enjoyed in Italy since World War II—a vogue that was heralded by such writers as Pavese, Cecchi, and Vittorini. Montale has written about Edgar Allan Poe, Emily Dickinson, Robert Frost, and Theodore Roethke. In his article on Poe (*Corriere della sera,* 23 March 1956), Montale traces the nature and impact of what he calls "the contagion of Poe" both in and outside the field of post-Baudelairian literature in Europe. Not only are Poe's poems considered "one of the components of early French symbolism of more or less Baudelairian derivation," but by virtue of his very personality Poe is regarded as a *poète maudit* who exercised a considerable fascination for

—if not real influence on—a number of artists. Although in England and America he has long ceased to be considered anything more than a minor artist, he still enjoys practically the same vogue in Italy and France today as before. And certainly as far as Italy is concerned, Poe and Whitman have exercised a greater influence than Emily Dickinson, whom Montale regards as "the Christina Rossetti of New England." Montale's essay on Emily Dickinson (*Corriere della sera,* 4 May 1957) is one of the most comprehensive critiques of a foreign poet that he has ever written. It combines a sensitive and even sympathetic appreciation of the real virtues of her art with a drastic assessment of her limitations. Her profuse poetic output, Montale finds, is lacking in "the minimum *labor limae."* And he sees a link between her secluded and uneventful life and, paradoxically enough, "the exuberant psychological and emotional charge of her verse." She embodies "the extreme example of a life *written,* not lived; and written with a particular intensity precisely because it was materially or physically not lived." As to the question of literary influences and affinities, it is strange, Montale observes, that while she studied Browning, Sir Thomas Browne, and the Metaphysical poets with particular interest, she should not have been drawn to Blake, "since there is an affinity between the two, especially with regard to the feline, almost bestial way in which they both attack the divine mystery."

Montale's brief note on Robert Frost (*Corriere della sera,* 30 January 1963) was written as an obituary. He calls Frost "the patriarch of American poetry and undoubtedly its most authentic voice," and analyzes the essential characteristics of his poetry as being his "moral sanity" and his "religious disquietude," which does not, however, disturb the sober surface of his art.

In his comment on Theodore Roethke (*Corriere della sera,* 3 June 1966), Montale describes him as being "a real professional lyricist" and typically American in virtue of "his effusion and his capacity for perennial stupor," which contrasts so sharply with the later Yeats. For if, in the end, Yeats turns out to be an incomparably *miglior fabbro,"* it is because of his different cultural background and a "more concentrated vision."

Among the American novelists, Montale has written on Melville, Hawthorne, Hemingway, Faulkner, F. Scott Fitzgerald, and Sinclair Lewis. The occasion for writing on Melville was the publication of Montale's own translation of *Billy Budd* (1942), for which he wrote a preface. Together with Hawthorne and Poe, Melville belongs to "the great period, the heroic period of American literature," that is to say, the period between 1845 and 1855. And of these three writers, he is the one closest to us, because "in him that obscure sense of being condemned which the puritan Hawthorne modified and channeled into an honorable literary career, not however without its compromises, rises to biblical heights and at times explodes with Manichean violence." In *Billy Budd,* "the flower and the crowning achievement of Melville's output," this feeling finds consummate expression.

But the American novelist on whom Montale has written more than once is Hemingway who, like Pound, knew and loved Italy and spent a lot of time there. It is in Italy that one of Hemingway's latest novels, *Across the River and into the Trees,* is set. In the obituary notice published after the false rumor of Hemingway's death in an air crash,[23] Montale referred to Hemingway's life as that of "a profoundly 'vital artist,' " who was not exactly D'Annunzian, but who was nonetheless inclined to consider life as the best of the possibilities of art. A few months later, when Hemingway was awarded the Nobel Prize, Montale wrote about him again (*Corriere della sera,* 29 October 1954), pointing out that his earlier novels were the most successful and that *The Sun Also Rises* was "one of the best books of this century." In these works Hemingway "seemed to have snatched from Chekhov and Hamsun the art of expressing the inexpressible in the simplest possible words, but in reality with the most sophisticated orchestration which, he continues, is at once the delight and the despair of his numerous imitators." However, the besetting weakness of all Hemingway's writings, which is also their strength, lies in their being "proof against any form of spiritualism." This shortcoming was counterbalanced by what Montale calls in another article (*Corriere della sera,* 4 July 1961) "that sense of plain, almost infantile humanity which is furiously rejected and buried in the depths of one's consciousness as unworthy of a man 'of our times,' as his best books bring out." Instead of being a novelist in the accepted sense of the term—a novelist with "a traditional repertoire of characters, incidents, and situations"—Hemingway was "rather a reporter, a great reporter of life; and therein lay his originality, which is easy to misunderstand today when a false spontaneity and a facile photographic abandon are out to destroy the form and pattern of the contemporary novel."

Montale's last article on Hemingway (*Corriere della sera,* 16 May 1965) was a review of *Across the River and into the Trees* in which "the identification of the author with the hero was carried to the furthest limits." The whole book is "a musical game of Hemingway's best syncopated phrases," and Renata, the female protagonist in the novel, is "one of the most beautiful of Hemingway's women, beautiful as truth and with a firm naturalness of

23. See Montale's poem on his meeting with Hemingway in Venice in *Satura.* It is the second of the *Due prose veneziane:* "Visse ancora qualche anno," Montale tells us of Hemingway, "e morendo due volte / ebbe il tempo di leggere le sue necrologie."

soul." But Montale's evaluation of this novel in particular and of Hemingway's work in general is accompanied by important critical reservations:

> Faced with this and other works by Hemingway, as for instance the much discussed *A Movable Feast,* one must take it or leave it: there is no other alternative. The writer was moving toward a precious decomposition altogether congenial to the childlike nature of a man who had not grown up, of a man *manqué.* But an art like his, which must retemper the data of culture—and there was no lack of such data in Hemingway—in a perennial bath of irritated and flashy sensuality, can never become a profoundly thoughtful and meditative art. A certain basic immaturity is common to all the writers of Hemingway's generation. Perhaps for the first time in such writers *l'art pour l'art* in the most immediate sense of the term, and with its rich possibilities, but also with its limitations, revealed its potentialities in the field of narrative writing.

Writing about Sinclair Lewis in his obituary notice (*Corriere della sera,* 11 January 1951), Montale contrasted him with "the school of those difficult realists of the last group [from Faulkner on] who write only for the few and who create for themselves exasperated and often exasperating problems of style. Lewis wrote for everybody in a language that everybody could understand." Although not always a master in the art of creating characters, Lewis nonetheless "excelled in the study of ambient and often in satire; in his writings the outline devoured the work and became the principal argument and the most living theme."

In his obituary notice on F. Scott Fitzgerald (*Corriere della sera,* 7 March 1951) Montale observes that the decisive factor which guarantees "the solidity of Fitzgerald's work" is his "capacity to make moral judgments," and hence the fundamental difference between him and Hemingway is that "he still dares to say what Hemingway doesn't." Fitzgerald's appeal as a modern writer lies in the fact that he shed a disquieting light on one of the most dramatic aspects of his age, namely, that of "the ebbing away of vitality."

In his comments on Faulkner (*Corriere della sera,* 9 July 1962) Montale again makes a comparison with Hemingway. While Hemingway's chief aim was to "render sharp and subtle 'the artistic mode of writing,' Faulkner's prose tends to be condensed and clotted in his attempt to relive the memories and fantasies of the ancestral South which was, in his case, a living experience before it became a literary one." Nevertheless he remains a "writer who is more famous than read" and who represents "a pure primitive vitality, without symbols and without any occult significance."

The most important French writers Montale has written about are Paul Valéry, Valéry Larbaud, François Mauriac, Paul Éluard, and Albert Camus. Montale's first article on Larbaud was published in *Il Baretti* (15 January 1925). He finds various influences on him of writers such as Montaigne and Whitman, Choderlos de Laclos, Walter Savage Landor, and James Joyce, whom Larbaud considered to be "the only begetter" of "the inner monologue." Moreover, there is in his writings the pervasive "myth of the European man" and the kind of reality that embodies this myth "sustains all his work and gives it resonance." Nevertheless, Larbaud's writings are lacking in "that technical coherence which would have given them a more solid character."

Montale's article on Mauriac (*Corriere della sera,* 7 November 1952) appeared when the latter was awarded the Nobel Prize. Describing him as a Catholic writer, Montale notes that the Catholicism of his novel is a type in which "the devil and holy water play an equal part," and he himself is "a Goncourt who ends up in Bourget, a writer destined to be torn by the conflict between art and the intellectual demimonde" and at the same time one "who could afford the luxury of being an *homme de gauche* within certain limits, which enabled him to take sides openly against Phalangism without frightening his numerous admirers too much."

As to Mauriac's style, Montale praises him for his ability to hide "his vital contradictions under a mantle which seems poor, but which is in fact richly embroidered." However, Mauriac's genuine style and artificial stylization not only coexist but are almost inseparable, so that it would be difficult for his future critics "to single out his absolute masterpiece."

In his obituary article on Éluard (*Corriere della sera,* 19 November 1952) Montale sums up his merit and originality by describing him as "the most authentic lyricist" after Valéry. And insofar as Éluard is above all a love poet, what Montale admires most in him is the way in which he combines the traditional and the modern in his treatment of love.

On Camus, Montale wrote more than once. His last two articles (*Corriere della sera,* 17 October 1957 and 5 January 1960) were written on the occasion of the awarding of the Nobel Prize and on Camus's death, respectively. In *La peste,* which he regards as Camus's masterpiece, he finds "a narrative of classical composure, more a *récit* than a novel, a chronicle rather than a work of imagination." In *L'homme révolté,* on the other hand, as well as in some of Camus's essays, we have "a sort of *engagement* which is personally rewarding by virtue of its authentic stoicism *après le déluge.*" In the second article Montale stresses that rare kind of strength and individuality in Camus which earned him fame both with the public and the critics.

Outside of English, American, and French literature, Montale's most important articles are on Chekhov, Pasternak, and Cavafy. His article on Chekhov (*Corriere d'informazione,* 31 July–August 1954) came out on the fiftieth anniversary of Chekhov's death and examined the nature and extent of Chekhov's influence on European narrative literature—especially the short story—comparing it with Baudelaire's influence on poetry. The essence of his artistic singularity no less than his individual personality, according to Montale, lies in "his inexhaustible power of communication," in the "insubstantial character of his art, which makes one think of natural breathing" and which is "almost independent of the weight of words." As to Chekhov's dramatic compositions, Montale considers them to be the work of the last great poet in Europe who wrote for the theater:

> Chekhov is the first European writer who attained greatness without being affected by the rhetoric of Titanism, and without conceding anything to the nineteenth-century cult of the measureless and colossal . . . Even in the works of writers like Henry James, Joseph Conrad, and Thomas Mann, along with the presence of genius we feel something forced, out of season, nobly out of date. . . . Then came Joyce and Proust—giants in a minor key—masters of language, poets who cannot be translated . . . but the only way of giving a face and a voice to the hero of our times, the unknown man who lives and dies without leaving a trace, is the way that Anton Chekhov adopted.

Montale's first article on Pasternak (*Corriere della sera,* 23 October 1958) was written when he was awarded the Nobel Prize. He finds Pasternak at once unmistakably European and characteristically Russian. While discussing the novel *Doctor Zhivago,* Montale makes some subtle evaluative and analytical comments. Pasternak, he tells us,

> has intentionally avoided the problem of the so-called novel in order to give us a long poem open in all directions and susceptible even to a symbolic interpretation—a poem in which the characters sacrifice the prominence they would have had in a great naturalistic novel in order to reveal themselves to be what they are—dry leaves caught up in the vortex of a great storm. Hence there are no longer any characters or situations that can be exploited for the sake of a representation meant to dole out the effects. Instead, one finds the great atony and the quasi indifference on the part of him who lives his history (a great page of history) by annulling himself in it, at once a witness and a victim of a shipwreck which is perhaps the last will of an unknown and terrible God.

Doctor Zhivago, Montale adds, not only represents a further stage in the development of the traditional historical novel, but also maintains "that sense of the long wave which the narrative had never known before Proust . . . with the difference, however, that Proust, no less than Gogol, concentrates on his characters, whereas Pasternak lets all his characters and objects, facts and episodes be leveled and equalized by an inexorable tide." The final impression that Pasternak's masterpiece leaves on a reader like Montale (and in considering the type and quality of reader that Montale himself represents it is pertinent to bear in mind what he says about the universality of a writer, namely that it is not to be "deduced statistically from the number of his readers," but from the fact of his being accessible "only to those who have a culture similar to his own") is that it is the book "of an enlightened spirit, of a great Russian who looks to the future without renouncing his country and his people, and yet without letting himself be entangled by the miseries of the present."

On the modern Greek poet Constantine Cavafy, Montale has written two articles (*Corriere della sera,* 13 April 1955 and 5 June 1962). Although he finds a superficial resemblance between Cavafy on the one hand and Pascoli and Rilke on the other, inasmuch as the Greek poet has also written "convivial poems" or "long poems of neoclassical intonation, even though with a modern sentiment," he is, both in body and spirit, a true Alexandrine and "altogether alien to those humanistic reflections which are always at the root of every poetic neoclassicism." In his revocation of the Hellenic world, Cavafy shows himself to be "an absolute pagan," although his bond with the ancient world was a matter of "luxury and not of a rational and religious consensus." If he peoples his world with historical characters, he does so as an iconoclast, so that he treats Caesar and Cleopatra, for instance, as his contemporaries. And although he does not swim with the current of the modern lyric, he is "an epigrammatist endowed with the taste of a Landor, a poet of late Latinism, a decadent in the historical (that is to say, classical) sense of the term."

From a general survey of Montale's critical pronouncements on the more important Italian and foreign writers of this century what emerges is the free play of a vigorous, independent, and analytical intelligence in full possession of itself and buttressed by an ever vigilant awareness of the political, social, and cultural aspects of the *Zeitgeist,* which he interprets in his triple capacity as poet, critic and journalist. The ease and naturalness of the prose style is itself an index of the depth of Montale's sincerity and knowledgeableness about what he is discussing. His wide range of reading in modern European classics, coupled with an intellectual curiosity and perceptiveness, gives his critical formulations an air of stimulating liveliness as well as of authority, which much academic or professional criticism in Italy conspicuously lacks. Thus, by applying his mind to the cultural and social as well as literary problems of the day, Montale has enlarged the scope and frontiers of creative and critical sensibility. For his approach to those problems is not only that of a practitioner in verse, but also of a whole man and critic whose strength and originality are inseparable from the realized fullness of being.

8: Montale and the *Zeitgeist*

If in Montale's poetry the sense of moral and political involvement in the events and dilemmas of his age figures only implicitly, in his prose writings it finds a well-defined, reasoned, and polished formulation. As a result of this, even in his most journalistic pieces Montale appears to be a sharp and perceptive observer and a qualified interpreter of the *Zeitgeist* and its various trends, assumptions, and dogmas, which he himself has influenced in a decisive way.

Auto da Fè is the first collection of Montale's articles and essays which he has published over the last forty years or so and which cover the various aspects of the *Zeitgeist*. Most of them were published in *Corriere della sera* and the rest in the literary and cultural periodicals of this period as well as in other newspapers.[1] In his brief prefatory note Montale refers to the "two different times separated by a long interval" in which these articles were written, so that "the chronological time doesn't always coincide with the psychological." The range of themes is very wide and varied indeed, including in its ambit politics, literature, painting, Marxism, psychoanalysis, opera, aesthetics, and atheism.

In the essay "Fascism and Literature" ("Il fascismo e la letteratura") Montale traces the genesis, causes, and nature of fascism insofar as it made an impact on Italian literature. But this impact was very limited. In fact, apart from Marinetti and D'Annunzio—he calls the latter a "poet-prophet . . . the spirit incarnate of imperial fascism"—fascism did not produce any writer of first-rate calibre. Not only that, but there was, generally speaking, something quite mediocre about the writers who were zealous champions of the Fascist ideology. For all its blatant incentives and rewards, fascism merely engendered "skepticism, moral indifference, and base opportunism." There were, however, other writers who were more men of action than pure artists—writers like

---

1. Apart from *Corriere della sera* and *Corriere di'informazione,* Montale's articles appeared in *Primo Tempo, Il Baretti, La fiera letteraria, Solaria, Il Convegno, Pan, Pegaso,* and *Il Mondo* (of Florence, as distinguished from the Rome edition edited by Mario Pannunzio).

Gobetti, Gramsci, and Rosselli—who fought against fascism, and Montale is full of praise for them.

In another essay, while reviewing Corrado Alvaro's book *L'Italia rinunzia,* Montale touches on some aspects of contemporary Italian life that have a special bearing on southern Italy and on the mentality of the people there. To what extent can one attribute to the North the political, economical, and social backwardness of the South? Alvaro's book, Montale points out, seems to lay too much stress on the North being responsible for the state that the South is in. According to Alvaro, the latter has been kept deliberately in colonial conditions in order to provide a cheap market for the surplus industrial products of the North. On another matter, too, Montale and Alvaro do not see eye to eye; it is when the latter points out how fascism was backed "almost exclusively by reactionary bourgeois forces." On the contrary, Montale points out, it was from the bourgeois and intellectual classes that the most effective opposition to fascism came.

In another article, "The Wheel of Fortune" ("La ruota della fortuna"), Montale wonders whether or not the popular view of success, "Good politics is what succeeds and bad politics what fails," and its corollary, the spirit of opportunism, have much to do with the general political attitude of contemporary Italians, whom Montale calls the "late grandsons of the men of the Renaissance." There is no doubt that such attitudes contributed to some extent to the rise of fascism.

However, most of the articles in *Auto da Fè* deal with nonpolitical topics, and interspersed throughout them are observations, comments, and evaluations of books, personalities, and events which are at once sensitive and thought-provoking. One of the most interesting articles is on "The solitude of the artist" ("La solitudine dell'artista"), where Montale displays a firm analytical grasp of the essential factors in the artist's sense of isolation and his instinctive need to communicate.

> Our times have the merit of having discovered or accentuated as never before the full dramatic character of an artistic experience. The attempt to pin down the ephemeral, to render the phenomenal nonphenomenal, to make the individual "I," which is not so by definition, communicate—in short, the attempt to rebel against the human condition (a rebellion dictated by a passionate *amor vitae*) is behind the artistic as well as philosophical search of our times.

And paradoxical though it may seem, the only way of achieving "communication," Montale tells us, is not through "engagement," but through "isolation" —isolation that sharpens one's awareness and sense of perspective.

The neopositive humanism of science and technology, and the resultant betterment—at least in the material sense—of the masses is, of course, an important factor. Nevertheless, it is the destiny of the artist to be aware of a profound spiritual vacuity in the midst of material prosperity, and his privilege to make others feel that there is

> behind the isolated voice [of artists] an echo of the fatal isolation of each one of us. In this sense only the isolated speak, only they communicate; the others—men of mass communication—repeat, echo, vulgarize the words of poets, which at present are not words of faith, but which could perhaps turn out to be so one day.

This leads to Montale's reflections on art and literature in general, both in their relevance to modern times and to a hypothetical future. His preoccupation with the concept of time—past, present and future—dates back to his early interest in Bergson's philosophy. In "Mutations" ("Mutazioni"), for instance, he talks about old, or relatively old, classical writers like Fogazzaro, Kipling, Proust, Castoldi, or Stendhal as authors to be read during the holidays, and adds how in "the age of cubism and surrealism" people show a secret predilection for the works "in which time, the psychological sense that unites us to the past, is still perceptible." Montale goes on to analyze what he considers to be the tragedy of our times:

> . . . we react to new phenomena with old instruments, we have discovered arms, objects, and thoughts of which we know neither the why nor the wherefore nor the range. We see many a thing perish, and many another come to life, but the sense, the direction of the change escapes us. For instance, if men, all men, could be cured of their complexes, would art still have a *raison d'être*—art as it is understood today?

The awareness of the existential actuality of the present and the desire to realize it before it slips irrevocably away, leads Montale to ponder the condition of the intellectual in modern society, in the article entitled "Odradek":

> To live his life always on the alert is all that a man can do today, the man who boasts and is at the same time ashamed—and rightly so—of the dubious and discredited qualification of an intellectual. We cannot imagine other short-term solutions, whereas it is possible to advance many long-term hypotheses concerning the means to destroy or domesticate Odradek or to arrive at a complete identification with him.

As if anticipating what was to come a few years later as an era of general protest, Montale makes another diagnostic comment about the commitment of the artist, in the article entitled "Caught in the trap" ("Presi 'nel giro' "). He goes to the heart of the matter when he shows how the cultural industry conspires with the most radical and revolutionary aspects of contemporary protest in order to destroy what remains of "humanistic civilization."

Although the tenor and spirit of these articles is largely journalistic, the quality of Montale's prose, especially in its freedom from academic, technical, or professional jargon and in its analytical and explicative lucidity, raises them to the level of a higher and more complex interest. Judged from the point of view of what Matthew Arnold would call the element of "high-seriousness," a number of the pieces included in *Auto da fè* may be found to be lacking. Nevertheless, running through them all we can detect a vein of moral and intellectual honesty, vigor, and purposefulness as well as a stylistic maturity and austerity that one doesn't habitually associate with journalism. Take, for example, what Montale says in "No fear but . . . " ("Niente paura ma . . .") about the transient nature of a work of art achieved under modern conditions.

> The idea of a work that can resist the march of time is becoming more and more anachronistic day by day; a work should burn itself out the moment it has fulfilled a demand and has been enjoyed by the client: the needs of the clientele cannot be left to mature in *bainmarie*. They must be perpetually prodded by an apposite cultural industry. Critics, good-intentioned teachers, journalists, lecturers, angry young men, and philosophers, who are no longer innocuous, contribute to this industry without taking into account the mechanism in which they are caught.

Here the logic of the argument and the aptly metaphorical nature of the expression are so closely interwoven as to enrich the moral and psychological quality of what is being said. But it is not so much the presentation as the way of looking at everyday things and events that brings out the creative vitality of Montale's prose. Discussing the problem of the place and relevance of art in modern times and in the future, Montale observes:

> I am not one of those who would like to take a leap back to the centuries that condemned men to the stake for mere theological cavils. I am not one of those who would like to abolish industry, compulsory education, and universal suffrage. I don't even wish (though I fear it) that a tremor from an unknown God, a great sweep of the broom might annihilate, in the course of a few years or a few hours, a civilization which, carried by a *tapis roulant,* considers itself to be progressive; I don't wish for anything and I accept the age in which I live. The only thing I would

wish is that that rare subspecies of human beings who keep their eyes open might not become totally extinct. In the new visual civilization it is this species that is most threatened.

Another moral and psychological predicament in the life of modern man is his sense of alienation,—his sense of being a marginal man, an outsider. This theme has been elaborately exploited in art and literature. "Without a sense of alienation," Montale observes in "Alienated Man ("L'uomo alienato"),

> how could one exploit the splendid feminine examples of the human race, endowed with everything except mind and ideas? [2] The film industry takes care of that. One of these beings is taken, put alongside a man or two, and one is left to watch what will happen. They love each other or they don't; leave each other or don't; accept each other or don't: this is all that the game is about: this is a living representation of the drama of modern alienation. If you ask why nearly all the stories based on the lack of human communication are nine times out of ten stories of *couchages,* you will be told that this is precisely where drama begins—from the incapacity to love—and that you have put your finger where it hurts. And if this operation is also lucrative, so much the better; it is not necessary that the artist should be alienated from money; it's enough that he is not alienated from . . . alienation.

Such criticism of the values—or nonvalues—of modern life derives its force from the intellectual acumen, psychological insight, and ethical irony that are so effectively operant in these articles.

For instance, in "The Market of Nothing" ("Il mercato del nulla"), referring to the crisis of language which, according to a modern school of philosophy, "does not grasp real entities but phantasms," Montale observes how a follower or expounder of such a philosophy "can obtain a university chair and achieve worldwide fame," just as by "destroying the hypothesis of every possible art, an artist today can achieve great fame and live at the expense of the very bourgeois world he detests."

Terms like *reform, renovation, avant-garde,* and *protest* have been used to characterize the social, political, and literary ferment in Italy over the last few

2. Cf. Leopardi:

> Che se più molli
> E più tenui le membra, essa la mente
> Men capace e men forte anco riceve.
>
>   "Aspasia"

years. And insofar as this phenomenon impinges on contemporary literature and especially on the use of language, necessitating violent and radical alterations and upheavals in the hands of the avant-garde champions, Montale contemplates it with concern and perplexity. In such a state of affairs even the ultratechnical and almost incomprehensible language of some literary periodicals is bound to be superseded by something even more incomprehensible.

One of the most penetrating essays in *Auto da fè* is "In the Flow of the Current" ("Sul filo della corrente"). Its quasi-scientific language admirably conveys the ironic essence of Montale's thought. In the sphere of politics, philosophy, art, and religion, people in the past, Montale observes, used to delegate power to those few they had elected, which means that they had no individual existence of their own and were content to remain "the raw material of history." [3] But now millions of beings "want to be represented, want to live and explode individually." They want to live their lives on the only plane possible for them—the plane of emotions and sensations. And because such a "sensual egotism" does not, and by its very nature cannot, make for anything durable, it is "precisely the concept of duration that is being discredited." In the course of such a drastic transformation of values, it is only natural that even the very notions of what is good and evil should undergo a profound change. For his own part, however, Montale has this to say:

> I love the age in which I was born, because I prefer to live in the flow of the current rather than vegetate in the marsh of a timeless age: namely, the age which we mistakenly call the age of our forefathers. I prefer to live in an age that recognizes its evils rather than in the interminable age where evils are covered with the cloak of hypocrisy. After all, without denying the infinite impostures that submerge us, one gets the impression that today men have opened their eyes as never before—not even in the time of Pericles. And yet, even with their eyes open, they see nothing. Perhaps one would have to wait for a long time, but for me and for all those who are alive, time is running short.

In the following essay, "Man in the Microgroove" ("L'uomo nel microsolco"), the autobiographical note merges with a sort of prose symbolism. Man is compared to a sailor who is continually voyaging, carrying about with him a shoehorn which becomes the symbol of personal identity.[4] He then goes on to reflect on the course of history, both in the individual and in

---

3. For Montale's reflections on history, see poems like "La storia," "Fanfara," and "Che mastice tiene," in *Satura.*
4. See "L'abbiamo rimpianto a lungo l'infilascarpe," *Xenia* II.

the universal sense, and the reflections that he offers form the substance of some of the poems in *Satura*.[5]

One of the major preoccupations of modern art is the theme of time—time in its existential, metaphysical, and psychopoetic reality. In the face of what has been achieved by various sciences—biology, physics, sociology, and economics—it is not so much the modern artist, but the modern nonartist who knows that

> Time is irreversible, that the tridimensional character of objects is a provisional conquest already outdated by science; he also knows that the only reality is the incessant and ever new flux of vital energy. There is no longer any dualism between external and immobile reality and the phenomenon of transience, between the idea (or Reason, or God) and the act of sneezing.

And what has happened in the field of art in general comes out in an even more dramatic or sensational form in the fields of contemporary poetry and music. In registering and assessing the impact of this change Montale again shows himself to be endowed with a penetrating insight into contemporary civilization. In "The gagged mouths" ("Le bocche imbavagliate"), for instance, he expounds his views on what modern poetry and music have come to mean. In "From the Museum to Life" ("Dal museo alla vita") light music is described as "a pleasant optical-acoustic hell," "a music of gestures," or "the manifestation of the only individual that counts: the collective." It is a kind of music that resolves the aesthetic problem of whether art should express the individual or the universal, and resolves it "in the sense that it has rendered subjectivity anonymous and impersonal." Similarly, the theater is also affected by "the industrialization of culture and mass media." Nor has literary criticism remained immune from the radical changes undergone by music and literature. To the extent that writers, poets, and critics are all involved in bringing about these changes and exploiting their results, they may be said to have been engaged in what Montale calls the "breaking operation." The article entitled "Breaking operation" ("Operazione di rottura") is one of the most drastic appraisals of neo-avant-garde tendencies in art, literature, and culture. At the root of the concept of what is avant-garde or neo-avant-garde Montale finds a basic moral contradiction. For, while wanting to destroy "en bloc our neocapitalist society," the avant-garde artists do not hesitate to accept "the advantages of the literary industry, mass media, and cultural planning, thereby putting a positive, not a negative, mark on how much there is of the tribal in present-day mass civilization." Moreover, they

5. See note 3.

also favor a new form of surrealism ("anarchy on the surface, comfort at the bottom"), and wish to bring about an order in which "modernity and a bad conscience are perfectly compatible."

Auto da fè thus offers a substantial body of illuminating and cogently argued comments on the various aspects of contemporary civilization—a comment that has at least this in common with Montale's poetry, that it constantly weds the edge and intensity of a personal view or observation with the force and gravity of something impersonal and at the same time morally pregnant.

Fuori di casa, which came out in 1968, is another book of essays dealing for the most part with Montale's travels as a journalist in countries like England, France, Portugal, Greece, Syria, and Israel. It also displays the same degree of psychological acumen, intellectual wit, and moral irony as *Auto da fè,* as well as the same stylistic and linguistic qualities. Among the more interesting pieces are "Le Cinque Terre" (which evokes the "mysterious local mythology" embodied in Montale's poetry and *Farfalla di Dinard*), "Baffo E. C.," "Two Irresistible People" ("Due irresistibili," impressions of a twentieth-century Italian in England), and "On the Way to Damascus" ("Sulla strada di Damasco"). In some pieces, such as "A Powerful Clique" ("Una potente consorteria"), Montale's journalistic flair combines most effectively with his critical acumen as he offers us the pen-portraits of modern French writers like Mauriac, Bourdet, and Malraux. Claudel is described as a writer "whom few like but nearly everybody admires," and Saint-John Perse as one whom one can't understand without understanding his "sense of plurals." When dealing with Camus, Montale makes a caustic diagnosis of the ephemeral nature of the avant-garde industry in France and elsewhere, and of the phenomenon of the best-seller: "Camus's seven or eight books," he tells us, "are considered a very light *bagage* by the young people who at the age of twenty have already published two or three novels. Authors who do not publish anything for a few years are spoken of as if they were already dead. It is commonly said, so and so was important in '49."

From the point of view of narrative and creative qualities, "The Countess of Sarre" ("La Contessa di Sarre"), "Visit to Brancusi" ("Visita a Brancusi"), "Mistral and the Provence" ("Mistral e la Provenza") and "The singular case of Charloun" ("Il singolare caso di Charloun") are among the most significant. The articles on Spain, Portugal, and Greece are exercises in literary and geographical discoveries, which only a poet of Montale's stature could have saved from the kind of glib journalism or travelogue they all too often turn out to be. One of the most rewarding and characteristic pieces in *Fuori di casa* is "The House of Flaubert" ("La casa di Flaubert"), in which a lyric delicacy of descriptive detail, a wealth of literary reminiscences and associations, and a subtle undercurrent of pathos and nostalgia serve to present some of the themes and motifs of Montale's poetry as well as of *Farfalla di Dinard,* in a new light and context. Describing such places as Honfleur, Deauville, and Trouville in Normandy, which are now both fashionable resorts and literary centers, Montale tries to picture to himself what they must have been like at the end of the nineteenth century.

> Up to fifty years ago these beaches must have been—apart from the climate—rather like the old Forte dei Marmi: places of long sojourn where one could lead the life of a clan, at once rustic and elegant. I haven't seen in the parks any probable Albertina to play like the devil, though. Instead, new sports that I don't even know the names of flourish like mushrooms; and each one has its international champions and tournaments. All in all, these little towns give the coast a Nordic, almost English, appearance; in fact they are only a few minutes by air from Brighton or from Eastbourne.

Honfleur is "a refuge for countless artists, many of whom manage to preserve themselves as best they can from its 'too picturesque' character by having recourse to abstract compositions. In its less agreeable aspects the town may remind one of the life of Ascona and Capri, rendezvous of the Nordic nudists and misunderstood geniuses." The description of Octeville-sur-Mer belongs to the same class as some of the best pieces in *Farfalla di Dinard,* and pinpoints certain themes and details which Montale was to exploit in *Xenia:*

> The steep wall of impervious rock that extends to the northwest from Cap da la Hève lets the sea in only from deep narrow fissures where it is risky to venture. The sea had receded far, leaving behind stretches of *varech* and darkish seaweed. I am left with more than an hour to watch a flock of young falcons' first feeble attempts at flying from the top of an embankment. The falcons, *le mouettes,* the big cormorants, and even the magpies that sometimes leave the fields and come as far up as here have all a different way of flying, almost a different language. I thought I was alone, but then toward dusk the *estivants* started moving inland like a long line of ants climbing the whole length of the cleft. They appear one at a time along the steep slope, tired, sweating, equipped with cages, bags, thermos flasks, and sticks. They are real *estivants,* not holiday-makers in the true sense, because almost no one here has a house or a villa. It is a strange human fauna which joins the other and complements it. In these vast regions which seem deserted even at holiday times, but which are in

fact very crowded, the practice of camping has assumed inconceivable proportions. Wherever one looks one can see perfectly habitable tents, more or less uniform, and in places where camping is allowed, temporary villages spring up, almost always cleverly camouflaged in the woods so as not to spoil the harmony of the landscape.

To stand on the ridge and observe the world that swarms, in Indian file, from the impervious gorge, is a spectacle that so far, if I am not mistaken, no neorealist cinematographer has really exploited. The children, above all, tousled, playing with crayfish and seaweed, are often incomparable actors. The tricks and cunning they employ in order to get a lift and so save themselves the journey back to the paternal tent are incredible. One gets the impression that in this place the *enfants prodiges* worthy of going on the stage are the rule rather than the exception.

Fuori di casa ends with a piece that finds Montale "at home" in Venice. It is dedicated to Stravinsky on the occasion of a performance of *The Rake's Progress* for which W. H. Auden wrote the libretto. The libretto, according to Montale, contains perhaps the most beautiful poetry Auden ever wrote.

Conclusion

While summing up the grounds for Montale's stature as the most important twentieth-century Italian poet, one finds oneself laying stress on what T. S. Eliot claimed that only a man of genius can do—i.e. alter expression. But the altering of expression is not a simple matter. It calls forth in a poet a complex variety of powers and capabilities—moral, psychological, and intellectual— together with a wide range of emotional and imaginative sympathies that give meaning to his personal experiences and constitute the sum of individual destiny while at the same time reflecting the universal one.

Through an impressive combination of realism and naturalism on the one hand and symbolism on the other, Montale not only delves deep into and exploits the hitherto untapped resources of the Italian language, but also enriches the domain of poetic metaphor and imagery. The peculiar intensity of tone and timbre in his use of a word or an image results from, as it in turn leads to, the quality of crystalline concreteness and sharply marked specificity or "thisness" which characterizes his poetic diction without, nevertheless, depriving it of a delicate nuance of evocativeness and symbolism. Montale's reaction against the courtly tradition of the Italian language led him to use a ruggedly prosaic diction, underlying which there is, however, a particular depth of lyricism that Italian poetry had not known since Leopardi.

Few modern Italian poets have followed more rigorously and with more impressive creative results what Pound meant by his salutary dictum, "Go in fear of abstractions." [1] For Montale's poetry assiduously avoids, from first to last, what is vague, generic, and abstract and not sharply pinpointed in utmost precision and concreteness. Even while expressing what is deeply rooted in his personal experience, he always succeeds in striking a cogent balance between what is personal or individual and what he himself calls the "transcendental ego, which is hidden in all of us and which recognizes itself in others;" [2]

1. "A Retrospect," *Literary Essays of Ezra Pound,* ed. T. S. Eliot, p. 5.
2. See the Montale essay "La solitudine dell'artista," in *Auto da fè,* p. 54.

in other words, between what is movingly and intimately subjective and what is strikingly impersonal and universal.

Moreover, Montale's originality emerges no less in the way he widens or "deprovincializes" the cultural and linguistic as well as the philosophical range of the Italian lyric, while remaining at the same time as rooted in his native tradition as Pascoli, D'Annunzio, or Cardarelli. For instance, his interest in English literature—especially in Elizabethan drama, the English essayists, the poetry of Keats, Browning, Pound, and Eliot—provides him both with a perspective and a measuring-rod for assessing the inherent worth of the Italian poetic tradition while at the same time enriching and changing it. In this respect he may be compared with T. S. Eliot, although there is a fundamental difference between the two. Eliot's poetry—and in particular his religious or philosophic poetry—indicates a frame of mind and a mode of exploring reality, as well as of interpreting one's own experience, which are on the whole extraneous to Montale. For one thing Montale's poetry seldom parades ethical, philosophical, or religious concepts for their own sake. For another, there is no nisus toward an explicitly or implicitly professed dogma at the core of his thought as there is at the core of Eliot's. In other words, Montale's poetry is rich in what Keats calls "Negative Capability"—the capability, that is, of being "in uncertainties, mysteries, doubts, without any irritable reaching after fact and reason." [3] It was the lack of this capability that Pound had in mind when he observed that Eliot was "too weak to live with an uncertainty." [4] Montale's "Negative Capability" gives the "criticism of life" or "critical corrosion of existence" in his poetry the vigor and sharpness, as well as the poignancy, of a personal experience. This quality is pervasive in all Montale's poetry, but it is more pronounced and more artistically effective in *Ossi di seppia*. In a substantial number of lyrics in this volume, especially under the group entitled "Ossi di seppia" and the series called "Mediterraneo," Montale's art achieves an impressive degree of maturity, depth, and originality, which was to change the face of the Italian lyric and which his own later poetry seldom surpassed.

3. *The Letters of John Keats*, ed. Maurice Buxton Forman (Oxford, 1935), p. 72.
4. Quoted in the introduction to *New Approaches to Ezra Pound*, ed. Eva Hesse (Berkeley and Los Angeles: University of California Press, 1969), p. 18.

Appendix 1:
Montale's Early Poems

Before the publication of *Ossi di seppia,* Montale had already published eight poems in the periodical called *Primo Tempo* (no. 2, June 1922): "Riviere" (1920) and "Corno inglese" (this poem was included in *Ossi di seppia*); and "Violini," "Violoncelli," "Flauti-fagotti," "Oboe," and "Ottoni," collectively called *Accordi.* In the first edition of *Ossi di seppia* there was another earlier poem of Montale's, "Musica sognata," which was excluded from subsequent editions. In 1960 *Accordi* (including "Corno inglese" and "Musica sognata") reappeared in *L'espresso mese* (Rome, vol. 1, no. 6 [Oct.]), and two years later they were published again in a limited edition of three hundred numbered copies. In the same year another group of four hitherto unpublished poems appeared in a private edition, together with "Musica sognata," which was renamed "Minstrels." These four poems are "A galla (1919), "Nel vuoto" (1924), "Botta e risposta I" (1961) (this is the only poem which was to be included in the fourth volume of Montale's poetry, *Satura*), and "Ventaglio per S. F." (1962).

The most significant and characteristic of these poems is "Nel vuoto," which, as I have gathered in the course of my conversations with him, is also Montale's own opinion. Hence one wonders all the more why this poem was not included in *Ossi di seppia,* where it would have belonged just as appropriately as "Corno inglese" or an even earlier poem, "Meriggiare pallido e assorto" (1916). It heralds and indeed illustrates in a more than rudimentary or tentative manner those qualities of style and technique which were to characterize Montale's later and more mature verse—qualities like pictorial neatness, verbal tautness, and rhythmic freshness and dynamism, no less than the effective and well-organized use of realistic and metaphorical detail. The element of poetic suspense and surprise is also so dexterously interwoven within the fabric of the poem as to affect us in a most delicate and convincing way:

The sun's mane lay entangled
in the dry orchard twigs
and a few lazy sloops
lay drowsy on the bank.

Under the bright arch
the day gave out no sound,
nor did pine cone splash, or bud
split beyond the wall.

Everything was immersed in silence,
our boat kept cutting across
the sand unimpeded,
and a sign that had long been suspended
in the air—fell plumb.

Now the earth was an overflowing brim,
a weight melted into a dazzle,
and the blaze was the dark's white foam.
The ditch kept widening and widening,
until it was too late for anchoring
and for us.

Then all of a sudden
something happened.
the rampart closed its openings,
nothing was lost—and everything.
I woke up at the sound
of your hitherto mute lips.
And since then we both lie imprisoned
in the crystal's vein waiting
invisibly for its day.

La criniera del sole s'invischiava
tra gli stecchi degli orti e sulla riva
qualche pigra scialuppa pareva assopita.

Non dava suono il giorno
sotto il lucido arco,
nè tonfava
pigna o sparava boccio
di là dai muri.

Il silenzio ingoiava tutto,
la nostra barca non s'era fermata,

tagliava a filo la sabbia, un segno a lungo
sospeso in alto precipitava.

Ora la terra era orlo che trabocca,
peso sciolto in barbaglio,
la vampa era la spuma dell'oscuro,
il fosso si allargava, troppo fondo
per l'àncora e per noi

               finché di scatto
qualcosa avvenne intorno, il vallo chiuse
le valve, nulla e tutto era perduto,
ed io fui desto al suono del tuo labbro
prima muto—da allora imprigionati
tutti e due nella vena che nel cristallo,
invisibile, attende la sua giornata.

Appendix 2:
Montale's Translations of Poetry

Montale's verse as well as his prose translations are for the most part from English. Translations of poems are included in *Quaderno di traduzioni* (Edizioni della Meridiana, 1948). It concludes three sonnets by Shakespeare (22, 33, 48) and some passages from *A Midsummer-Night's Dream*, three poems by T. S. Eliot ("A Song for Simeon," "La figlia che piange," and "Animula"), two by James Joyce ("Watching the Needleboats at San Sabba" and "A Flower Given to My Daughter"), and one poem each from William Blake ("To the Muses"), Emily Dickinson ("The Storm"), Gerard Manley Hopkins ("Pied Beauty"), Herman Melville ("Billy in the Darbies"), Thomas Hardy ("The Garden Seat"), W. B. Yeats ("The Indian to His Love"), and Dylan Thomas ("Poem Fifth"). With the possible exception of Eliot, there is nothing in these translations to suggest that Montale was drawn to these poets by any particular interest based on any sense of affinity with them or influence of their work on his own work or development, or that he intensively studied any one of these poets with any particular aim in mind. All that this miscellany does suggest is that in the course of his browsings in English and American literature Montale must have been struck by certain poems for their own intrinsic charm as well as for the possibilities of a creative rendering into Italian that they offered. The translations are both creatively impressive and faithful to the text and achieve that rare balance between beauty and fidelity which Croce thought a metaphysical impossibility. (Other poems in *Quaderno di traduzioni* are: Joan Maragall's "Cant Espiritual"; O. V. De L. Milosz's "La berline arretée dans la nuit"; Jorge Guillén's "Los Jardines," "Rama del otoño," "Arbol del otoño," "Advenimiento," "Presagio," and "El cisne"; and Leonie Adams's "Lullaby.")

Appendix 3:
Montale's Metre

In his use of metre, too, Montale makes an eclectic and personal use of traditional metres, applying the principle of making a rule of exceptions. With a distinct awareness of what has been achieved or invented by other poets from Leopardi to D'Annunzio, he achieves a remarkable degree of suppleness and variety in matching or juxtaposing what is new with what is traditional. However, in Montale as in Eliot, the sense of metrical freedom or inventiveness goes hand in hand with a relentless discipline and control, so that whenever he takes liberties, say, with a traditional "endecasillabo" or "settenario" or whatever variations he chooses to play upon their structure and combination with other metres, there is always a technical, artistic, or structural necessity behind it. Another important factor in Montale's metrical innovations is the frequent use of prose structure and cadences, as a result of which not only single paragraphs but also some poems in their entirety can be made to read as a prose passage with minimal or even without any alterations in the syntax. Conversely, there are certain passages in *Farfalla di Dinard* which can be made to read as poetry. Besides the penetrating observations of Solmi and Contini in their critical essays on Montale an exhaustive treatment of Montale's use of metre is to be found in Giorgio Bàrberi Squarotti's article, "Montale, la metrica e altro" (*Letteratura,* no. 51, 1961, pp. 53–66) and in Ottaviano Giannangeli's article, "Il significante metrico in Montale" (*Dimensioni,* June 1969, pp. 15–49).

Bibliography

PRIMARY SOURCES

1. Poetry

Ossi di seppia
  1st ed. Turin: Gobetti, 1925.
  2d ed. Turin: Ribet, 1928. With six new poems and an introduction by Alfredo Gargiulo.
  3d ed. Carabba: Lanciano, 1931.
  4th ed. Carabba: Lanciano, 1939.
  1st ed. Turin: Einaudi, 1939. 2d, 3d (definitive edition), 4th, 5th, 6th eds., 1942. 7th ed., 1943. The 6th and 7th editions contain some minor changes in some poems from the text of the 5th edition, itself a revised version of all previously published non-Einaudi editions.
  1st ed. Milan: Mondadori, 1948.
La casa dei doganieri e altri versi. Florence: Edizioni dell'antico Fattore, 1932.
Le occasioni
  1st ed. Turin: Einaudi, 1939.
  2d ed., 1940 (Four new poems added.), 3d ed., 1942. 4th ed., 1943. 5th ed., 1945.
  1st ed. Milan: Mondadori, 1949.
Finisterre
  1st ed. Lugano: Quaderni della Collana di Lugano, 1942.
  2d ed. Florence: Barbera, 1945. *Finisterre* is now to be found in *La bufera e altro.*
La bufera e altro. Venice: Edizione Neri Pozza, 1956.
  1st ed. Milan: Mondadori, 1957.
Accordi e pastelli. Milan: Scheiwiller, 1962. (Contains six pastels and eight poems by Montale).
Satura. Verona, 1966. Privately printed. (Contains five poems. "Minstrels" was included in the first edition of *Ossi di seppia,* but excluded from the subsequent editions.)

Xenia. Text with translation and preface by G. Singh (each copy signed by Eugenio Montale). Los Angeles: Black Sparrow Press and New York: New Directions, 1970.

Satura. Milan: Mondadori, 1971. (It includes *Xenia* I and *Xenia* II.)

Diario del '71. Milan: Scheiwiller, 1971 (a limited edition of 100 copies of Montale's most recent poems.)

2. Prose

Farfalla di Dinard. Venice: Neri Pozza, 1956.
    1st ed. Milan: Mondadori, 1960.

The Butterfly of Dinard. Translated by G. Singh, with a preface by Montale. London: Alan Ross, 1970. An American edition of this translation was published by Kentucky University Press, Lexington, 1971.

Auto da fé. Milan: Il Saggiatore, 1966.

Eugenio Montale–Italo Svevo: Lettere. Bari: De Donato, 1966 (contains Montale's critical essays on Svevo as well).

Fuori di casa. Milan: Ricciardi, 1969.

3. Translations by Montale

Steinbeck, John. *La Battaglia.* Milan: Bompiani, 1940.

Melville, Herman. *La Storia di Billy Budd,* with a preface by Montale. Milan: Bompiani, 1942.

Parker, Dorothy. *Il mio mondo è qui.* 2d ed. Milan: Bompiani, 1943.

O'Neill, Eugene. *Strano interludio.* Preface by Eugenio Montale. Rome: Edizioni Teatro dell'Università, 1943.

Steinbeck, John. *Al Dio sconosciuto.* Milan: Mondadori, 1946.

Shakespeare, William. *La Commedia degli errori. Racconto d'inverno. Timone d'Atene.* In *W. Shakespeare: Teatro,* ed. Mario Praz. 3 vols. Florence: Sansoni, 1947.

Hawthorne, Nathaniel. *Il Volto di pietra.* Milan: Bompiani, 1947.

Shakespeare, William. *Amleto, principe di Danimarca.* Milan: Cederna, 1949.

Marlowe, Christopher. *La tragica storia del dottor Faust.* In vol. 1 of *Teatro elisabettiano,* ed. Alfredo Obertello. Milan and Rome: Bompiani, 1951.

Del Carlo, Omar. *Proserpina e lo straniero.* Milan: Ricordi, 1952.

Wilson, Angus. *La cicuta e dopo.* Milan: Garzanti, 1956.

Jorge Guillén tradotto da Eugenio Montale. Milan: All'Insegna del Pesce d'Oro, 1958.

Corneille, Pierre. *Le Cid.* In *Teatro francese del grande secolo,* ed. G. Macchia. Turin: Edizioni RAI, 1960.

T. S. Eliot tradotto da Eugenio Montale. Introduction by Eugenio Montale. Milan: Scheiwiller, 1963.

Quaderno di traduzioni. Milan: Edizioni della Meridiana, 1948 (Contains verse translations of some sonnets and songs by Shakespeare, as well as of poems by

Blake, Emily Dickinson, Melville, Hardy, Joan Maragall, Joyce, O. V. de L. Milosz, Yeats, Eliot, Jorge Guillén, Leonie Adams, and Dylan Thomas.)

4. Prefaces

Vita e avventure di Robinson Crusoe, Daniel Defoe, Milan: Universale Economica, 1951.
Liriche cinesi 1753 a.C.–1278 d.C. Edited by Giorgia Valensin. Turin: Einaudi, 1952.
Il Decamerone di Giovanni Boccaccio ("Settima giornata") ed. Mario Fubini, Milan: Collezione del Canguro, Universale Economica, 1952.
Poesie, Eugenio Montale. Swedish translation by Gösta Andersson, Stockholm: Casa editrice Italica, 1960.
Canti barocchi e altre liriche, Lucio Piccolo, Milan: Mondadori, 1956.
Poesie di Thomas Hardy. Edited by G. Singh. Parma, 1968.
Farfalla di Dinard, English translation by G. Singh (see section 3).
Selected Poems, Eugenio Montale. Edited with notes and introduction by G. Singh, Manchester, England: Manchester University Press, 1973.

5. Notes

Porticello piccolo (anthology). Ed. Giacomo Prampolini, Milan: All'insegna del Pesce d'Oro, 1959.
Clemente Rebora, Iconografia. Edited by Vanni Scheiwiller, Milan, 1959.

6. Introductions

Caterina II racconta la sua vita. Milan, 1954.
Genova come era 1870–1915. Luciano Frassati, 1960.
Le poesie di Guido Gozzano. Milan: Garzanti, 1960.

7. Selected Criticism

(Other than that published in *Corriere della sera* and referred to in chapter 7)
"Emilio Cecchi," *Primo tempo,* October 1923.
"Stile e tradizione," *Il Beretti,* January 1925.
"Presentazione di Italo Svevo," *Il Quindicinale,* January 30 1926.
"Umberto Saba," *Il Quindicinale,* June 1926.
"Dubliners" [of Joyce], *La Fiera Letteraria,* 19 Sept. 1926.
"T. S. Eliot," *Circoli,* Nov.–Dec. 1933.
"Sulla poesia di Dino Campana," *L'Italia che scrive,* Sept.–Oct. 1942.
"Intenzioni : intervista immaginaria," *La Rassegna d'Italia,* January 1946.
"Ragioni di Umberto Saba," *Solaria,* May 1928.
"Pietro Pancrazi e la critica del buon senso," *Lettura,* 12 Sept. 1946.
"Palazzeschi, ieri e oggi," *Immagine,* March–July, 1943.
"Eliot e noi," *Immagine,* Nov.–Dec. 1947.

"Dante ieri e oggi," in *Atti del congresso internazionale di studi danteschi,* vol. 2, Florence: Sansoni, 1966.

"L'estetica e la critica di Croce," in *Benedetto Croce. (Cultura e Realtà* series). Milan: Comunità, 1963.

"Italo Svevo nel centenario della nascità," *Umana,* nos. 1–4, Trieste, 1962.

"Lo zio Ez" (Ezra Pound), *Nuova Corrente,* Milan, June 1956.

SECONDARY SOURCES

1. Books

Avalle, D'Arco S. *"Gli Orecchini" di Montale.* Milan: Il Saggiatore, 1965.

———. *Tre saggi su Montale.* Turin: Einaudi, 1970.

Bonora, E. *La poesia di Montale.* 2 vols. Turin: Tirrenia, 1965.

Jacomuzzi, Angelo, *Sulla poesia di Montale.* Bologna: Cappelli Editore, 1968.

Manacorda, Giuliano. "Montale," *Il Castoro,* vol. 26 (February 1969). Florence: La Nuova Italia.

Nascimbeni, Giulio. *Eugenio Montale.* Milan: Longanesi, 1969.

Pipa, Arshi. *Montale and Dante.* Minneapolis: University of Minnesota Press, 1968.

Ramat, S. *Montale.* Florence: Vallecchi, 1965.

Ramat, Silvio, ed. *Omaggio a Montale.* Milan: Mondadori, 1966. (Various old and new articles, essays, and tributes by diverse hands, collected in this volume and presented to Montale on his seventieth birthday.)

2. Articles

Anceschi, Luciano. "Dai Rondisti agli Ermetici." *Le poetiche del Novecento in Italia,* pp. 209–14. Milan, 1962.

Antonielli, S. "Eugenio Montale." *Aspetti e figure del Novecento.* Parma: Guanda, 1950.

———. "Farfalla di Dinard." *Belfagor,* no. 44 (1961), pp. 512–14.

Barberi Squarotti, G. "Montale, la metrica e altro." *Letteratura,* no. 51 (1961), pp. 53–56.

Bigongiari, P. "I tre tempi della lirica montaliana." *Poesia italiana del Novecento.* Florence: Vallecchi, 1965.

Bo, C. "Della poesia di Montale." *Otto Studi.* Florence: Vallecchi, 1939, pp. 175–206.

———. "Il terzo Montale." *Lettere e arti,* no. 4 (1946), pp. 30–35.

Bonfiglioli, P. "Pascoli, Gozzano, Montale e la poesia dell'oggetto," *Il Verri,* no. 4 (1958), pp. 34–54.

———. "Dante, Pascoli, Montale." *Nuovi studi pascoliani,* pp. 35–92. Bolzano and Cesena: Centro di cultura dell'Alto Adige e della Società di studi romagnoli, 1963.

Cambon, G. "Montale dantesco e l'altro," *Lotta con Proteo,* pp. 113–37. Milan: Bompiani, 1963.

————. "Eugenio Montale's 'Motets': the Occasions of Epiphany." *PMLA* 82, no. 7, (1967): 471–84.

Cattaneo, G. "Montale e la linea italiana." *Palatina*, no. 2 (1957), pp. 20–29.

Cecchi, E. "Alla ricerca della gioventù." *Il Secolo*, no. 1 (1925).

Contini, G. "Introduzione agli 'Ossi di seppia.'" *Corrente*, June 15, 1939. Reprinted in *Esercizi di lettura*, pp. 75–87. Florence: Parenti, 1939.

————. "Dagli 'Ossi' alle 'Occasioni.'" *Esercizi di lettura*, pp. 88–119. Florence: Parenti, 1939.

————. "Di Gargiulo su Montale." *Corrente*, April 30, 1940. Reprinted in *Un Anno di letteratura*. Florence: Le Monnier, 1942.

————. "Montale e *La Bufera*." *Letteratura*, December 1956.

De Robertis, G. "Montale, 'Ossi di seppia.'" *Scrittori del Novecento*, pp. 50–56. Florence: Le Monnier, 1940.

————. "Le occasioni," "La bufera e altro" and "La Farfalla di Dinard." *Altro Novecento*, pp. 308–24. Florence: Le monnier, 1962.

Donini, F. "Montale e Leopardi." *La cultura*, no. 3. (1969), pp. 328–31.

Ferrata, G. "La casa dei doganieri." *Solaria*, no. 12 (1934), pp. 46–51.

————. "La ristampa degli 'Ossi di seppia.'" *Primato*, no. 17 (1942), pp. 325–26.

Flora, F. "Eugenio Montale." *Scrittori italiani contemporanei*. Pisa: Nistri-Lischi, 1952, pp. 119–59.

Gargiulo, A. "Introduzione agli 'Ossi di seppia.'" *Ossi di seppia*. Turin: Ribet, 1928.

————. "Eugenio Montale, 'Le Occasioni.'" *Nuova Antologia* (April 1, 1940), pp. 294–97.

(Both are now in *Letteratura italiana del Novecento*, pp. 453–58, 633–42. Florence: Le Monnier, 1958.

Giannangeli, Ottaviano. "Il significante metrico in Montale." *Dimensione* (June 1969), pp. 15–49.

Leavis, F. R. "Xenia." *The Listener* (London, December 16, 1971), pp. 845–46.

Pancrazi, P. "Eugenio Montale, poeta fisico e metafisico." *Scrittori italiani del Novecento*, pp. 268–76. Bari: Laterza, 1934. Reprinted in *Scrittori d'oggi*, ser. 3. Bari: Laterza, 1946.

————. "Le Occasioni' di Eugenio Montale." *Scrittori d'oggi*, ser. 4. Bari: Laterza, 1946.

Pasolini, P. P. "Montale." *Passione e ideologia*. Milan: Garzanti, 1960, pp. 205–98.

Praz, M. "Eliot and Montale." In *T. S. Eliot, A Symposium*. London: PL Editions, Poetry, 1948.

Sanguineti, E. "Da Gozzano a Montale." *Lettere italiane*, no. 2 (1955), pp. 188–207.

————. "Documenti per Montale." *Il Verri*, nos. 2, 3 (1962), pp. 68–75.

Segre, C. "Invito alla 'Farfalla di Dinard.'" *Letteratura*, nos. 79–81 (1966), pp. 184–93.

Singh, G. "Eugenio Montale." *Italian Studies*. Cambridge: 1962, pp. 101–37.

———. "Montale e la critica." *Le Parole e le idee,* nos. 3–4 (Naples, 1965), pp. 163–86.

———. "Lyrikern Montale." *Horisont,* no. 3 (Vasa and Stockholm, 1968).

———. "Il 'drammatico monologo' di Montale." *Nuova antologia* (Rome, July 1971), pp. 338–44.

Solmi, S. "Ossi di seppia." *Il Quindicinale,* no. 3 (1926). Reprinted as "Montale 1925" in *Scrittori negli anni,* pp. 19–24. Milan: Il Saggiatore, 1963.

———. "Poesie di Montale." *Primato,* no. 4 (1940). Reprinted as " 'Le Occasioni' di Montale" in *Scrittori negli anni,* pp. 192–201.

———. "La poesia di Montale." *Nuovi argomenti,* nos. 5–6 (1957). Reprinted in *Scrittori negli anni,* pp. 278–314.

Spender, Stephen. "The Poetry of Montale," *New York Review of Books,* 1 June 1972.

General Index

Index to Montale's Poetry and Prose

Montale's prose is only selectively indexed.